The Heart of the City throws light on the global impact of the important but often neglected 1951 CIAM VIII Conference at Hoddesdon, UK that marked the shift from modernism to postmodernism in European architectural and urban design. Zuccaro Marchi weaves a rich conceptual tapestry of many threads that unfolds brilliantly into current issues for architects, planners, historians and teachers alike.

David Grahame Shane, Columbia GSAPP, USA

In this pioneering book, Zuccaro Marchi has traced a map of the confused urban thinking in the post-war period – during which the most important discussions seemed centered, rather surprisingly, on Venice, Milan and Amsterdam. While the unresolved conflict between the city as an organism and the city as an automaton featured in much of that crucial discussion, it still resonates with twenty-first century concerns. The book will therefore be essential reading for anyone concerned with our cities and their future.

Joseph Rykwert, University of Pennsylvania, USA

533 243 46 9

The Heart of the City

The Heart of the City concept, which was introduced at CIAM 8 in 1951, has played an important role in architectural and urban debates. The Heart became the most important of the organic references used in the 1950s for defining a theory of urban form.

This book focuses on both the historical and theoretical reinterpretation of this seminal concept. Divided into two main sections, both looking at differing ways in which the Heart has influenced more recent urban thinking, it illustrates the continuity and the complexities of the Heart of the City.

In doing so, this book offers a new perspective on the significance of public space and shows how The Heart of the City still resonates closely with contemporary debates about centrality, identity and the design of public space. It would be of interest to architects, academics and students of urban design and planning.

Leonardo Zuccaro Marchi is an Italian architect, encompassing and tackling the ambiguous complexity and different ambassadorial roles and practices of architecture, both relying on fundamental historical-theoretical references and inspiring the advancement of innovative approaches. He graduated from A.S.P. Alta Scuola Politecnica, Politecnico di Milano and Politecnico di Torino. He received his PhD at IUAV and TU Delft Universities. He has been Post-doctoral Fellow at KTH University. He is currently Visiting Lecturer at TU Delft, Netherlands.

This publication has been made possible in part
by funding from the Chair of Methods and Analysis at TU Delft
and a grant from the Creative Industries Fund NL.

stimuleringsfonds creatieve industrie

creative industries fund NL

The Heart of the City

Legacy and Complexity of
a Modern Design Idea

Leonardo Zuccaro Marchi

Routledge
Taylor & Francis Group

LONDON AND NEW YORK

First published 2018
by Routledge

2 Park Square, Milton Park, Abingdon, Oxfordshire OX14 4RN
52 Vanderbilt Avenue, New York, NY 10017

Routledge is an imprint of the Taylor & Francis Group, an informa business

First issued in paperback 2020

British Library Cataloguing-in-Publication Data
A catalogue record for this book is available from the British Library

Library of Congress Cataloging-in-Publication Data
Names: Zuccaro Marchi, Leonardo, author. | Avermaete, Tom, writer of
    foreword. | Viganò, Paola, 1961– writer of foreword. | Gregotti, Vittorio,
    writer of afterword.
Title: The heart of the city : legacy and complexity of a modern design idea /
    Leonardo Zuccaro Marchi.
Description: New York : Routledge, 2018. | Includes bibliographical
    references and index.
Identifiers: LCCN 2017035017 | ISBN 9781472483041 (hardback) |
    ISBN 9781315557298 (ebook)
Subjects: LCSH: Public spaces. | City planning—Philosophy. | International
    Congresses for Modern Architecture (8th : 1951 : Hoddesdon,
    England)—Influence.
Classification: LCC NA9053.S6 Z83 2018 | DDC 720.1—dc23
LC record available at https://lccn.loc.gov/2017035017

ISBN: 978-1-4724-8304-1 (hbk)
ISBN: 978-0-367-50203-4 (pbk)

Typeset in Sabon
by Apex CoVantage, LLC

MIX
Paper from
responsible sources
FSC C013985

Printed in the United Kingdom
by Henry Ling Limited

To my son Edoardo
and to our family.

Contents

Figures

Foreword

Bodily metaphors and urban metamorphosis: the vicissitudes and potentials of an organic figure

> The notion that the city might be thought of as an organism, a notion that came with the rise of biology in the eighteenth and nineteenth centuries . . . is the most prevalent among planning professionals today, and the enthusiasm for this outlook is spreading daily among lay citizens.[1]
>
> Kevin Lynch, *A Theory of Good City Form*

In one of his well-known publications, *A Theory on Good City Form*, the American urban planner and theorist Kevin Lynch noticed several decades ago that he had long felt drawn to the tempting idea to analyse the city as if it were an organism. He added that he found it regrettable "that the world may not be so."[2] Others, like the historian François Bédarida, put it more strongly: "the idea to consider the city as a body is irresistible."[3]

In common language, metaphors as the "arteries of the city" and "urban lungs" are well established and understandable, but also in the professional discourse on the architecture of the city there is a long pedigree of conceiving a parallelism or isomorphism between the body and the city. If we disregard Plato for a moment, who did compare the work of city officials with the care of doctors for the human body (Plato, Republic V), thinking in organic metaphors of the city seems to start around 1500 in the work of the Italian architect and theorist Francesco di Giorgio Martini. He postulated that the parts of which the city is composed hold similarities to body parts. A century later, his compatriot and colleague Vincenzo Scamozzi developed this analogy by specifying that the streets of the city are its veins.[4]

According to Richard Sennett, subsequent centuries saw an increasing projection of anatomic and physiological knowledge on the city and urban life. Sennett recalls, for example, that correlations can be discovered between reflections on skin and urban cleaning, between William Harvey's discovery of blood circulation at the beginning of the seventeenth century and new traffic circulation patterns in various nineteenth century cities as well as between new insights about healthy respiratory systems and the emergence of new types of city parks.[5] The Parisian water supply and sewer system which was developed by Baron Haussmann in the second half of the nineteenth century – and wherefore much of the medieval town was destructed – is, according to the historian David P. Jordan, a direct result of his thinking in organic metaphors. Haussmann held that just as the outside of a body does not reveal how the digestion proceeds, so the beauty of the city should not be affected by the functioning of its digesting organs that are hidden under her skin.[6]

The nineteenth century British town reformers such as Ebenezer Howard were also fascinated by the analogy of the functioning of the human body and that of rapidly developing cities. Graeme Davison and Martin Melosi have shown that different experts such as planners, hygienists, statisticians and economists relied time and time again on bodily metaphors. They considered cities like bodies, of which the whole was greater than its constituents, which were subject to processes of growth, change and decay, adaptation and homeostasis. Such processes regulated the urban-social health as temperature, blood circulation, digestion and breathing do in the body.[7] The most radical interpretations were based on the assumption that society, because it is composed of individuals, could in structure and function be compared with an organism.[8] The attraction of the organic analogy seems to have been fuelled by the large developments in the field of biology and evolutionary theory in the second half of the nineteenth century.

Kevin Lynch claims,

> Giants created the organic theory of settlement in the 19th century and carried out is development in the twentieth: men like Patrick Geddes and his successor Lewis Mumford; Frederick Law Olmsted, the American landscape architect; the socialist reformer Ebenezer Howard; regionalist like Howard Odum and Benton McKaye; Clarence Perry who set forth the neighborhood unit idea; Arthur Glikson, the ecologist who dreamed of human communities and regional landscapes as harmonious wholes; and a number of designers who applied these ideas in detail, such as Henry Wright and Raymond Unwin.[9]

The statement of Lynch makes it clear that we are not dealing here with the first and best way of urban thinking. The organic metaphor seems to be a perennial and robust *modus* of the *logos* and *praxis* of urban design and planning. Time and time again, this *modus* has offered designers and planners a conceptual base to understand existing urban conditions and to imagine new figures of urban development.

It is against this background that the introduction of the metaphor of the "Heart of the City" needs to be situated. The eighth *Congrès International d'Architecture Moderne* (CIAM) in 1951 in Hoddesdon, titled "The Heart of the City," was the culmination of a series of CIAM in which the original ideal of the functional city had been questioned. This initial ideal was, among others, based on the zoning of urban functions and on a perspective of unlimited urban expansion. In the post-war CIAM, several serious debates were held on the way to create centrality and cohesion within the ever-growing city, but also on how new urban neighbourhoods would install a sense of identity. These new considerations were paired within the CIAM, with a growing attention for the monumentality of the city and for its historical dimension, which had been largely expelled from CIAM discourse before the Second World War.

The renewed attention for centrality, cohesion and identity cannot be disconnected from the specific historical matrix from which it emerged. It is no coincidence that the devastation caused during the Second World War to the inner cities of Europe functioned as a backdrop for the ideological and conceptual definition of the Heart of the City. In addition, the entire debate on the Heart of the City should be situated against the horizon of a growing awareness of the symbolic significance of the city as the embodiment of human values. The attempts to design the city centre as a place of the community, as well as the quest for urban identity, were nothing new in 1951. Voelker Welter has argued that its roots go back to the Scottish planner Patrick Geddes and the investigations into the "city crown" of the German architect and urban planner Bruno Taut. The metaphor of the Heart of the City bares resemblances to, but also differs from, these historical precedents.

It is the contribution of Leonardo Zuccaro Marchi that offers an in-depth exploration of one of the most central organic, or more precisely corporal, metaphors of urban thinking: the Heart of the City. Zuccaro illustrates how the long-standing tradition of organic urban thinking was, once again, reinvigorated in the second part of the twentieth century within the discourse on the modern architecture of the city. The notion of the "Heart of the City" would at once become a sharp instrument of internal critique *vis-à-vis* pre-war planning ideals and a powerful design concept for future urban planning in modern avant-garde organisations such as the CIAM. Also beyond this high modernist discourse the metaphor of the heart would play a central role. This was, for instance, the case in the work of Victor Gruen, who used the notion of the heart to fashion his own position, which was simultaneously compliant with and critical of the dispersed model of urban development in North America.

The Heart of the City, however, not only served as a lens and mode of critique. Quite on the contrary, it also became a *modus cogitandi et operandi* for new urban developments. This is especially what the architects that contributed to the CIAM illustrated: in their work, the Heart of the City is not an abstract and detached construct but offers a metaphorical frame to conceive and design new urban environments. Worldwide, many CIAM architects designed new cities and urban extensions based partially on the concept of the heart. Meanwhile, the notion of the "Heart of the City" became gradually a part of everyday discourses on the development of towns, among others, in the debate on urban redevelopment in the Netherlands.

Specific for the metaphor of the heart is that it suggests the presence – *in absentia* – of an entire set of other urban organs. It is impossible to conceive of the metaphor without taking into consideration the veins, arteries, lungs and other organs that complement the urban body. In other words, the heart metaphor introduces centrality but only on the condition that it is thought as part of an entire organism surrounding it. Kevin Lynch formulates this as such:

> Perhaps, it is the holistic view which is the most important contribution of organic theory: the habit of looking at a settlement as a whole of many functions, whose diverse elements (even if not strictly separable) are in constant and supportive interchange, and where process and form are indivisible.[10]

This ontological interrelatedness might also explain the contemporary interest for the heart metaphor in ecological discourses on the city.

Organic metaphors, such as the heart, did not remain without criticism. The American sociologist Peter Langer, for instance, has compared four categories of metaphorical thinking on the city: bazaar, jungle, organism and machine.[11] Langer argues that the organic metaphor focuses mainly on macroscopic issues and leaves the small-scale characteristics of the city out of sight. He also claims that organic metaphors as the heart are too often used as exclusively positive tropes, while others such as "jungle" and "machine" mainly as negative ones. On the use of the organic metaphor, Langer suggests that it paradoxically mainly focuses on general and comprehensive planning and on "the characteristics of the system in the making," and much less on the "processes by which individuals create the city."[12] The heart metaphor, though intentionally introduced to correct urban visions and developments that were considered negative, does not seem to be exclusively positively charged or value free. Quite the contrary.

As a big proponent, Kevin Lynch also did not refrain from commentary. He claimed that the organic metaphor of the city would be

> even more apt if it could divest itself of its preoccupation with simple plant and animal associations, with limits, stabilities, boundaries, hierarchies, autarchies, and inevitable biological responses. Incorporating purpose and culture, and especially the ability to learn and change, might provide us with a far more coherent and defensible model of the city.[13]

If one critique can be uttered vis-à-vis the thinkers of "Heart of the City," it would be that they started to conceive some of these cultural and adaptive dimensions but did not fully develop them. This might be considered a flaw, but it can also be understood as a challenge for contemporary urban thinking and practice that needs – once again – to rearticulate the productive resonance between the body metaphor and urban metamorphosis.

In the contribution of Leonardo Zuccaro Marchi, the contemporary relevance of the Heart of the City metaphor is highlighted through the rigorous reconstruction of its utilisation by a group of "actors" that crosses the second half of the twentieth century: the First Urban Design Conference held in Harvard in 1956, the CIAM Summer School in Venice and Jaap Bakema, a Dutch architect connecting two worlds and two different discourses, those of CIAM and Team 10. In the reconstruction of non-obvious relations among these actors, Zuccaro Marchi reveals some underinvestigated continuities among them which help to understand the great stability of the Heart of the City as a metaphor and as a concept able to structure the city project until very recent times. It is the case of Richard Rogers' contribution to the *Grand Paris de l'agglomération parisienne* (2009) which has reproposed a reading of the big city as a body provided with organs to support the need to reconnect the different parts of the *banlieue* (Great Paris) to its Heart (the "small" Paris).

Easily communicable, easily visualised, easily discussed, the Heart of the City is, nevertheless, highly ideologically charged: it advocates the social role of public space and mix-use; it associates the notion of heart to urbanity, with high density and continuity as media. No heart without relatively high densities, no heart without streets and squares, spaces ever more distant from the open configurations of the civic centre elaborated by Modern Urbanism and well represented by Le Corbusier's St Dié project, its most famous prototype.

Without a critical distance in approaching and using the metaphor, today the Heart of the City can easily lead towards the design of nostalgic or mimetic spaces, simulacra of communitarian aspirations.

The organic metaphors and analogies to which the Heart of the City belongs contain a strong deterministic vision and are easily used as a legitimisation of design choices which might be totally inconsistent with any other point of view.

Different from evolutionist models, organic and corporal metaphors are not useful to understand and interpret urban-social change. In fact, evolutionist models, although inspired by life, do not assume, as organic metaphors do, that society and the city behave as organisms (rise and decline are not mandatory, for example), or be composed like a body. In their static and deterministic representation lie the Heart of the City limits.

Leonardo Zuccaro Marchi critically considers the return of the Heart of the City in the contemporary debate and, out of the metaphor, he observes it from the point of view of some of the projects generated by it, in particular, through the three actors he patiently follows. More interesting, in fact, is the idea of studying the outcome of such a strong metaphorical and ideological construction and to consider the importance that metaphor-inspired design explorations can tell us today.

The shift is to recognise that the Heart of the City has also been a concrete urban material, a fundamental brick in the construction of the city. We do not need to adhere to the entire metaphorical system to develop a proposal for new centralities, places of social exchange and recognisability. From this point of view, the book opens up to a contemporary reflection on the civic value of space: that space the heart tries to symbolise with its own strong image.

In the words of Le Corbusier at Hoddesdon, the idea of civic centre constitutes the "problem" to which modern architects, urban designers and urbanists had to give form. This same problem exists today, in a more extended and diffuse urban condition and with a weaker legitimation of designers to actually design and realise the Heart of the City. The metaphor is increasingly forced into a space inevitably tied up with consumerism and leisure culture, still part of a contemporary possible spatial translation of terms as collective, public, civic.

In the always provisional and incomplete quest for civic space, Giedion's questions about the concrete nature of such a space – how is it composed and constituted? where did it emerge spontaneously? what form does it have? – are still relevant today. It is not only the single episode that counts, but also the idea of city the heart can help to realise. It is the occasion, as proposed by Le Corbusier in Hoddesdon, to rethink the structure of urban space.

When we assume the radical transformations of the urban space (radical if we compare the contemporary city to that of the Modern Movement), we fully understand the difficulty of reintroducing such an almost obsolete theme as the "civic centre," or Heart of the City, and not only because of the harsh criticism that followed the initial enthusiasm created by the Hoddesdon Congress.

How can the fragmented and scattered metropolis cope with the expression, in space, of values that are not solely individual, but contain the aspiration to become common? How can design imagine a civic space for individuals, or molecular groups only occasionally playing as society? These are the questions that contemporary architecture and urban design have pushed aside and deserve more attention and effort. If the extended and diffuse city is the expression of the subject's autonomisation, the ambition to represent the innovation in social practices as a civic centre, a core, or a heart remains a "problem." Probably more complicated than in the past.

The revelation of a space of differences advocated by Henri Lefebvre,[14] the idiorrhythmic configurations of small groups in search of separation and distinction, described by Roland Barthes[15] can partially explain the flaws of many Hearts of the City, where architecture and urban design had difficulties to absorb and represent the evolving and innovative practices of urban space in too abstract or too general ideas of community.

The Heart of the City is a challenging topic to reconsider today, where the possibility for the coexistence of populations, differences, practices is probably the most critical object to imagine a space for. The work of Leonardo Zuccaro Marchi is an important contribution towards a critical reconsideration of the Heart of the City metaphor and its multifarious relations to urban material.

Tom Avermaete,
Professor of Architecture at the
Chair of Methods & Analysis
at TU Delft.

Paola Viganò,
Professor for Urban Theory and
Urban Design at EPFL and Professor
in Urbanism at IUAV University.

Notes

1 Kevin Lynch, *A Theory of Good City Form* (Cambridge, MA: MIT Press), 89.
2 Ibid., 88.
3 François Bédarida, "The French Approach to Urban History: An Assessment of Recent Methodological Trends," in *The Pursuit of Urban History*, ed. Derek Fraser, Anthony Sutcliffe (London: Edward Arnold, 1983), 395–407.
4 Albert Erich Brinckmann, *Platz und Monument: Untersuchungen zur Geschichte und Asthetik der Stadtbaukunst in neuerer Zeit* (Berlin: Ernst Wasmuth, 1912), 30.
5 Richard Sennett, *Flesh and Stone: The Body and the City in Western Civilization* (New York: Norton, 1994), 255–271.
6 David P. Jordan, *Transforming Paris: The Life and Labours of Baron Haussmann* (New York: The Free Press, 1995), 271.
7 Graeme Davison, "The City as a Natural System: Theories of Urban Society in Early Nineteenth Century Britain," in *The Pursuit of Urban History*, 357. Martin V. Melosi, "The Place of the City in Environmental History," *Environmental History Review*, 17, no. 1 (1993): 1–23.
8 Elizabeth Grosz, "Bodies-Cities," in *Places Through the Body*, ed. Heidi Nast, Steve Pile (London: Routledge, 1998), 31–38.
9 Lynch, *A Theory of Good City Form*, 90.
10 Ibid., 98.
11 Peter Langer, "Sociology – Four Images of Organized Diversity: Bazaar, Jungle, Organism, and Machine," in *Cities of the Mind*, ed. Lloyd Rodwin, Robert M. Hollister (New York and London: Plenum Press, 1984), 97–118.
12 Ibid., 110.
13 Lynch, *A Theory of Good City Form*, 98.
14 Henri Lefebvre, *La production de l'espace* (Paris: Anthropos, 1974).
15 Roland Barthes, *Comment vivre ensemble*, Cours et séminaires au Collège de France (1976–1977) (Paris: Seuil, IMEC, 2002).

Preface

The book focuses on both the historical and theoretical reinterpretation of the Heart of the City Idea, which was introduced at CIAM 8 in 1951 and has played an important role in architectural and urban debates ever since. It is a comparative history-theory, which traces the social-spatial role and character of transdisciplinary encounters and migrations on the concept of the Heart of the City.

The main aim is to illustrate the continuity and the complexity of this pivotal theme, highlighting a new perspective on the significance of public space in our contemporary urban condition as well.

In an age of rapid urbanisation and fast transformations of the public realm, the book is also of interest to compare to our current attempts at planning and thinking about the city. Indeed, the Heart of the City has many links and resonances with our contemporary debate about the centrality and the identity and with the right public space design. It is a theoretical discourse which has been often exposed as a specific post-war debate; on the contrary, its complex interpretations have many layers of significance which have many reflections on the contemporary social, physical structure of the city.

Furthermore, within the dissolution of the contemporary urban elements, or their legibility, we need to go back and study the essentials that lie at the foundations of the urban structure. The Heart of the City is certainly one of them. It is a Constituent Element at the basement of the urban structure dealing with the balance between the private and the public spheres, between the social and physical structure of the city. The issue of the Heart of the City is the question of the symbolical and physical reform of the structure of the city through the creation of centres of social life.

After the first chapter that reveals the debate which occurred at CIAM 8, three actors are used in order to dissect the complexity of the Heart of the City theme, similarly to the sections of a complex project or territory. These sections reveal three different relationships: the First Urban Design Conference at Harvard in 1956 and Victor Gruen, and the Heart as Urban Design and Invention of the City; the CIAM Summer School in Venice in the 1950s and the Heart of the City as Continuity; Jaap Bakema and the Heart of the City as Total Relationship. The failures, successes and contradictions of the theories and projects of the three actors are important key studies for contemporary design of the City.

Acknowledgements

This book is the result of a reinterpretative and rewriting process of my PhD thesis, presented and defended at both IUAV and TU Delft University in 2013.

Therefore, I owe my greatest debt first of all to my advisors. I must express my profound appreciation to Tom Avermaete for his continuous, precise and encouraging advice, reviews, references and support. Probably, this book would not be possible without him. Some topics discussed in the book are coherent with and profoundly linked to his chair of Methods and Analysis at TU Delft where I taught. I am also grateful to Paola Viganò and Bernardo Secchi who always engaged me in useful and insightful critical debates about the city. The death of Secchi made me reflect upon his ideas and I was impressed to recognise how much his influence affected me. Alessandro De Magistris deserves my deepest thanks for his enthusiasm and support on the topic of the research from the beginning. I also wish to thank Michiel Riedijk and the members of the PhD commission for their critiques and help in deepening concrete and particular issues about the Heart.

I am also grateful to Joseph Rykwert for the breakfast discussions we had in Venice, to David Grahame Shane for our tours in Padova and his important comments and help. Moreover, I was honoured to discuss some topics of this research with Vittorio Gregotti who enthusiastically participated in a conference I organised at IUAV in 2013 on the subject of CIAM 8. He also generously agreed to write the afterword of this book, as a direct witness of CIAM 8 whose legacy influenced his Architect life.

Furthermore, my research on the Heart of the City has deeper roots than the PhD program. I started to study and interpret Gruen and his legacy during my Master thesis at Politecnico di Milano. Therefore, I am grateful to the professors and friends who (in)directly influenced my research, while framing my first period of development as an Architect. Although they are probably not aware of it, I am deeply indebted to Ivo Covic, Cino Zucchi, de Magistris again, Sergio Crotti, Guya Bertelli, Gianluca Catellani, Luigi Trentin, Rossella Salerno, Anna Zaretti and others.

Regarding the archive material, my work was facilitated by several archives and institutions. I am particularly grateful to Ines Zalduendo who allowed me to visit Frances Loeb Archive at GSD Harvard, and she continued to help me until the end of the book. During my research, I have enjoyed the hospitality of the Canadian Centre for Architecture (CCA), so I wish to thank Mirko Zardini and Phyllis Lambert. My research relied also on other archives such as gta/ETH in Zurich, Archivio Progetti at IUAV, ArkDes Stockholm and Het Nieuwe Instituut in Rotterdam. I express my gratitude to all the archivists who were patient with my inquiries and who generously gave their time helping me with curiosity and passion.

I would like to express my appreciation also to private foundations who financed my PhD research, such as Onaosi, Rotary International and in particular to *Stimuleringsfonds Creatieve Industrie*, thanks to which the costs of this book were partially covered. I also wish to thank Angela who helped me with my English errors.

Finally, my deepest thanks go to my family, from my grandfather, the most acculturated person I have ever met who couldn't read all his books before the end of his life, to my son Edoardo who gave me new energy for everything, including this book. I express my gratitude to my parents, to my brother and to Gabriella for their help and for the importance they always gave to the cultural-artistic aspects in life. I thank Giulia, my wife, who lovingly and patiently waited for the end of my PhD research and this book now, always thinking that wind turbine blades would be a more useful research.

Abbreviations

Abbreviation	source
AA	Library of the Architectural Association, London.
Arkdes	The Swedish centre for architecture and design, Archive, Stockholm.
Bake	Bakema Archive, Het Nieuwe Instituut, Rotterdam.
BROX	Architectenbureau Van den Broek en Bakema/Archief, Het Nieuwe Instituut, Rotterdam.
CCA	Canadian Centre for Architecture, Montreal.
FLC	Fondation Le Corbusier, Paris.
GSD	Archive, Frances Loeb Library, Harvard Graduate School of Design, Cambridge, Massachusetts.
gta/ETH	Archive, Institut für Geschichte und Theorie der Architektur (gta), ETH Zurich.
IUAV archive	Archivio Progetti, fondo Egle Renata Trincanato, IUAV University, Venice.
JLS	The Josep Lluís Sert Collection, Frances Loeb Library, GSD Harvard.
JT	Jaqueline Tyrwhitt Archive, gta/ETH, Zurich.
RIBA	British Architectural Library, Royal Institute of British Architects: Manuscript and Archives Collection, London.
SG	Sigfried Giedion Collection, gta/ETH, Zurich.
TTEN	A. en P. Smithson. Archiefdeel Team 10/Archivalia, Het Nieuwe Instituut, Rotterdam.
TyJ	Jaqueline Tyrwhitt Archive, RIBA, London.

Part I

Preamble

The heart and the CIAM's discourse

Introduction

The heart and the city

HERE IS . . .
A new book about people
And the space around them
And how the space has been filled . . .
And you – the architect, designer, city planner – are also trying to make the city the best possible to live in, which is why you will want to read this book.[1]

Russell F. Neale, Introduction to *The Heart of the City*,
Pellegrini and Cudahy edition, 1952

This book is centred on the complex and ambiguous relationship between an abstract organic metaphor and its interpretative use and influence on the corporeal urban structure: the Heart of the City.

This encounter between the city and the heart, the "palpable and [the] verbal, [the] 'objectal' and [the] semantic"[2] is a spirally recurrent topic in the history of urbanism and still affects our contemporary urban and social condition. The strong association between the city and the human body is archetypical and it is so insightful that in antiquity the secret and inaccessible structure of the body was interpreted and understood through the structure of the city rather than the contrary: "the human body was as a city,"[3] as the urbanist Bernardo Secchi remembered. Hence, also the heart of the City can be assumed as one of the "certain continuous things running through history,"[4] as an archetypical idea of public space, a preconscious a priori, universally recognised or even "the eternal present."[5]

As far as our condition is concerned, the image of the heart remains a contemporary "central organ of internalized humanity in the dominant language games of our civilization,"[6] thanks to its "capacity for relationships – in all places at all times" according to the well-known philosopher Peter Sloterdijk.

Consequently, when attributed to the city, the heart refers to the innermost essence of its public life, to the identity and rights of the public realm, to the proper balance between the private and the public, to the ideal conjunction between the social and physical structure of the city, which are still important, unresolved contemporary issues: "We shall start out from the one point accessible to us, the one eternal center of all things." – Jacob Burckhardt claimed as early as 1868, and Giedion recalled in his discourse about the Heart in the 1950s – "We shall study the recurrent, constant, and typical as echoing in us and intelligible through us."[7]

The Heart of the City is certainly part of this intangible echo, becoming of paramount importance in the face of the fear of the vanishing city, or its legibility, and the dissolution of the contemporary urban elements, as described by Secchi who radically highlighted the contemporary need to go back and study the socio-spatial "elements which lie at the foundations of the urban structure."[8] The Heart of the City is certainly one of them; it is a Constituent Element at the base of the urban structure. Christopher Alexander recently described it as "positive space"[9] or "necessary binding force that creates the core of every city"[10] and its social-spatial relationships.

With reference to these topics, the book critically illustrates the continuity and the complexity of the theme of the Heart of the City, as a multifaceted social and spatial category which lies at the crossroads of the intellectual-theoretical and architectural-design worlds. The aim of the book is to unearth the different levels of significance of the Heart of the City, historically and theoretically analysing its concepts within the post-war architectural debate, and to detect the links and brand new perspectives on the significance of public space in our contemporary urban condition. As Michel Foucault stated when describing his idea of the "history of the present":

> The game is to try to detect those things which have not yet been talked about, those things that, at the present time, introduce, show, give some more or less vague indications of the fragility of our system of thought, in our way of reflecting, in our practices.[11]

Today's urgency to tackle our contemporary political, social fragility of system of thought through "Elementarism"[12] and the constituent elements of the public sphere, through the "Fundamentals"[13] of our practice and everyday life embraces the ambition of this book about the Heart of the City.

This is clear if we really look back at and analyse the issues relating to the formation of our modern structure of society and the city in the post-war period and consider the topic of the Heart as the "question of the reform of the structure of the city," through "the creation of centres of social life"[14] as Le Corbusier had already proposed it under the elitist umbrella of CIAM – "*Congrès Internationaux d'Architecture Moderne*," in 1951.

From CIAM to CIAM 8

CIAM was the most institutional, highly cultural and exclusive group of the last century. In the 1960s, Banham defined it "the official Establishment of architecture in our time."[15] Founded in 1928 in the castle of Mme Hélène de Mandrot in La Sarraz, CIAM was officially disrupted in 1959 in Otterlo by the progressive ideas of a younger generation of architects who had been raised in its womb and were later called the Team 10. In its thirty-year life, CIAM had certainly played a pivotal role in framing and contaminating architectural-urban thinking worldwide. Within the CIAM, the "C" standing for "Congress" was first used and selected for its original sense of collaboration, of "marching together"[16] as described by the Swiss historian Sigfried Giedion. It soon shifted into a trench[17] of avant-garde, as "the basis of a new architecture"[18] which was destined to influence both the theoretical debate on the city and its physical, corporeal configuration up until the present day.

In particular, CIAM's last period of life coincided with the base for worldwide theoretical and urban design activity of the last sixty years. Therefore, studying the

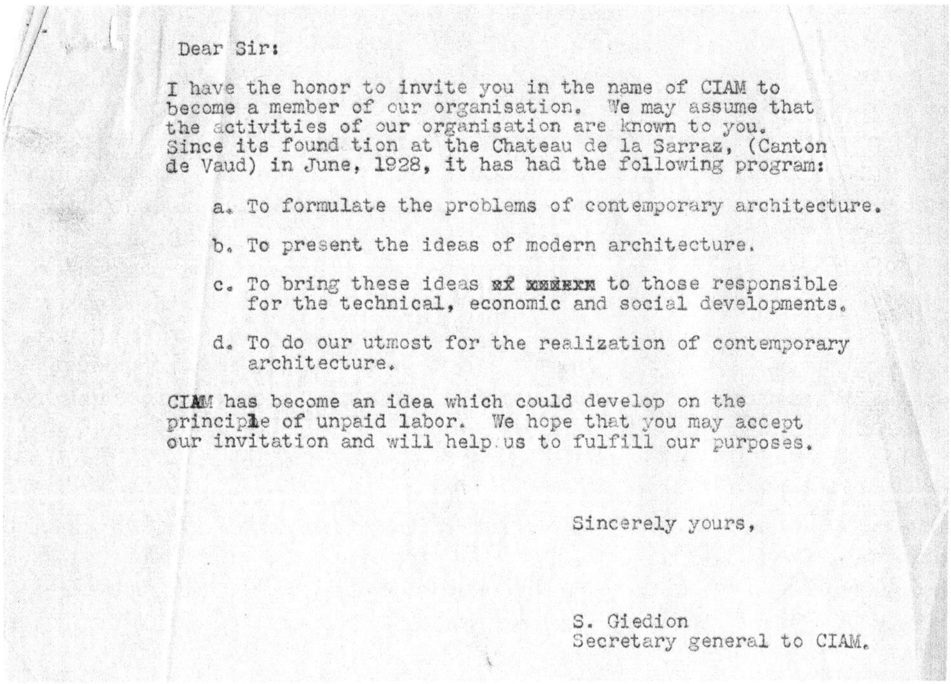

```
      Dear Sir:

      I have the honor to invite you in the name of CIAM to
      become a member of our organisation.  We may assume that
      the activities of our organisation are known to you.
      Since its found tion at the Chateau de la Sarraz, (Canton
      de Vaud) in June, 1928, it has had the following program:

          a. To formulate the problems of contemporary architecture.

          b. To present the ideas of modern architecture.

          c. To bring these ideas xx xxxxxx to those responsible
             for the technical, economic and social developments.

          d. To do our utmost for the realization of contemporary
             architecture.

      CIAM has become an idea which could develop on the
      principle of unpaid labor.  We hope that you may accept
      our invitation and will help us to fulfill our purposes.



                                      Sincerely yours,




                                      S. Giedion
                                      Secretary general to CIAM.
```

Figure I.1 CIAM, Invitation Letter to New CIAM Members.

Source: CIAM Collection C7. Courtesy of the Frances Loeb Library, Harvard Graduate School of Design.

last CIAM movement means studying our nearest origins and their current influence on our profession. This thesis is supported by Vittorio Gregotti who, as pupil of the Italian CIAM member Ernesto Nathan Rogers, stressed that the post-war CIAM has transmitted the essence of the Modern, offering the basic work materials for the younger generations, which are still working and sharing their values and criticisms.[19]

As far as the CIAM 8 is concerned, the years after the Second World War coincided within CIAM with a passage from orthodox functionalism to open humanism, from the abstract machine-age interpretations to other "regional variation, history, and politics as well as socio-economic and anthropological interpretations"[20] (Grahame Shane). This critical passage was already evident in 1951 during the CIAM 8: the debate on the contradictory and pervasive figure of speech of the Heart traced the shift from the analytical, "universalist and exclusive approach"[21] (Pedret) of both theoretical and urban compartmentalisation of the orthodox pre-war CIAM to a comprehensive synthetic idea of anthropological habitat.[22] Indeed the Heart became part of the new humanism and existentialism, as already highlighted by de Solà-Morales and Curtis.[23] It even "represented the collapse of Modern Architecture"[24] according to Grahame Shane, becoming a counterforce to the zoning method of planning, of the division into four functions (dwelling, work, recreation and transport) of the Charter of Athens, to the rational development methods of "The Functional City" of the 1930s which emphasised and mythologised the heroic first decades of CIAM. CIAM's discourse on the Heart also became the "precursor"[25] of the later discourse on Urban Design in the US and it activated an "epistemological shift towards the ordinary everyday life"[26] which became central in the notion of habitat as later discussed by Team 10.

Therefore, CIAM 8 embodied a deep complexity of values and significance that can be hardly compressed within the mere issue of post-war reconstruction, as generally – and erroneously – thought.[27] The same issue of reconstruction enhanced different arguments about the commercial, political, sculptural and symbolical aspect of the heart. Furthermore, its complex interpretations have many layers of significance which have many reflections on the contemporary social and physical structure of the city. Its influence is still present today, "as a reference point for the new forms of public space,"[28] as already highlighted by Mumford. This has already been highlighted by several historians in the recent decades, but without a complete frame of interpretation of the theme.

Moreover, the need for a discipline for the appropriate design of public space seems as valid today as it was in the 1950s. "The elements of social life, the associative life, are in decay. Where can the masses gather?"[29] Giedion asked in the 1950s while a similar question can also be posed in the contemporary debate about the design of public space. The heart undeniably seems to be recognised as a valid humanistic idea and urban design concept which needs to be uncovered today.

Two decades of transatlantic flows of ideas of the Heart

The CIAM 8 discourse had direct and indirect influences in different urban contexts around the world. The flow of ideas starting from the meeting at Hoddesdon, which have not yet been fully described, was particularly intense in Europe and in the US. The case studies given in this book mostly concern these two continents, though other contexts might be part of the discourse too.[30]

This is evident also from the sites of the projects presented in Hoddesdon in 1951. As shown in the map published in 1952, seven projects were situated in America, twelve in Europe and only one in India and in Japan. Of course, this geography of the Cores is due to the preponderant participation of the European and American architects at CIAM 8. Moreover, this transatlantic discourse about the Heart of City even preceded CIAM 8, as Konstanze Domhardt previously highlighted when analysing the influences between the CIAM discourses on the city centre and the American neighbourhood unit theory, from 1937 until 1951.[31]

Finally, the investigated flows of ideas starting from CIAM 8 are mostly concentrated within the twenty years after the Hoddesdon Congress. Russell Hitchcock considered these two decades, the 1950s and 1960s, as the outstanding ones for the production of urban and suburban structure within which we are destined to continue to live.[32] We can then consider the heart theme as part of this urban production we are still interacting with. The clear references to CIAM 8 will be less evident or even interrupted at the beginning of the 1970s, due to different new urban conditions which will focus the attention of critics and architects on different issues.[33]

Heart as in-between: metaphor and symbol

The heart was hailed as the sun, indeed as the king,
yet closer inspection reveals no more than a muscle.

Niels Stensen, Opera philosophica[34]

As far as the conceptual role of the Heart and its "imponderable nature"[35](CIAM 8) are concerned, the Heart of the City is characterised by interesting and contradictory conditions that define and cause its complexity of definitions. One of these conditions, which is stressed throughout the book, is its Janus-faced semantic load, both as functionalist metaphor and humanist symbol. We can therefore consider the Heart of the City as a double entity, which is probably one of the main reasons for its theoretical ambiguity.

As an organic metaphor (from Greek "*Metaphoria,*" which meant "to transfer"),[36] the urban structure mirrors the presumed physical properties of the organ: the urban heart is compared with an organ of limited size and growth, with a precise position and relationship with other organs, and whose function is to pump blood.[37]

As a symbol (from the Greek "*Symbolon*" meaning "to throw together"),[38] the heart becomes "an intellectualized image"[39] (Ricoeur), with a social and humanist aim. It is focused on the relationship between physical space and society, always implying "an emotional investment."[40]

This ambivalence between metaphor and symbol, which was brought to the fore at CIAM 8, is somehow mirrored in the historical concept of the Heart itself which is ambiguously divided between Descartes' mechanistic approach and Harvey's vitalistic belief, between a pure mechanistic process of actions and reactions and the reinterpretations of "pre-ideas" of the soul. Thomas Fuchs, who analysed this ambiguous issue, concluded that the synchronic overlapping perspectives on this polarity and ambivalent points of view remain open even today.[41] Similarly, the Heart of the City is also a pervasive contemporary topic and its metaphorical-symbolical substance is often merged together. Moreover, when the image of the Heart is grounded and applied to the structure of the city, its interpretations become even more complex and indefinite.

In spite of the abstract essence, the cultural domain of the Heart persists. This was already stressed at CIAM 8 by the Dutch Opbouw Group, who primarily described the Heart of the City as an Idea and it has recently been reiterated by Tom Avermaete who depicted the Heart of the City as "an element of urban culture,"[42] which neither purely refer to the physical matter, nor only to the social issue.

Finally, these dual essences affect the relationship between the social and physical presence of the public space, contradictorily shifting between antagonistic expressions of Power-Control and Freedom-Democracy, and vice versa. Indeed, the cultural and semantic interpretation, the abstract and physical translation of the Heart, imply a contradictory reading and design of the city. This contradiction and complexity within the Heart, which have varied over the centuries, are analysed and reinterpreted via their etymological meanings, several case studies and some most intriguing reflections on the organic city in this book.

As far as the carried metaphorical image of the human organ is concerned,[43] many authors have highlighted its critical use in a potentially misleading and open-to-criticism discourse, as "an elusive concept"[44] (Kevin Lynch), as a reassuring and conservative analogy within a "system of knowledge or power that are in decline"[45] (Henri Lefebvre), where functionalism and organicism share "a common root and the cause of their weakness,"[46] as uncovered by Aldo Rossi. Indeed, within the city as a human body, "the most pervasive and powerful metaphor in any discourse about the city"[47] since the Renaissance, the form, location and role of the organs of the human body are predetermined without a real conjunction with existing life. As a result, the possible harmony of the body of the city could degenerate into an uncontrollable "monster"[48] rather than a harmonious human relationship.

A relevant historical example is the "nonetheless delightful project"[49] proposed by architect Pierre Rousseau in 1760 and unearthed by Foucault in "Security, Territory and Population" in 1978. Rousseau considered the reconstruction and beautification of Nantes through a boulevard-promenade with a heart-like form ensuring the circulation of the blood: the problem of urban mobility was supposed to be resolved using a "good form having to be the support of the exact exercise of the function."[50] The post-structuralist philosopher uncovered this functionalist interpretation of the heart, the Saint Simonian metaphor[51] of urban circulation as an arterial flow, emphasising its expression of power within society. Within the functionalist town of the eighteenth century, Foucault was interested in the heart-like form of the circulatory system of Nantes as the main characteristic at stake in this functionalist notion of "*milieu.*" Its relationship with the human being became a determinant and critical factor for the freedom and social activity of each individual.[52]

The Heart as Power has also been recently analysed by the philosopher Peter Sloterdijk. In his book *Bubbles-Spheres I*, the author highlighted, on the one hand, the emotional-spiritual symbol of the Heart through the domain of Christianity and, on the other, its dictatorial image.

With regard to this latter image, the philosopher compared the "Platonic image of the sun's kingship' in the cosmos with the heart as the monarch in the world of animal-human bodies."[53] Until the first decades of the seventeenth century, the Sun-King corresponded to the Heart-King, both "absolute givers,"[54] since the Sun and the Heart functioned in the manner of radiation, from the centre to the extremities without return, as considered by the coeval anatomical studies. Hence, the Heart of Power did influence not only the physical and social structure of the city but also the scientific anatomical research on the human body itself. This cardiological power, typical of the monarchy, was then first opposed by the anatomists who tried to ground and mechanise the heart from its absolute image of the Sun to mere machine, "demoting it from a king of the organs to a leading functionary in the blood circulation."[55] In "*L'homme machine*" (1747), Julien Offray de La Mettrie finally celebrated the enlightened human machine as an expression of the satisfaction of human freedom from the previous cardiological power of the monarch.

Interestingly, this liberation and the relationship between Heart and Machine with regard to Power were destined to be inverted three centuries later at CIAM 8. If in the eighteenth century a new human machine concept played the role of freeing humans from the temporal and spiritual dictatorship of the Heart-king, then three centuries later in Hoddesdon the Heart was conversely considered as the renovated humanist symbol against the "tyranny of mechanical tools,"[56] a symbolic counterforce of the "mechanized killing"[57] which led to the horror of the Second World War, as stressed by Giedion in 1951.

The Heart turned into a positive image which resembled, in the words of Hannah Arendt, the "proper place for human excellence;"[58] it was a new symbol of post-war humanism which responded as a counterforce to totalitarianism and mass destruction.[59] The book of CIAM 8, *The Heart of the City*[60] with the subtitle "Towards the humanisation of urban life," already stressed this real symbolical aim of the CIAM 8: it embodied a new rising humanism, instead of a mere comparison of the city with an organic structure.

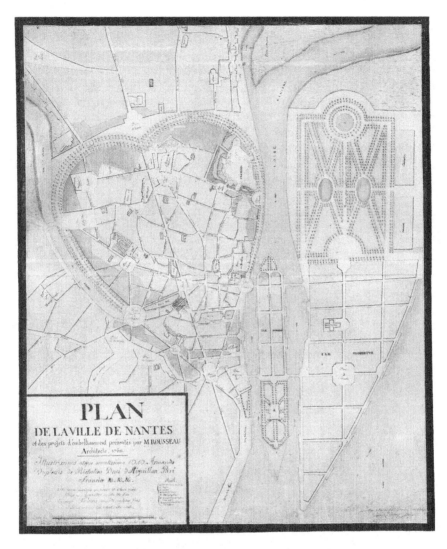

Figure I.2 Rousseau Pierre, *Plan de la ville de Nantes et des Projets d'Embellissement Présentés par Mr Rousseau Architecte*, 1760.

The plan shows the relationship between functionalism and organic metaphor. The form of a heart ensures the circulation of blood-traffic.

Source: © ArchivesNantes – Plan II157/13.

Some of the CIAM members, such as Sigfried Giedion, underlined this abstract interpretation during CIAM 8 in 1951. While many participants tarnished the symbolical meaning of the Heart with unclear definitions and project proposals on centralities, centres or functionalist divisions, Giedion hardly made any considerations about the physical form of the heart. This latter became a new social symbol of an appropriate relationship between the private and public realm, between collective and individual activities, or simply between "You and Me."[61] Giedion did not confuse a

direct translation of abstract social and humanist values with the physical characteristics of the human organ: if the organic metaphor might presume a predetermined
dimension, scale, growth, function and relationship with other organs, then the symbol of the heart is linked to an abstract idea of social public well-being which has to
be translated and interpreted by the architect, without any prearranged physical form,
dimension or role.

Finally, in front of this ambivalence between the functionalist metaphor and the
humanist symbol, a general frame of interpretation of the Heart theme is still lacking,
and there is still a narrow use of the "Heart of the City" theme in some contemporary
urban theories and projects. Hence, this book aims to shed light on the productive
theoretical ambiguity which first occurred in Hoddesdon, focusing particular attention on the continuity and complexity of the idea of the Heart by analysing three main

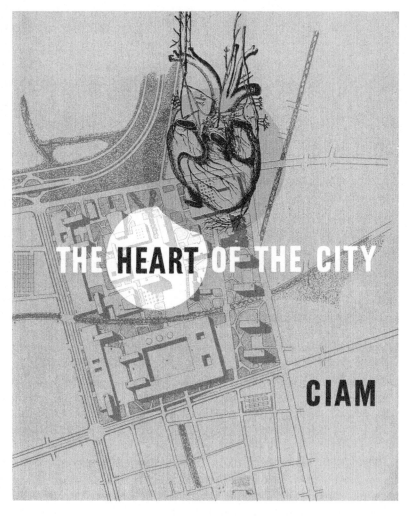

Figure I.3 Book Cover, CIAM 8, *The Heart of the City: Towards the Humanisation of Urban
Life*, 1952.

Source: CIAM Collection B6A. Courtesy of the Frances Loeb Library, Harvard Graduate School of Design.

actors: The Urban Design Conference and Victor Gruen, Jaap Bakema and the CIAM Summer School in Venice.

Anatomy of the heart: three actors

As far as the theoretical influence of CIAM 8 is concerned, we can consider the different layers of significance of the heart theme, or arteries of the heart if we want to keep the metaphor alive, as branches of a cultural phylogeny tree. Defined by the anthropologist Kroeber, the phylogeny tree differs from a classical tree structure due to its overlapping branches which melt, hybridise with the others, similarly to the semi-lattice structure outlined by Christopher Alexander.[62] The difference is well described by Carlos Martí Arís in his book "*Le variazioni dell'identità. Il tipo in Architettura,*"[63] where the author describes the natural tree as the "biological phylogeny" compared with the "cultural phylogeny,"[64] symbolising the complexity of "the mechanism of the human creation." For Arís, "biological phylogeny" represents the classification of elements while "cultural phylogeny" is the transformation of the typological forms and culture.[65] As a cultural and typological tree, the "cultural phylogeny" tree therefore seems to perfectly represent the stratification and interaction of the different arteries of meaning of the heart Idea, deriving symbolically from a main trunk, the CIAM 8, and melting together through history.

Since it is not possible to describe each single branch of a tree, even of a natural tree, three main "actors" have been identified in order to horizontally dissect the symbolic branches, intersecting the most important ideas and issues regarding the Heart of the City, in the same way as sections of a complex project or territory.

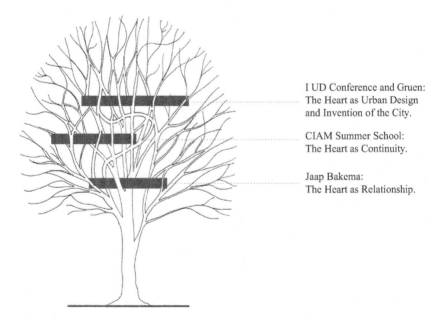

I UD Conference and Gruen:
The Heart as Urban Design
and Invention of the City.

CIAM Summer School:
The Heart as Continuity.

Jaap Bakema:
The Heart as Relationship.

Figure I.4 Scheme, Three Main Actors and the Cultural Phylogeny Tree by Kroeber (redrawn and modified by the author).

Source: Redrawn and modified with the three actors by the author, from Carlos Martí Arís, *Le variazioni dell'Identità. Il tipo in Architettura*, 49.

The three actors have been selected because they best stress the continuity or legacy of CIAM 8, with all its contradictions, exposing an insightful balance between the theoretical apparatus and the design experimentations on the Heart of the City. Moreover, their failures and successes have become important lessons for present-day Urban Design. Indeed, they help specify the context of the Heart theme, delineating some of the theoretical issues and project devices which still concern contemporary urban planning.[66]

Each of these actors represents a main theme or process of the city in the last sixty years. The Urban Design Conference and Victor Gruen represent the renewal of the city in America through urban design (the Heart idea as Urban Design and invention of the city). The CIAM Summer School in Venice represents the rising importance of tradition, of Rogers' continuity, of the recognised role of history and its context within the modern project (the Heart as continuity). Last, Bakema represents the physical interpretation of an abstract Idea of the heart, relying on the relationships between the urban factors as the main issue for the city's sociological and physical structure (the Heart as relationship). The Invention of the City, the Continuity of the City and the Relationships within the City might therefore be considered the three main themes stemming from the Heart Idea, and which connect the other main arteries of interpretation, as discussed in the book, with many contemporary resonances.

Three actors: flows of ideas and contemporary legacy

I actor: I UD conference and Victor Gruen

THE HEART AS URBAN DESIGN AND INVENTION OF THE CITY

The First Urban Design Conference at Harvard, 1956   In the second half of the 1950s, while Team 10 was dissolving and rescinding CIAM, as well as questioning the concept of the Core, the continuity of the CIAM discussion was assured overseas, as Eric Mumford had already described.[67] The CIAM president, Josep Lluís Sert (1902–1983), was appointed Dean at Harvard University in 1953 and many other CIAM members were engaged there too, basing their research directly on the CIAM 8 discussion. In 1956, Sert organised the First Urban Design Conference at Harvard, reiterating many issues that had been discussed in Hoddesdon, such as the need for a three-dimensional design of the city, the need for a synergy between different professional figures acting on the city structure, the rights of the pedestrian and the need for centralisation of the city.

As far as the passage from CIAM 8 to the First Urban Design Conference is concerned, the CIAM President and Dean Sert focused his attention on two specific opposite urban conditions: the reconstruction and recentralisation of the city. The debate about the Heart of the City tackled the resilience of the decontextualised social-spatial tabula rasa created by the dangerous mechanical progress which led to the horror of the War. But it also dealt with the resilience of embracing, stemming and compressing the "real scandal of Galileo's work . . . , [the] constitution of an infinite, and infinitely open space,"[68] (Foucault) which was, for the first time, mirrored in the urban American sprawl. This latter concern became of paramount importance within the discourse at Harvard in 1956 on the constitution of the discipline of Urban Design.

Finally, this post-war critical urban condition, of both bombed centres and infinite sprawl, became an impressive work-ground on which to rebuild another society, to analyse theoretically the central issues of the city and to propose experimental projects which are now at the basis of our architectural knowledge and contemporary Urban Design. This link with our contemporary condition was particularly brought to the fore in 2006, on the occasion of the fiftieth anniversary of the First Urban Design Conference, when many critics and historians discussed its consequences and, more generally, the role of Urban Design today.[69]

For instance, Richard Marshall stressed that the struggle of Sert and his contemporaries to define the terms of the urbanism problem within CIAM and Harvard "has never really ended."[70] Eric Mumford highlighted too that the issues formulated during the 1950s and 1960s are still current, even the "Heart of the City" theme.[71] In particular, there is "a direct linear development from this post-war CIAM focus on the urban core to more recent thinking about pedestrian-based urban design"[72] as Eric Mumford believes.

Contrariwise, Christopher Alexander claimed that some of the positive proposals discussed in the 1950s and directly linked to the heart theme have totally failed during the last sixty years because of a lack of "a significant invention of new structure in the realm of urban space."[73] In his essay about the Heart of the City, Alexander began, not by coincidence, by describing and criticising the 1956 First Urban Design Conference, and consequently CIAM 8 as its "precursor":[74] "One might say the brutal landscape of modern urban design and modern city-building, was largely caused by the kind of thinking which was articulated at the 1956 conference."[75] Alexander dramatically accused the 1956 Conference for its unawareness, its incapacity to focus attention on public space as the generator of the city, leading to the crisis of contemporary public space, which still affects our everyday life and still needs to be tackled. Indeed, if the twentieth century CIAM members failed in the reorganisation of the structure of the city toward the "positive space" of the Heart of the City, as "a genuinely new concept requiring the remaking of space," then this remains "what we 21st-Century architects, now must deliver,"[76] claimed the Austrian-born architect, underlying the importance of contemporary discourse about the Heart of the City. Hence, facing the failure of the First UD Conference, the complexity of the Heart of the City still remains a vibrant and open theoretical idea which needs to be developed further, both as a theoretical concept and physical public urban reality.

Victor Gruen   The American discourse of Urban Design in the 1950s also intersected with the commercial design of the "mall maker"[77] Victor Gruen (Vienna, 1903–1980). Gruen participated in the First Urban Design Conference in 1956 and, not by coincidence, wrote *The Heart of Our Cities: The Urban Crisis: Diagnosis and Cure* in 1964, a decade after the book about CIAM 8 *The Heart of the City: Towards the Humanisation of Urban Life* was released.

This chapter investigates the hidden encounters and influences between the avant-garde of CIAM and the mass consumption of Gruen's theories and projects. It reconsiders the effects on society by exploring some ideas shared by both post-war CIAM and Gruen, such as the need for centralisation, the symbolical and functionalist split between vehicular and pedestrian flows. This transatlantic flow of ideas and references were developed until the 1970s in Gruen's far-sighted manifesto – "Die Charta von Wien" (The Charter of Vienna). Fifteen years later at the moral death of CIAM in Dubrovnik at the hands of the young Team 10 members, Gruen raised the legacy of CIAM, detecting a possible continuity of the Modern Movement and developing the commercial architectural principles experimented in the American context into ecological urban planning proposals.

As far as Gruen's practice is concerned, in the US he explored a dialectic profession between the architectural and the urban scale, between private commercial spaces and public spaces; he highlighted and developed a crucial interaction between the design interest and the theoretical one, care for the environment and "high-culture" modernist references. These latter radically influenced the design of his shopping centre which however "quite never escaped a second-class architectural citizenship"[78] in the history books, as Smiley already commented. This seems too profoundly in contradiction with Gruen's pivotal role regarding the commercial evolution of the public sphere and its contradictory relationship. If, in 1987, Fishman affirmed that the future of the great metropolis "will dwindle to what we would today call a massive shopping mall"[79] and a few years later Margaret Crawford stated that "the world of the shopping mall . . . has become the world,"[80] then Victor Gruen was certainly one of the main actors of this contemporary realised utopia.[81]

II actor: Venice CIAM Summer School

THE HEART AS "CONTINUITY"

The second actor is focused on the relationship between CIAM 8 and the CIAM Summer Schools in Venice. During CIAM 8, the education committee decided to move the summer school from London to Venice, where it was held five times, from 1952 until 1957. The young participants included some of the most important modern and contemporary architects, such as Denise Scott Brown, Vittorio Gregotti, John Turner and Reima Pietilä, while many of the architects and tutors who were present in Venice were members of both CIAM and Team 10.

"Venice" as Tafuri later described the city – "she can be seen as the place in which antitheses have been removed, in which dialectics has no function, in which there is no contradiction between tradition and innovation, development and memory, continuity and renewal, sacred and mundane."[82]

Apropos of this unique urban condition, lying between tradition and innovation, nature and pre-existence, suspended memory and lack of antithesis, between the old obsession to build everything, "even the ground and the water,"[83] and its fragility in front of nature itself, the CIAM Summer School in Venice became a pivotal opportunity to either demonstrate, uncover or criticise the ideologies of the main congresses.

During the summer school, Venice became a fertile, concrete, common laboratory where the abstract ideas of CIAM were grounded, situated[84] and negotiated for the first time through the analysis and projects of the younger generation and its confrontation with the older CIAM generation. In the encounter with the neutral platform of CIAM, Venice, the "heart of a dispersed and complex city"[85] immersed in the "amniotic liquid"[86] of the lagoon, radically turned into the "City of the new Modernity"[87] – as later described by Tafuri and Gregotti. Venice became an important lesson and experience for Modernity and the Modern Movement, which needed Venice more than the contrary, an excellent contemporary "place of history[88] . . . , as idea of the project as dialogue."[89]

Indeed, the CIAM Summer School of Venice was proof of the renewed interest of all CIAM in history and context, which became a main issue during the following decades, and still is today.

This theme has been well described since 1950s within the Italian cultural milieu, in particular by Ernesto Nathan Rogers in *Casabella Continuità*, and it was emphasised for the first time at international level at CIAM 8. In fact, according to Gregotti, the Hoddesdon meeting became the embryonic moment for a broader international debate about continuity, modification, context and contextualism, about "listening to the context and of the project seen as a dialogue with the context as a deposited form of the history of a specific place."[90]

III actor: Jaap Bakema

THE HEART AS RELATIONSHIP

The third and last actor is the Dutch architect Jaap Bakema (1914–1981), whose presence was relevant both for his theoretical contribution to and administrative organisation of CIAM, and later at Team 10.

The most relevant aspect of Bakema highlighted in the book is that he radically tackled the problem of extracting the "language of the city" from the purely abstract symbolical stage – a problem also stressed by Roland Barthes in his discourse on urban semiology[91] – translating and actively reinterpreting the idea of the Heart into a physical project. Among the CIAM members, Bakema was able to both propose the most non-figurative, intangible aspect of the heart and to later transpose and ground his idea into the physicality of the urban structure, also providing a pivotal lesson to our contemporary role of the architect.

As far as the abstract Heart is concerned, unlike other CIAM members, Bakema considered the total "relationship" as the main characteristic of the Heart. Indeed, he revealed the "moment of the Core" as a pure system of "relationship between man and things,"[92] highlighting the rising role of relationship and relativity as a basic theoretical concept, main "common ground" and "paradigm of the twentieth-century culture"[93] (Kuhn, 1962; Strauven, 1998) in architecture as well as in philosophy, and also in other disciplines such as physics and art. Moreover, the Heart was conceived as representative or a symbol of a collective social "abstract idea . . . fluctuating from one place to another"[94] (Opbouw Group) which had to be actively translated by the architect into physical form.

His abstract and provocative idea of the Heart – Bakema mentioned the Asplund cemetery in Stockholm as first example of Heart – was later interpreted and grounded in the US. The main case study is his project for the "humane core"[95] of St Louis in 1960. Almost ten years after CIAM 8, Bakema reconsidered the Heart theme, stressing the importance of its historical background, its three-dimensionality and the relationship between the social and physical urban structure of the City.

In St Louis, the Heart was mentioned in order to highlight the proper and resilient overlaying of the social and physical structure and to symbolise the ideal "architecture of the city as the structure of society."[96] The final master plan was a translation of this overlapping interpretation of the Heart Idea without any direct representative or functionalist references to organic form or structure. The project is an intriguing example of an accurate and sophisticated translation of the abstract idea of the heart into an urban physical and social form. It reveals a prolific and useful *praxis*, a process of realised theory, for our contemporary method of design and thinking.

Finally, the Heart relied on a contradictory discourse which enhanced and stimulated urban design and thinking when faced with the radical urban transformation of the city which occurred globally during and after the War. From the tangible binomial reconstruction-recentralisation of the urban Core and the symbolical abstract resilience of the Heart as a constituent element at the foundation of the urban structure, the heart introduced an anthropological idea of Habitat as an integrating part of the human settlement, later developed within Team 10.

If the failures of CIAM (Frampton)[97] and of the First Urban Design Conference (Alexander)[98] were surprisingly caused by the incapacity of a "significant invention of new structure in the realm of urban space,"[99] then the idea of Heart with its countless interpretations remains a theoretical ground that is still fertile and open for further interpretation and investigation.

Notes

1 Russell F. Neale, Introduction "The Heart of the City" to Pellegrini and Cudahy, GSD, CIAM collection B6A.
2 Eleonore Kofman, Elizabeth Lebas, Henri Lefebvre, Stuart Elden, ed., *Henri Lefebvre: Key Writings* (New York: Continuum, 2003), 126. Originally published in French: Lefebvre Henri, "Foreword" to *L'Habitat pavilionaire*, ed. Henri Raymond, Nicole Haumont, Marie-Geneviève Raymond, Antoine Haumont (Paris: CRU, 1966).
3 "Since antiquity the human body and the city have been metaphorically linked; but in antiquity, when the human body was the difficult entity to understand, it was the body to be like a city." Bernardo Secchi, *La prima lezione di urbanistica* (Roma: Laterza, 2000). Bernardo Secchi, "A New Urban Question 3: When, Why and How Some Fundamental Metaphors Were Used," in *Metaphors in Architecture and Urbanism: An Introduction*, ed. Andri Gerber, Brent Patterson (Bielefeld: Transcript Verlag, 2013), 125.
4 Sigfried Giedion, "Historical Background to the Core," in *The Heart of the City: Towards the Humanisation of Urban Life*, ed. Jaqueline Tyrwhitt, Josep Lluís Sert, Ernesto N. Rogers (London: L. Humphries, 1952), 18.
5 The interpretation in Giedion of the core as an eternal element is already underlined by Francis Strauven. He affirms that Giedion's discourse about the Heart "ties in closely with the research into 'the eternal present' he was engaged in at the time, a search for the original archetypes of art and architecture, for the primal, prehistoric forms that he saw simultaneously reemerging in the art of the contemporary avant-garde. He regards the core as an urban archetype, as the place where the individual can participate in public life." Francis Strauven, *Aldo van Eyck: The Shape of Relativity* (Amsterdam: Architectura & Natura, 1998), 238. See also Sigfried Giedion, *The Eternal Present: I. The Beginnings of Art* (New York: Bollingen Foundation, Pantheon Books, 1962). Sigfried Giedion, *The Eternal Present: 2 The Beginnings of Architecture* (New York: Bollingen Foundation, Pantheon Books, 1964).
6 "The heart has by no means been equated with the deepest interior of humans – one could also call it the source of their sense of self and their capacity for relationships – in all places at all times." Peter Sloterdijk, *Bubbles: Spheres Volume I: Microspherology*, trans. Wieland Hoban (Los Angeles: Semiotext(e), 2011), 101 originally published as Peter Sloterdijk, *Sphären I: Blasen, Mikrosphärologie* (Frankfurt: Suhrkamp, 1998).
7 Jacob Burckhardt, *Force and Freedom, Reflections on History* (New York: Pantheon Books, 1943), 81–85. Quoted in Giedion, *The Eternal Present: The Beginnings of Art*, iv. Sigfried Giedion, *Architecture You and Me* (Cambridge: Harvard University Press, 1958), 109.
8 Bernardo Secchi, *Conversation During PhD at IUAV Venice* (26 March 2012).

9 The positive space "is coherent space which has the attribute that people want to be there, choose to be there. It has the quality that people feel well in themselves when they are there, and they are capable of experiencing their own life when they are there."

Christopher Alexander, "The Heart of the City. The Necessary Binding Force that Creates the Core of Every City," in *Center for Environmental Structure*, ed. Maggie Moore Alexander (2006), 5. Accessed on July 8, 2016, www.livingneighborhoods.org/library/the-heart-of-the-city-v18.pdf

See also Christopher Alexander, Sara Ishikawa, Murray Silverstein eds., "Pattern # 106," in *A Pattern Language* (New York: Oxford University Press, Center for Environmental Structure, 1977), 517–523.

10 "This essay invites a journey of non-traditional thought about architecture and urban design, and proposes a science of context-sensitive, harmony-seeking, shape-forming process focused on generating and shaping positive space in all public places, so that the overall urban process will be able, in the hands of thousands of professionals and users – to generate inspiring, useful space throughout the city and throughout the region." Alexander, *The Heart of the City*, 2.

11 Sylvere Lotringer, ed., *Foucault Live: Collected Interviews, 1961–1984* (New York: Semiotext(e), 1996), 411.

12 See Paola Viganò, *La città elementare* (Milano: Skira, 1999), 7.

13 OMA's "Fundamentals" at the Venice Biennale 2014 was mainly focused on the elements of architecture, such as the balcony, the window, the door, the toilet and so on. Here we state the urban fundamentals are even more relevant and urgent to study for our contemporary fragile condition.

14 "*The question of the Core – of the creation of centres of social life – is really the question of the reform of the structure of the city*" Le Corbusier, "Conversation at CIAM 8," in *The Heart of the City: Towards the Humanisation of Urban Life*, ed. Jaqueline Tyrwhitt, Josep Lluís Sert, Ernesto N. Rogers (London: L. Humphries, 1952), 39. Quoted also in Viganò, *La città elementare*, 87.

15 Reiner Banham, *The Architecture of the Well-Tempered Environment* (Chicago: University of Chicago Press, 1969), 143.

16 "The association then formed was called the *Congres Internationaux d'Architectyure Moderne* – in abbreviation, the C.I.A.M. The word 'congress' was used in its original sense of a 'marching together'. It is a congress based on collaboration, not a congress in which everyone merely contributes circumscribed knowledge from his own special field, as in the nineteenth century."

Sigfried Giedion, "Introduction," in *Can Our City Survive? An ABC of Urban Problems, Their Analysis, Their Solutions*, ed. Josep Lluís Sert (Cambridge: The Harvard University Press, Cambridge, 1944), ix.

17 According to Martí Arís, the word "avant-garde" stems from war-terminology, referring to the invasion in enemy territory, in order to occupy strategic positions. When the avant-garde reaches its goal, it disappears and it is replaced by other forces which are able to consolidate the result. See Carlos Martí Arís, *Silenzi Eloquenti* (Milano: Christian Marinotti, 2002), 29.

18 Joseph F. Hudnut, "Foreword," in *Can Our City Survive?*, iv.

19 Vittorio Gregotti, "Editoriale – Gli Ultimi CIAM," *Rassegna*, 52, no. 4 (1992): 5.

20 David Grahame Shane, "The Street in the Twentieth Century. Three Conferences: London (1910), Athens (1933), Hoddesdon (1951)," *The Cornell Journal of Architecture* 2 (1983): 41.

21 Annie Pedret, "Representing History or Describing Historical Reality?: The Universal and the Individual in the 1950s," in *Universal Versus Individual: The Architecture of the 1960s* (Finland: Alvar Aalto Academy; Alvar Aalto Museum: Helsinky; University of Art and Design: Jyväskylä, 2002), 82–85. Accessed on February 25, 2017, www.alvaraalto.fi/conferences/universal/finalpapers/annie.pedret.rtf

22 Later CIAM and Team 10's discourse about Habitat reiterated the Heart's multidisciplinary approach, its anthropological definition and its critiques to the factionalist analytical urban division. The discourse about Habitat fostered the complex topic of the human relationship with its social-spatial context, whose research already started with the Heart of the City-CIAM 8 discourse.

23 See Barry Curtis, "The Heart of the City," in *Non-Plan: Essays on Freedom, Participation and Change in Modern Architecture and Urbanism*, ed. Jonathan Hughes, Simon Sadler (London and New York: Architectural Press, Routledge, 2000), 52–65.
     Ignasi de Solà-Morales,"Architecture and Existentialism," in *Differences: Topographies of Contemporary Architecture* (Cambridge: MIT Press, 1997), 41–56.
24 Grahame Shane, "The Street in the Twentieth Century," 41.
25 Eric Mumford, "Sert and the CIAM 'Heart of the City': Precursor to Urban Design, 1947–52," in *Defining Urban Design: CIAM Architects and the Formation of a Discipline, 1937–69* (New Haven and London: Yale University Press, 2009), 80.
26 See Tom Avermaete, *Another Modern, the Post-War Architecture and Urbanism of Candilis: Josic-Woods* (Rotterdam: NAi Publishers, 2005), 142. "With the term epistemology I refer to the way that architectural knowledge concerning the built environment is acquired, treated and applied." Ibid., 384.
27 Volker M. Welter, "From Locus Genii to Heart of the City: Embracing the Spirit of the City," in *Modernism and the Spirit of the City*, ed. Iain Boyd Whyte (London and New York: Routledge, 2003), 36.
28 For instance: CIAM 8 "was perhaps the first expression of what would become major preoccupations with architect-designed public gathering places in the work of Victor Gruen, Kevin Lynch and many others in the following decades. CIAM 8 can be seen as a reference point for the new forms of public space, including Shopping malls." Eric Mumford, *The CIAM Discourse on Urbanism, 1928–1960* (Cambridge: MIT Press, 2000), 215.
29 "*Gli elementi della vita sociale, della vita associativa, sono in disfacimento. Dove si riuniscono le masse?*" Sigfried Giedion, *Breviario di Architettura* (Milano: first ed. Garzanti, 1961. Torino: Bollati Boringhieri, 2008), 68. Originally published as *Architektur und Gemeinschaft* (Reinbek: Rowohlt, 1956).
30 For instance, the Japanese Metabolist Movement, born in 1960, has many links and resonances with CIAM 8 too: in particular, for Kenzo Tange's participation in the congress in Hoddesdon and the recurrent use of the organic metaphor as a leitmotiv. Tange talks in the 1960s about "core spaces . . . of visual communications spaces" directly referring to the Core of the city, though from a structuralist point of view. See Kenzo Tange, "Function, Structure, Symbol (1966)," in *Kenzo Tange 1946–1969*, ed. Udo Kultermann (Zürich: Verlag für Architecktur Artemis Zürich, 1970), 242.
31 Konstanze Sylva Domhardt, *The Heart of the City: Die Stadt in den transatlantischen Debatten der CIAM 1933–1951* (Zürich: Gta Verlag, 2012).
32 See Virginie Lefebvre, *Paris-Ville Moderne. Maine-Montparnasse et la Défense, 1950–1970* (Paris: ed. Norma, 2003), 19.
33 In 1984, Bernardo Secchi described three different styles of planning with particular attention to the Italian condition: the first, which dominates the 1950s, is concerned with the theory of the urban form and urban growth, repetitively using the organic metaphor; the second, in the 1960s, is more focused on the democratic decision, on the political mediation for the transformation of the territory; the third, in the 1970s, is centred on the social practices operating for the use of the territory. Bernardo Secchi, *Il Racconto Urbanistico. La politica della casa e del territorio in Italia* (Torino: Einaudi, 1984), 60–61.
34 Sloterdijk, *Bubbles*, 101.
35 CIAM, "A Short Outline of the Core," in *The Heart of the City: Towards the Humanisation of Urban Life*, 165.
36 In late fifteenth century: from the French *métaphore*, via Latin from the Greek *metaphora*, from *metapherein* "to transfer." *Oxford English Dictionary*, s.v. "metaphor."
37 See "Problems of organic theory" in Kevin Lynch, *A Theory of Good City Form* (Cambridge: MIT Press, 1981), 95.
38 In late Middle English (denoting the Apostles' Creed): from Latin *symbolum* "symbol, Creed (as the mark of a Christian)," from Greek *symbolon* "mark, token," from "*sun*" – with + "*ballein*" – to throw. *Oxford English Dictionary*, s.v. "symbol."
39 "The symbol is an intellectualized image. What is meant here is that the image provides the basis for 'reasoning by analogy, which remains implicit, but which is necessary to the interpretation of the statement.'" Paul Ricoeur, *The Rule of Metaphor: The Creation of Meaning in Language*, trans. R. Czerny et al. (London and New York: Routledge, 2010), 219. Originally published in Paul Ricoeur, *La métaphore vive* (Paris: Editions du Seuil, 1975).

40 "Symbols, on this view, always imply an emotional investment, an effective charge (fear, attraction, etc.) which is so to speak deposited at a particular place and thereafter 'represented' for the benefit of everyone elsewhere." Henri Lefebvre, *The Production of Space*, trans. Donald Nicholson-Smith (Malden, MA: Blackwell Publishing, 2010), 75–76. Originally published in Henri Lefebvre, *La production de l'espace* (Paris: Anthropos, 1974).

41 "It is not to be assumed that this interplay has found its end in the conceptions of today . . . Walter Pagel has written about Harvey: 'unification of what is today sound and relevant with its apparent opposite,' the attempt to tie together what appears self-contradictory, to allow a synchronic multiplicity of point of view – this could be a way to be fairer to the aspects of the heart and circulation." Thomas Fuchs, *The Mechanization of the Heart: Harvey and Descartes*, trans. Marjorie Grene (Rochester, NY: The University of Rochester Press, 2001), 229.

42 Avermaete, *Another Modern*, 71.

43 As an example of a strict functionalist metaphor of the Heart, in 2009, Richard Rogers proposed a project for the "Grand Paris" where the heart became a metaphor for the restoration of connections to external severed urban limbs, reconstructing the governance of the Ile-de-France with balanced districts.

44 "Optimum size also seems to be an elusive concept. No one has been able to confirm it, and the accepted figure shifts about (it usually rises)." Lynch, *A Theory of Good City Form*, 97.

45 "When an institution loses its birthplace, its original space, and feels threatened, it tends to describe itself as 'organic'. . . It 'naturalizes' itself, looking upon itself and presenting itself as a body. When the city, the state, nature or society itself is no longer clear about what image to present, its representatives resort to the easy solution of evoking the body, head, limbs, blood or nerves. This physical analogy, the idea of an organic space, is thus called upon only by systems of knowledge or an organic space, is thus called upon only by system of knowledge or power that are in decline." Lefebvre, *The Production of Space*, 274.

46 Aldo Rossi, *L'architettura della città* (Padova: Marsilio, 1966; Novara: Citta' Studi, 2006), 36.

47 Secchi, "A New Urban Question 3," 125.

48 Ibid., 125–126.

49 Michel Foucault, "Security, Territory and Population, Lecture One 11 January 1978," in Michel Foucault, *Security, Territory and Population, Lectures at the College de France 1977–78*, eds. Michel Senellart, François Ewald, Alessandro Fontana, trans. Graham Burchell (New York: Palgrave Macmillan, 2009), 17.

50 "I will skip the nonetheless delightful project of an architect called Rousseau who had the idea of reconstructing Nantes around a sort of boulevard-promenade in the form of a heart. It's true that he is dreaming, but the project is nonetheless significant. We can see that the problem was circulation, that is to say, for the town to be a perfect agent of circulation it had to have the form of a heart that ensures the circulation of blood. It's laughable, but after all, at the end of the eighteenth century, with Boullée, Ledoux, and others, architecture still often functions according to such principles, the good form having to be the support of the exact exercise of the function. In actual fact, the projects realized at Nantes did not have the form of the heart." Ibid., 33.

51 See Secchi, "A New Urban Question 3," 126.

52 The functionalist Town of the eighteenth century became the visible case study for the emergence of the relationship between the "naturalness of human species within an artificial *milieu* . . . within the political artifice of a power relation." The centrality within a circle of *Le Maître's Métropolitée*, the grid of the camp in the town of *Richelieu* and the heart-like form of Nantes, as proposed by *Rousseau*, are metaphors of a *milieu* where the circulation and spatial distribution are connected to the sovereignty and political Power. Foucault, "Security, Territory and Population, Lecture one 11 January 1978."

53 Sloterdijk, *Bubbles*, 119–120.

54 Ibid., 123.

55 Ibid., 130.

56 Giedion, "Historical Background to the Core," 17.

57 Giedion, *Architecture You and Me*, 35.

58 Hannah Arendt, *The Human Condition* (Chicago: University of Chicago Press, 1958; Second edition 1998), 49. Citations refer to 1998 edition.

59 See Curtis, "The Heart of the City," 52.

60 Rogers, Tyrwhitt, Sert, *The Heart of the City: Towards the Humanisation of Urban Life*.

61 Giedion, *Architecture You and Me*.

62 "The tree axiom states: A collection of sets forms a tree if and only if, for any two sets that belong to the collection, either one is wholly contained in the other, or else are wholly disjoint . . . The semi-lattice axiom is: A collection of sets forms a semi-lattice if and only if, when two overlapping sets belong to the collection, then the set of elements common to both also belongs to the collection." Christopher Alexander, "A City Is Not a Tree," in *Human Identity in the Urban Environment*, ed. Gwen Bell, Jaqueline Tyrwhitt (London: Penguin Books, 1972), 405–406. Originally published in *Architectural Forum*, 122, no. 1 (April 1965): 58–62.

63 Carlos Martí Arís, *Le variazioni dell'identità. Il tipo in Architettura* (Torino: Clup, 1990).

64 Ibid., 49.

65 Indeed, the overlapping of the semi-lattice structure, which represents the complexity of the structure of the society and of the old natural-cities, has a correspondence with the hybridisation of the types in architecture. The semi-lattice is therefore a valid model simultaneously for the structure of the society, for the structure of the city and for the architectural type as well. See Ibid., 49. See also Philip Steadman, *The Evolution of Design* (Cambridge: University Press, 1979). Alfred Louis Kroeber, *Anthropology: Race, Language, Culture, Psychology, Prehistory* (New York: Harcourt Brace Jovanovich, 1948).

66 As Paola Coppola D'Anna Pignatelli highlights: "The design of a Heart is also nowadays one of the most complex problems of urban planning, because of the lack of a definition specifying its contents." (In Italian: "*La progettazione di un cuore costituisce oggi uno dei problemi più complessi della pianificazione urbana, proprio per una mancanza di una definizione che ne precisi il contenuto.*") Paola Coppola D'Anna Pignatelli, "Cuore della città," in *Dizionario enciclopedico di Architettura e Urbanistica*, ed. Paolo Portoghesi (Roma: Gangemi; I edition 1968, II edition 2006), 120.

67 Eric Mumford, "The Emergence of Urban Design in the Breakup of CIAM," *Harvard Design Magazine* (2006): 15.

68 Michel Foucault, "Of Other Spaces, Heterotopias," *Architecture, Mouvement, Continuité*, 5 (1984): 46–49. Original Publication: *Conférence au Cercle d'études architecturales, 14 Mars 1967*. See also Bernardo Secchi, *La città del ventesimo secolo* (Bari: Laterza, 2005), 155.

69 For instance, Fumihiko Maki affirms that nowadays the issues of the meaning of the central district and of community, as discussed in 1956, are still important. Describing the complexity of Tokyo, he then affirms that Urban Design "*in reality remains a skill that demands their interpretation into three-dimensional space within a fixed time, budget and program.*" Fumihiko Maki, "Fragmentation and Friction as Urban Threats: The post-956 City," in *Urban Design*, ed. Alex Krieger, William S. Saunders (Minneapolis and London: University of Minnesota Press, 2009), 97.

70 "At the 1956 conference, Sert and his contemporaries were driven by the idea that the design professions should claim intellectual and practical territory around the problems of urbanism, but they struggled with how to define the terms of that claim. It seems to me that this struggle has never really ended." Richard Marshall, "The Elusiveness of Urban Design: The Perpetual Problem of Definition and Role," in *Urban Design*, 40.

71 "It is in fact at this time that many ideas about urbanism were formulated in ways that are still current. These ideas include the recognition of the importance the 'heart of the city' as a place of urban pedestrian life and cultural institutions, the need to better organize traffic circulation patterns, and the value of the natural environment as part of urbanism, as well as the absence of an overtly partisan political justification for strengthening the central city." Mumford, "The Emergence of Urban Design in the Breakup of CIAM," in *Urban Design*, 31–32.

72 Mumford, *Defining Urban Design*, 80.

73 Alexander, *The Heart of the City*, 3.

74 Mumford, "Sert and the CIAM 'Heart of the City': Precursor to Urban Design, 1947–52," in *Defining Urban Design*, 80.

75 He then lists all the problems or failures which he recognises in the last fifty years of Urban Design:

- "lack of positive urban space
- failure to resolve the car
- lack of variation
- gigantism
- a view of the city as a machine, not as an organism
- lack of attention on the suburbs
- lack of attention on 90% of the Earth which is in a state of poverty
- failure in the economy of cities
- failure in class and social divisions"

Alexander, *The Heart of the City*, 3.
76 Ibid., 25.
77 M. Jeffrey Hardwick, *Mall Maker: Victor Gruen, Architect of an American Dream* (Philadelphia: University of Pennsylvania Press, 2004).
78 David Smiley, *Pedestrian Modern. Shopping and American Architecture, 1925–1956* (Minneapolis: University of Minnesota Press, 2013), 5.
79 Robert Fishman, *Bourgeois Utopias: The Rise and Fall of Suburbia* (New York: Basic Books, 1987), 187, cited in Timothy Mennel, "Victor Gruen and the Construction of Cold War Utopias," *Journal of Planning History* 3 (2004): 140. Accessed on June 4, 2014, doi:10.1177/1538513204264755.
80 Margaret Crawford, "The World in a Shopping Mall," in *Variations on a Theme Park: The American City and the End of the Public Space*, ed. Michael Sorkin (New York: Hill and Wang, 1992), 6.
81 The utopia of the world as a commercial centre was already preannounced in 1900 by Bradford Peck who, influenced by the *utopian socialism* of Edward Bellamy, published in 1900 *The World a Department Store: A Twentieth Century Utopia*. In the novel, the department store metaphorically incorporated all the world until it absorbed all social and governative functions.
   See Bradford Peck, *The World a Department Store: A Twentieth Century Utopia* (Lewiston: B. Peck, 1900). See also Edward Bellamy, *Looking Backward 2000–1887* (Houghton Mifflin, 1888).
82 Manfredo Tafuri, *Venice and the Renaissance* (Cambridge: MIT Press, 1995), X. Originally published in Italian as *Venezia e il Rinascimento* (Torino: Einaudi, 1985).
83 Originally in Italian: "*L'ossessione di Venezia è stata per secoli quella del costruire; qui la terra è costruita, lo è anche l'acqua.*" Vittorio Gregotti, *Venezia Città della Nuova Modernità* (Venezia: Consorzio Venezia Nuova, 1999), 26.
84 This interpretation was first given by Tom Avermaete, Personal discussion.
85 Gregotti, *Venezia Citta' della Nuova Modernità*, 29.
86 (Originally in Italian: "*la laguna come liquido amniotico in cui Venezia vive.*"), Ibid., 25.
87 In 1993, the historian Manfredo Tafuri gave his lecture for the opening academic year: "*The forms of the time: Venice and the Modernity*" (in Italian: "*Le forme del tempo: Venezia e la modernità*") The architect Vittorio Gregotti refers to Tafuri's lecture as reference for his thesis of Venice as city of new Modernity. Ibid. 12.
88 "But I think that the slogan 'Venice city of the new modernity' has today another significance as well, since I believe that the modern architecture itself needs Venice, place of the history par excellence, since in the last thirty years both the nature and the significance of the notion 'modern' are deeply changed." (Originally in Italian: "*Ma io penso che lo slogan 'Venezia città della nuova modernità' abbia oggi anche un altro significato, perché credo che sia l'architettura moderna da avere bisogno di Venezia, luogo della storia per eccellenza, da quando sono profondamente mutate negli ultimi trent'anni la natura e il significato della nozione di 'moderno'.*") Ibid., 19.
89 (Originally in Italian: "*l'idea di progetto come dialogo*"), Ibid., 34.
90 (Originally in Italian: "*il problema dell'ascolto del contesto, del progetto come dialogo con esso in quanto forma depositata della storia del luogo specifico.*") Gregotti, *Editoriale: Gli Ultimi CIAM*, 5.

91 "The city is a discourse and this discourse is truly a language [. . .] Still the problem is to bring an expression like 'the language of the city' out of the purely metaphorical stage." Roland Barthes, "Semiology and the Urban (1967)," in *Rethinking Architecture: A Reader in Cultural Theory*, ed. Neil Leach (London and New York: Routledge, 1997), 168.

92 Jaap Bakema, "Relationship Between Men and Things," in *The Heart of the City: Towards the Humanisation of Urban Life*, 67.

93 "Relativity forms the common ground of the fundamental innovations of twentieth-century science and art – that to use Kuhn's term it is the paradigm of twentieth-century culture." Strauven, *Aldo van Eyck: The Shape of Relativity*, 423.

94 Opbouw Group, "CIAM 8 Describing the Core of Pendrecht, Responsible Rapporteur: W. Wissing," Het Nieuwe Instituut, Rotterdam, Bakema Archive, g. 18.

95 Jaap Bakema, *The Humane Core: A Civic Center for St. Louis, MO* (Washington, DC: Washington University Press, 1960).

96 Ibid., 2.

97 "CIAM failed and with it Team 10, not because of their formalistic or conflicted ideological projections but rather because there was ultimately no ground left upon which to continue any kind of rational discourse." Kenneth Frampton, "Foreword," in Mumford, *The CIAM Discourse on Urbanism, 1928–1960*, xv.

98 Alexander, *The Heart of the City*, 3.

99 Ibid.

1 CIAM 8

The Heart of the City, towards a new humanism

What Are you?
... You are a human being, living thinking, doing, ...
But, alas, you do nothing with your hands, with your legs,
with your head, with your voice, because you have nowhere
– neither a place nor a building – where you can make a noise,
where you can mess about,
where you can be quiet,
where you can be alone,
where you can be together.[1]

Le Corbusier, CIAM 8, 1951

The Heart of the City discourse at CIAM 8

Dealing with the topic "The Heart of the City," the third CIAM Congress after the War,[2] CIAM 8 took place at High Leigh, in a "lonely Victorian mansion in Hoddesdon,"[3] twenty miles from London, from July 7–14, 1951. The stay in Hoddesdon was combined with some architectural visits[4] to interesting Modern architectural and urban proposals in England, such as the Festival of Britain. The Festival had opened on the South Bank of London in May that year with the aim to celebrate British achievements and influence on civilisation using a festival as a "tonic to the Nation"[5] after the disasters of the wars.

The congress was attended by over 150 members from twenty-two countries, mainly from Europe and North America. The English MARS[6] Group (Modern Architectural Research Group), "the best and most active group in the Congress today,"[7] according to CIAM President Sert, was designated to organise the congress in its home country.

The topic of the Core, which was already proposed by the Dutch CIAM group in the previous meeting in Bergamo in 1949,[8] contradicted a previous desire of Le Corbusier, who instead urged first a discussion on the topic of the Charter of the Habitat[9] as early as 1949.[10]

Contrary to this desire, Sert considered the topic of the Core as more interesting while Gropius agreed to initially consider "the problem of the centers of settlements, you call it the hearts," as more urgent and "organically basic than housing as such." According to the German architect, the heart was conceived as a fundamental, attractive and necessary factor to discuss and design since, "within the whole cycle of human life . . . it reaches really the basic substance of all our doings."[11]

Figure 1.1 Le Corbusier, van Eesteren, Sert, Peressutti, Emery, Alaurant, at CIAM 8 Meeting, Hoddesdon, 1951.

Source: gta/ETH Archive, 42_JT_9_553.

Figure 1.2 De Vries, Chermayeff, Maekawa, van den Brock, at CIAM 8 Meeting, Hoddesdon, 1951.

Source: gta/ETH Archive, 42_JT_9_556.

Figure 1.3 Maekawa, Rogers, Sert with Students, at CIAM 8 Meeting, Hoddesdon, 1951.

Source: gta/ETH Archive, 42_JT_9_558.

Figure 1.4 Rogers at CIAM 8 Meeting, Hoddesdon, 1951.

Source: gta/ETH Archive, 42_JT_9_559.

Figure 1.5 Merkelbach, de Vries, Bakema, at CIAM 8 Meeting, Hoddesdon, 1951.

Source: gta/ETH Archive, 42_JT_9_561.

At the end of 1949, the English CIAM group sent the *"Plan Proposé par MARS pour CIAM 8"*[12] to the other CIAM members. This preliminary text stated that in the previous meetings the four elements, which were introduced in the pre-war CIAM (Dwelling, Work, Cultivation of Mind and Body, Circulation), were already deeply and widely considered. However, another element had to be analysed, "the element which makes the community a community and not merely an aggregate of individuals . . . This is the physical heart of the community, the nucleus, THE CORE."[13]

Hence, the Heart of the City was explained, in the first presentation by the MARS Group, as an added fifth element which completed the previous ones. Remarkably, this definition heightened the misunderstanding and confusion. It was a misleading definition of the Core, which allowed an immediate superficial criticism of the theme, without considering its deeper levels of significance. Indeed, the additional fifth element was contradictorily perceived either as a supplementary updated function or as a counterforce to the previous ones, undermining the entire idea of the Functional City itself.

On the one hand, in the 1950s, some of the young members of CIAM and Team 10, "who knew little or nothing of what had been discussed before the war years,"[14] later perceived this association and supplement of the Core as a mere addition, as a belated attempt to reexamine the analytical approach of the pre-war CIAM.[15]

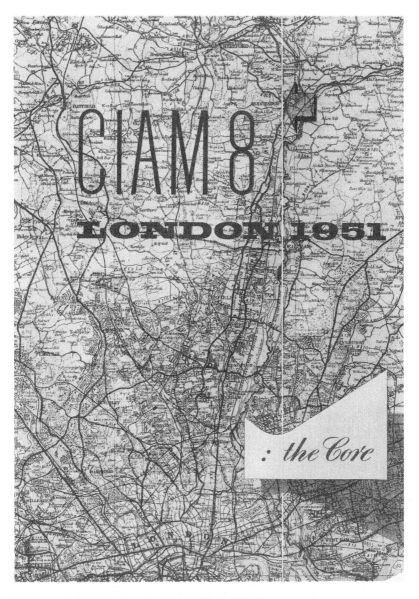

Figure 1.6 Cover, "CIAM 8, London 1951: The CORE."

Source: gta/ETH Archive, 42_JT_7_8.

On the other hand, the choice of Core fulfilled the critiques to the strict functional division of the city which did not "adequately cover the ground of city planning,"[16] as claimed for instance by Lewis Mumford. This latter, in 1940, even refused to write an introduction to Josep Lluís Sert's "Can Our Cities Survive?",[17] where the four functions were described and emphasised. As opposite to the four functions, the heart appeared instead coherent with the plea of the American historian for "the organs of political and cultural association" which embodied "the distinguishing marks of the city"; their negation or absence would merely guarantee "only an urban mass."[18]

Un-definition of the heart

The problematic issue of a correct definition of a single theoretical frame of the heart theme seemed continuously present during the debate at CIAM 8. Indeed, many of the architects present in Hoddesdon showed and expressed several personal and some-times contrasting, significant features of the discussed topic. At CIAM 8, the concept of the Heart of the City was somehow "elastic,"[19] as Grahame Shane already depicted it. The discussion sometimes concerned the right size of the city, the human scale, humanist values, social issues, the emotional feelings of the individual. But it also interpreted the topic of the heart as the background of spontaneity, the meeting place of the arts, the aggregation of individuals, the central square of the city, the function-alist traffic roads as veins and so on.

The heart was defined at different scales and it was characterised by either meta-phorical or symbolic meanings, abstract or physical entities, functionalist or humanist values, between centre or centrality, reconstruction and recentralisation issues.[20]

These contradictions within the productive vagueness of the debate were redeemed in the "Summary of Needs at the Core," at the end of the book in which the CIAM 8 proceedings were reedited by Sert, Tyrwhitt and Rogers. However, the seven points composing the summary were evidently not enough to consider and manifest all the facets of the theme presented in Hoddesdon, nor its deeper historical roots[21] and later influences on the urban worldwide discussion.[22] *De facto* the Core was merely summarised and compressed into a single element in the city, a man-made artefact for pedestrians only, with only controlled commercial advertising and some possible varying mobile elements, which should be designed by architects, in cooperation with painters and sculptors.[23]

Besides this partial summary, what was clearly stated in the conclusions was the somehow spiritual, invisible entity which estranged the discourse on the Heart from an analytical-scientific description[24] and form a strict and mere comparison with the cen-tre of the city or CBD – central business district. At CIAM 8, the simple and simplistic relationship between the "Centre of the City" and "Heart of the City" was not so unadulterated as shown, for instance, twenty years earlier by Le Corbusier in *Aircraft* (1935), where the bird's-eye view of the Philadelphia business quarter of Philadelphia, seen from one of the first flying airplanes, was labelled as "the Heart of the City."[25] Furthermore, even though the projects on the reconstruction of the bombed cities directly dealt with the urban centres (Coventry, Basle, Providence, Lausanne, etc.) and many images of centre squares such as Piazza Duomo in Milan, Piazza San Marco in Venice, Rockefeller Plaza in New York and so on, were largely shown in the publica-tion, the Heart of the City discourse of CIAM 8 did not completely overlap with the central square or with either of the city's historical or commercial barycentres:"The

Figure 1.7 CIAM 8, "Logo": Social Centrality.

Source: In *The Heart of the City: Towards the Humanisation of Urban Life*, ed. Jacqueline Tyrwhitt, Josep Lluís Sert, Ernesto N. Rogers (London: Lund Humphries, 1952), frontispiece.

word 'Core', in the sense we are using it, does not mean merely the centre of the urban agglomeration," – as stated in "A Short Outline of the Core" – "nor the busy heart of the city traffic or economic activity; sometimes it may be united with these areas, but the Core includes other elements, often of an imponderable nature."[26]This "imponderable nature," which was stressed for instance by the Dutch architect Bakema and the Opbouw Group highlighting the abstract, decentred image of the Heart, allowed the discourse to shift from the centre of the city, its downtown or historical centre to a more complex socio-spatial and cultural "centrality" of its social public life. Without this centrality, the human being is inert, as Le Corbusier introduced in his "chapeau" of the publication of CIAM 8: "You are a human being, . . . But, alas, you do nothing with your hands, with your legs, with your head, with your voice, because you have nowhere."[27]

Finally, the shift from a physical centre to a social centrality was also graphically interpreted in the CIAM 8 logo which appeared in the published book of the congress. The starting picture was taken from the top of Piazza Duomo in Milan, but the square and any physical manifestations were erased, leaving only the shapes and shadows of the gathering people as the only presence in a stylised red circle, representing a physical void, a centre of gravity of a humanising process in the City.

Heart as productive ambiguity: synonyms, metaphors and symbols

As already discussed in the introduction, the double entity of both metaphor and symbol concerning the Heart of the City and the possibility of a huge collection of interpretations stemming from these two rhetorical figures were evident at CIAM 8. As Lefebvre later stated in "*La production de l'espace*," while commenting on Nietzsche, the metaphors and metonymies are the attempt to substitute and to go beyond "a chaos of impressions and stimuli."[28] Even though the organic metaphor was not always considered and accepted by CIAM members, a chaos of impressions and interpretations, as described by Lefebvre, around the image of the Core or Heart was apparent at CIAM 8. This lack of clarity of the organic metaphor/symbol was already expressed by Gropius in December 1949, when responding to the MARS proposal, he admitted he had come across "a great confusion and misunderstanding of what the organic elements or heart organs should be."[29]

Besides the interpretative discourse of the organic element and its semiotic misunderstanding, another issue was the different languages at CIAM 8. This problem was mentioned, among others, by the young Christian Norberg-Schulz, who highlighted the difficulty of interacting with his young colleagues "speaking six or seven different languages."[30] The slippage through different languages made the debate difficult but at the same time productive. Although English was chosen as the official language in Hoddesdon,[31] multiple nuances given to the term of the Heart changed according to the language which was adopted and considered. The use of several synonyms and their dissimilar translations in English, French, Italian or other idioms made it difficult to understand even the sense of the term under discussion. Civic Centre, Core, Nucleus, Heart, Hearth in English became *Centre, Cœur, Accueil, rendez-vous* or *Noyau* in French or *Centro, Cuore, Focolare* in Italian, with many even smaller deviations of meanings and weight of concepts.[32] Suddenly, the international presence and character which enforced the idea of CIAM turned into an element of misunderstanding and confusion about the topic of discussion.

Moreover, the request to investigate its meaning, to delineate the architect's frame of intervention within its content, had to face the preconceptions, perceptions and references which were grounded and embedded in each regional cultural background. As recently defined by Topalov, "each language organizes the urban world in a way, by hypothesis, specific."[33] In other words, the issue of language translation was inevitably also a matter of culture, of specific ways to organise and conceive the world which made the understanding of the Heart of the City even more complicated and slippery.

Finally, this problem of a Babelic CIAM became even more crucial in the following years, in particular, during the cultural and generational "language dispute about the word Habitat,"[34] as described by Wogenscky referring to the preparatory CIAM meeting held in Sigtuna, only one year later in 1952.

Core-Heart, an editorial choice

"This was the center, the heart of the city or the core of the city, whichever you may like to call it,"[35] as CIAM's president Sert explained in one version of his Introduction at CIAM 8. The use of the term "Core" rather than "Heart" was indeed almost undefined during the entire congress. In 1950, the CIAM members discussed the pertinence of the term "Core." In a meeting held in June 1950, "it was agreed that the 'CORE' was not the happiest term for the theme." "Centres of Community Life" gave a clearer expression to the ideas, but it was suggested that the MARS Group should try to think of a new word. It was agreed that "'center,' 'nucleus,' 'focus' were all inappropriate."[36] Nevertheless, the MARS Group seemed not to consider this, employing "CORE" directly both in its invitation to CIAM 8 and in the cover page of the official congress material.

During the congress, only a few attempts were made to distinguish the terms "Core" and "Heart of the City." Moreover, the given definitions were almost contradictory, highlighting again the general vagueness of ideas present within CIAM 8. For instance, according to the published book of 1952, the Italian architect Ernesto Nathan Rogers rejected the term "Core" ("*nocciolo*" in Italian), interpreting it as "that part of the fruit that contains the seed, the potential energy of an organism." He admitted he instead preferred the direct human organic metaphor, the heart, because it "has more beats, and also implies the physiological and biological values of sentiment," since it is the "symbolic centre of love."[37]

Nevertheless, other CIAM members contradicted the choice expressed by Rogers. Indeed, at the end of the book, the historian Giedion affirmed that the term "civic centre" is an "over-employed term"; for this reason, "the old English word CORE," defined in the *Oxford English Dictionary* as the "central innermost part, the heart of all"[38] was preferred. The Core was therefore conceived with a more universal and general meaning than the heart; it represented the heart metaphor in all its aspects and all its scales, from the human body to the city itself. Nevertheless, Sert inverted the scale of representation given by the Swiss historian. Answering Batista's question about the difference between the "Core" and the "Neighbourhood Unit," he clarified that "there should be no Neighbourhood Unit without its own small Core, but this is only a local reflection of the main Core – the Heart of the City."[39] If it were possible to admit the presence of different cores in the city, in Sert's opinion, the heart was in this case considered as the main one, whose characteristics and values should be mirrored in different dimensions, inside the smallest cores. However, in the unpublished report on the Hoddesdon Conference proceedings, the word "heart" does not appear in Sert's answer, but is substituted by "the whole subject of Cores."[40]

To conclude, no substantial differences intervened between the two terms, which often fell within pure rhetorical discourses, without deep theoretical impacts and consequences. Looking at the published book in English edited by Sert, Rogers and Tyrwhitt in 1952,[41] "Core" appears more times (in 106 pages) than "Heart" (in twenty-two pages). Though, while the MARS Group entitled the theme of the congress "The Core," which was also mainly used in Hoddesdon, "The Heart" was preferred as the title of the official book of CIAM 8, which was aimed to universally promulgate and popularise the debate of CIAM 8.

Following the considerations about the inappropriateness of the term "Core" as already expressed in 1950, Josep Lluís Sert wrote a letter in September 1951 to Jaqueline Tyrwhitt where he reiterated his doubts about the title adopted by the MARS Group: "Haven't we finally agreed that the title of the book should be THE HEART OF THE CITY? I really believe that the 'CORE' is an unpopular and meaningless word and I definitely believe that it is a mistake to use it in the title."[42] Sert's insistence regarding the title "The Heart of the City" and its "more popular appeal"[43] was demonstrated in several letters to Jaqueline Tyrwhitt, sent during the last months of 1951. Sert's concern about the "Core" was certainly about the misleading problem of a too-direct association with the centre of the city, with its functional central business district, rather than its centrality and symbolical presence. The "Core" could have hidden the cultural, humanistic values which were instead embedded, though vaguely and contradictorily, in the organ metaphor and symbol.[44] The answer of the English planner was simply to choose "the title that will sell best,"[45] without changing the word "core" throughout the book.

Hence, at the end of 1951, the discussion about the Core and the Heart apparently declined into a banal commercial issue. On the contrary, the editorial choice preserved and clarified the humanistic symbolical value of the Heart which was of paramount importance for the editors.

Finally, the official book reporting the CIAM 8 discourses was published in 1952 in English[46] and a few years later in Italian and in Spanish. All the languages corresponded to the nationality of the three editors Tyrwhitt, Rogers and Sert. Moreover, all editions referred to the human organ of the heart (*"cuore"* in Italian, *"corazón"* in Spanish), with the main cover showing the image of the human heart drawn upon a master plan drawing. The heart became the main urban metaphor and image representing and popularising CIAM 8 to the rest of the world, with certain influences on the later Urban Design and theory practice. Finally, these editorial choices theoretically filtered the debate of Hoddesdon, also with differing weights and contents with regard to the meetings and their proceedings, adding other interpretative layers of complexity and somehow fostering our awareness of a certain impossibility to reconstruct a "true" and "complete history" of CIAM.[47]

Heart-hearth, a project of equipoise

Among the multiple interpretations, between metaphorical translation and symbolical rhetoric, functionalist and humanist ideals, the Heart can be arguably considered as a constituent element at the foundation of the urban structure dealing with the right balance between the private and public spheres, with the basic aim "to re-establish an equipoise between the individual and the collective"[48] as argued by Giedion. Indeed, the Swiss historian stressed the necessity to rethink and continuously reshape the labile, proceeding equilibrium, at the centre of the Heart of the City discourse, that Man experiences between "his inner and outer reality, . . . private life and community life, . . . methods of thinking and methods of feeling."[49]

In particular, the interaction between the private hearth of the house and public heart of the city, can be traced in many speeches at CIAM 8. For instance, Bakema and Le Corbusier underlined that all houses have a Core, originally the hearth of a home, but at that time perhaps it had shifted to a mechanised tool, such as a television or a kitchen equipped with modern appliances.[50] It was no coincidence that in the 1940s and 1950s the term "Utility Core" was already used in architectural vocabulary, as Jos Bosman reminds us,[51] referring to the mechanical and technological part of the house that makes it more functional. However, if on the one hand, the private Core had some links with the mechanical architecture, on the other hand, through the urban public interpretation of the Core, CIAM went completely against the idea of machine's supremacy over man, as discussed later.

The Swedish CIAM member, Gregor Paulsson (1890–1977), also focused his discourse on the private house which was considered the first centrality for the community, a point of reference even in a "Coreless community"[52] lacking both identity and centrality. The Swedish historian then went on to study the relationship between animals and plants and their natural sites; more precisely, he reminded participants that ecology is derived from the Greek word *"oikos"* (house) and that the town-planner's task was "to make a good habitat for man as an individual as well as for man as a social animal."[53] In this perspective, the private house and its hearth were the germs of the urban structure and cohesion. Moreover, as early as 1951, Paulsson already introduced the basis of ecology for a discussion on habitat and the house as the organic navel of the entire urban system. His address about the private house anticipated the "language dispute,"[54] which took place at the preparatory CIAM meeting held in 1952 in Sigtuna (Sweden), between "*habiter*" and "habitat," between its functionalist and socio-biological interpretation, its private and more collective conception, its analytical analysis and synthetic research of relationships.

Regarding the projects presented at CIAM 8 which mirrored the equipoise between hearth and heart, the pioneering experiment of Doctors Innes Pearse (1889–1978) and George Scott Williamson (1884–1953), the Health Centre in Peckham (1935–1951), was certainly the most significant one.

Williamson was personally invited to CIAM 8 to show the importance of the "heart theme" within his activities and therefore out of the canonical architectural circle. The doctors' architectural-scientific approach to the Heart of the City was positively received by all CIAM members. Giedion reported, in his book *Architecture You and Me*, that "no one at the eighth congress of CIAM was listened to with greater attention than Dr G. Scott Williamson, founder of the Peckham Health Centre in London, which was indeed a 'core' based on the spontaneous activities of people of all ages."[55] In fact, the presence of a doctor at the CIAM meeting was extremely important in order to enhance a transdisciplinary thinking within CIAM, avoiding "a sort of intellectual CIAM incest,"[56] the archi-centric perspective which was affecting the organisation slightly, as radically denounced by Gropius in 1952.

The Health Centre project was initiated within the welfare debate of Great Britain during the World Wars which also involved Modern architecture, as Elizabeth Darling already explained.[57] The main purpose was to give back a healthy existence to the population mixing social, spatial and medical welfare projects which considered the healthy modernisation of the urban environment. "The most important step towards revitalization of the masses of the people is improvement of their environment,"[58] as Richards affirmed in 1935.

In the 1920s, Doctors Williamson and Pearse sought to develop new care techniques for the health of the community. In 1926, they launched an experiment, founding a club, the Pioneer Health Centre, in Peckham, a small district whose working-class inhabitants became an integral part of the Centre's activity. The investigation into citizens' health was organised in different phases, from 1926 until 1950.

The doctors' "Idea behind the idea,"[59] which should be reflected in the architectural design of the new centre, was founded on the Family, considered as "the Core for human development,"[60] as "the basic unit of the society, the lowest common denominator into which all society can be resolved as well as the natural biological unit."[61] The family had always been considered central and pivotal also in the discourse on the Heart of the City. In the invitation text to the CIAM 8 in Hoddesdon, written by the MARS Group, the family was already depicted as the lowest scale of community which constitutes the Heart of the City. While Ling recognised, during an open session at Hoddesdon, that the "Individual is the root, the Family, the flower and Peckham Health Centre the fruit."[62]

In the doctors' minds the architectural design of the Pioneer Centre should perfectly correspond to this family-in-its-home ideal: it should represent the physical and environmental space for the good growth of family-communities, enclosed within an open building. The private hearth and the public heart should thus coincide in "a lively and directive energy"[63] in order to obtain the best medical and therapeutic results.

The final project proposed by engineer Owen Williams appeared as the right architectural answer to all the requirements for a common social collective sphere, for a "public gaze"[64] where, radically, the "individual members are non-existent."[65] Alienation was abhorred, circulation was not channelled. There was an internal flexibility on all levels, guaranteed by glass panels division and a structural skeleton[66] enabling a free plan. "Freedom, in fact, is the salient characteristic of the plan. The building, from inside, appears to merge into the open air; it is extrovert in character"[67] as Richards described it.

Interestingly, in the Peckham Centre, the Core was constituted by a central swimming pool, a 23 × 10m rectangle of water around which the entire plan is orientated, becoming the central place of social congregation. It is a central void, a three-floor high enclosed chamber, healthily regulating the temperature and humidity of the building through its glass roof and walls.

Dr Pearse defined the Peckham Centre as an "enabling environment,"[68] highlighting the influence of the architectural space on the health of its inhabitants (there were 800–900 households!), who experienced and felt the Centre as an extension of their own home, rather than a clinic, all in one huge single social hearth which is clearly shown in the architectural plan and axonometric sketch drawn by the students from AA, published in the CIAM 8 book.

Finally, this sort of twentieth century health phalanstery project highlighted the importance of the role of the public community within private architectural projects, avoiding a split between the private sphere and the public one. Among the projects

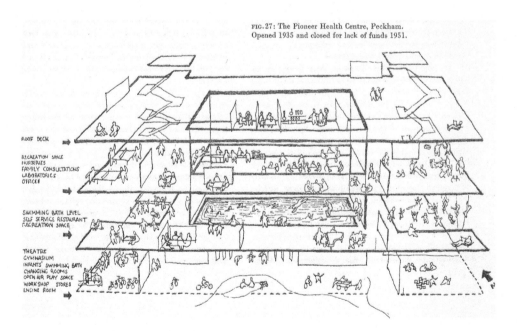

FIG. 27: The Pioneer Health Centre, Peckham.
Opened 1935 and closed for lack of funds 1951.

Figure 1.8 Sketch of Peckham Health Centre, Presented at CIAM 8, 1951. Drawn by Stephen Macfarlane.

Source: Courtesy AA School of Architecture, London. In *The Heart of the City: Towards the Humanisation of Urban Life*, ed. Jaqueline Tyrwhitt, Josep Lluís Sert, Ernesto N. Rogers (London: Lund Humphries, 1952), 30.

presented at CIAM 8, it was also a pivotal example of how the concentration and densification of the community into a well-defined structure with a gathering central point, even an empty one, could enhance the physical health and social relationships of the inhabitants. As already described by Richards in 1935, faced with a "centrifugal tendency of the present-day urban population" and the "lack of any cohesive nucleus within the town, round which the genuine urban life could evolve," the Pioneer Health Centre "provides a focal point at which the town as a workshop coincides with the town as a community."[69] Hence, the centre mirrored and anticipated the need for urban centralisation as a unique healthy and civic anchor, as vehemently praised by Sert and other CIAM members in Hoddesdon and later in a transatlantic discourse about Urban Design. Moreover, the urban hearth of the centre, the "fruit" of Doctors Pearse and Williamson, perfectly reflected and translated into medical method and architectural-urban structure, a certain social idea of community and relationship of the "Heart" described by Giedion as a "a bridge between private life and community life, . . . a place where human contacts between man and man can again be built."[70]

Heart as a symbol of new humanism

> "The *raison d'être* of symbolism . . . lies in the human
> need to represent what is unrepresentable."[71]

Giedion, 1950

Giedion and the symbol

In the published proceedings of the CIAM 8, "The Heart of the City," the subtitle "Towards the humanisation of urban life" highlighted the real aim of the CIAM 8 debate. In particular, it presented the symbolic value of the heart rather than its metaphoric translation: it embodied a new rising humanism after the tragedy of the Second World War, instead of a mere functionalist compartmentalisation or comparison of the city with an organic structure, or simple juxtaposition with the central business district of a city.

Sigfried Giedion, in particular, underlined the pivotal role of the abstract, humanist interpretation of the Heart during CIAM 8. He highlighted the Heart as a new social symbol[72] for an appropriate relationship between the private and public realm, between collective and individual activities, between "You and Me."[73]

The heart as an eternally present idea, as already noted by Strauven,[74] even became a symbol of the first reason for the civic existence of the city and of its social community. The city itself was thus "an arch-symbol of a diversified human society" which appeared at the beginning of civilisation and which "has continued throughout all periods."[75]

Giedion presented this *aporia*[76] of the Heart of the City during his lecture titled "Historical Background to the Core," at CIAM 8 in Hoddesdon. Remarkably, among the examples of the Heart, the Swiss historian mentioned Michelangelo's Capitol as a symbol of future democracy in parallel with the Greek Agora as a symbol instead of past freedom.[77] The physical presence and composition of both public spaces were symbolically interpreted as a social condition that was absent – either lost or yet to arrive. If the Agora still expressed freedom even after it vanished under the conquest of Greece at the time of Alexander and later, the Capitol was a manifestation of a better future social democratic development which was not yet under the despotism of the Pope, at the time of its construction.[78] Though perfect Hearts, both examples were not straight reflections of society, since they either foresaw or recalled a better one. In this perspective, the role and responsibility of the architect, of the "great artist," was to anticipate a better social condition through the design and physical interpretation of the symbol of the heart, rather than passively mirroring its social coeval presence. The Heart was considered as a pro-active symbolic idea, with a physical presence, aimed at improving the social structure of the city itself. From the Greeks to contemporary society, the architecture of the Core had to anticipate and educate the architecture of the society. "This is our task today,"[79] Giedion concluded.

The Swiss historian also showed different plans of the ancient Cores, the Greek Agora and Roman Forum, drawn with the help of his friend, the Hungarian-born artist György Kepes (1906–2001), who suggested working on grey papers and drawing the lines of the buildings at the Core in black and white.

Letters inside the drawing helped to show the four functions, which are in part different from the CIAM ones, and their variations in history (R: Recreation, M: Meeting Places, S: Sanctuaries, B: Business).

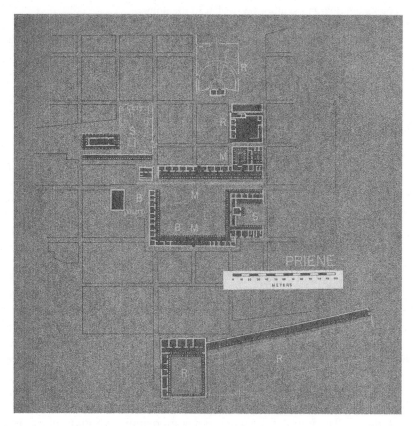

Figure 1.9 Giedion, Kepes, "The Agora of Priene."

Source: Courtesy MIT. In *The Heart of the City: Towards the Humanisation of Urban Life*, ed. Jaqueline Tyrwhitt, Josep Lluís Sert, Ernesto N. Rogers (London: Lund Humphries, 1952), 24.

Giedion explained that the human right of simply gathering in public space can first be found in the Greek Agora. As described by the Swiss historian, the Agora was bounded by simple standardised elements that form the *stoa*, a covered path where the public full of ideas and opinions could flourish in rainy or sunny weather. All public buildings are close to the square although they were always designed behind the *stoa*, behind the gathering place.[80] The Roman Forum was instead a disordered place where the prison, temples and *comitium* fit together. Nevertheless, the right of the pedestrian persisted. "This was sacrosanct," as Giedion nostalgically stressed. "Decay, decay, decay, through centuries!" later led to the ordered, coherent separation between public and private to sink while the gathering place for the community turned into a market place. In medieval cities, traffic also started flowing inside the public square, the street gained a shopping function and, later, the human right of the pedestrian consequently perished under the pressure of machine traffic.

Interestingly, this overlap and friction at the urban scale between pedestrian and vehicles flows, which was historically examined by Giedion, was also abstractly and broadly interpreted by the Swiss historian. The anxiety for the human right of the pedestrian as in the ancient Agora and its functionalist necessary split from car traffic was mirrored in the symbol of the heart as a continuous tension and struggle between "the human being as such – the bare naked man" and the "tyranny of mechanical tools"[81] which led to "the blood and horror" of the Second World War.

The Heart of the City consequently also symbolised regaining a social, emotional and human scale of the city, dismissing the dangerous primacy of the machine at all scales which had already been denounced by Giedion in "Mechanization Takes Command" (1948).

In this perspective, CIAM progressed from the austerity of functionalism, which was the major theme of the first meetings, to the symbolic translation of a human organ inside the city. From function to passion, as summarised by de Solà-Morales,[82] CIAM 8 became the highest point reached by the "pendulum"[83] which, between the 1940s and 1950s, rapidly swung towards a humanising process which sought the supremacy of the human scale in the city and the counterforce to the horror of "recent experiences of totalitarianism and scientifically planned mass destruction."[84] It was a radical shift towards the "City of Man,"[85] as described by Ernesto Nathan Rogers at CIAM 8, avoiding any Universal supremacy: it was a city in tension and labile equilibrium between the "Utopian and totalitarian city of the Sun" (the perfect city of the solar civilisation narrated by Tommaso Campanella in 1602) and the "transcendent City of God"[86] (described by St Augustine in the early fifth century AD, in contrast to the City of Man, the Pagans' City, immersed in the cares and pleasure of the present). In contrast to these high Utopias, the Heart of the City was instead one of the "utopias related to the revolution of humanism"[87] according to Tyrwhitt. It was a Utopia grounded in the everyday life and in the human being. It was a humanist equipoise that embodied the place of emotions and "emotional life."[88] If in the 1970s Lefebvre affirmed that "symbols, on this view, always imply an emotional investment, an effective charge,"[89] then as early as the 1950s, Giedion stressed the necessity to reconsider the emotions and "the revolt of the humiliated human instinct"[90] as the basic elements for the existence of the city itself. According to him, the major purpose of the century was to overcome the differences between the methods of thought and the methods of sentiments: their synergy was even considered as the universal conception of the world.[91] Culture was also a consequence of the relationship between the objects of knowledge and the emotional structure.[92] In this perspective, considering sentiments and emotions as a central role in our life meant perceiving the Heart of the City as an element of paramount importance in the built environment, as "symbolic centre of love"[93] as claimed by Ernesto Nathan Rogers.

Similarly, CIAM member Jaqueline Tyrwhitt, the "ardent disciple of Patrick Geddes,"[94] later described the Core as the "expression of common emotions," as "a space that can be filled by human emotion."[95] Interestingly, according to her, this emotional presence could manifest itself only in a "hollow core,"[96] made by "no-thing – . . . emptiness"[97] as the ultimate, main essence. Nevertheless, this physical void should not turn into a desert, a desolate landscape; it was supposed to become a human centrality, a gathering place, an urban space. The Geddesian "supreme organs of the city's life, its acropolis and forum, its cloister and cathedral"[98] which catalyse and develop "the true town plan," reverberated in this vision of Tyrwhitt's hollow core.[99] This continuous resonance of Geddes in Tyrwhitt's idea of Heart was so strong that enhanced the shift of CIAM 8 towards "a new humanism and post-modern globalism,"[100] according to Shoshkes.

Finally, three main basic components were described by Tyrwhitt in order to socially charge the void of the Core: the "human scale" as the range of the standing and walking man; the "visual dynamism" which is adoptable thanks to the use of light, colour and movement; the "spontaneity"[101] and "anonymous friendliness"[102] which free people to vent their feelings.

Regarding this last element of the Core, "spontaneity," the heart of the city as a symbol[103] requires simplicity, immediacy, instant recognisability and insight. Embedded in the action of direct "throwing" as etymological meaning of "symbol," the Heart represents the straight and honest "echo of the interior sentiment of Man."[104] *Vis-à-vis* this spontaneous nature of the Core, "we need today signs and symbols which spring directly to the senses without explanation,"[105] without any filters, any obstacles as Giedion urgently claimed at CIAM 8. This insightful quote was originally proposed by the French philosopher Jean-Paul Sartre, and it referred to psychologists' experience of the school of Würzburg.[106] It was a clear reference to a cultural humanist debate which developed beyond the close circle of CIAM and which radically affected the Idea of the Heart of the City.

In particular, Sartre, one of the main exponents of existentialist-humanism of the mid-twentieth century, compared two different kinds of humanism, in "*L'existentialisme est un humanisme.*" The first considered Man as a superior value, but "this humanism is absurd" since it is not possible to evaluate ourselves from an objective point of view from outside and, ironically, only a "dog or horse might judge all about man."[107] In contrast, the French philosopher proposed a humanism which considered the human being constantly outside of himself, beyond himself, central in the centre of the transcendent over-run. The final proposal was a universe which could not be anything other than a human universe, the universe of subjectivity. With this belief, the human heart was not a mere functionalist, spatial matter in the centre square of the city, but mankind itself, the individual subjectivity which suddenly turned out to be the heart of the urban issue. It was a humanism that did not refer to a Renaissance Man at the centre of the universe as the measure of everything. The major focus was the subjective individual who lives in an ever more complex collectivity, immersed in a lack of urban structure and social connections.

This second humanism precipitated the rise of brand new attention to everyday life, an epistemological shift[108] to an anthropological understanding of human life, to broader ecological conceptions of dwelling, to informal and spontaneous practices, to the autonomy of the individual and the subjectivity, which were already embedded at CIAM 8 and further revealed throughout the 1950s in the debate on the Charter of Habitat.

Monument and symbol

Giedion stated in *Architecture You and Me* that "monumentality springs from the eternal need of people to create symbols for their activities and for their fate or destiny."[109] The CIAM member then denounced the loss of the capacity to build monuments for his contemporary society, in parallel with the "dethroned symbolism" as already mentioned by Lewis Mumford in "Monumentalism, Symbolism and Style."[110] Nevertheless, Giedion specified in a footnote that this critique was written in 1943, only a few years before Le Corbusier's project for St Dié appeared. This latter master plan, also presented at CIAM 8 in Hoddesdon, was contemplated by Giedion as the first attempt of his period at a new form of representation of "a crystallization of community life" with the same potentialities of "the Greek meeting place."[111] Hence, between "the Death of the Monument,"[112] as enshrined by Mumford, and "The Need for a New Monumentality,"[113] as praised by Giedion, Le Corbusier's St Dié project was considered by the Swiss historian as the first modern example where monumentality and symbolism gained a modern connotation, an expression of the spirit of the time. St Dié embodied the symbol of the heart in the mid-twentieth century, similarly to the Agora in the fifth century BC. Moreover, it embodied and symbolised the right of the pedestrian, "*la royauté du piéton*"[114] (Le Corbusier), and consequently humanity over the tyranny of the machines that invaded urban centres.

This was achieved by separating pedestrian and car traffic, which was one of the main requisites assumed in Hoddesdon for the definition of the Core, tackling the chaotic and shapeless growth of the urban mass.

Indeed, in St Dié, the huge open pedestrian square was positioned on top of an artificial platform hosting parking garage, which was partially embedded in the hillside of the valley.[115] A tower, dedicated to municipal offices, police station and business, rose above the square along a central axis, which connects the Meurthe river and the old cathedral. On the same square, entirely organised for the pedestrian, there was a horizontal slab containing shops and cafés, a community centre and the famous museum with its spiralling design of unlimited growth.

At CIAM 8, Le Corbusier presented also the well-known plan for Chandigarh.[116] William Curtis already described "The symbolism of Chandigarh"[117] highlighting the monument of the "Open hand" as the "very symbol . . . of international peace, transcending politics, caste, religion, race,"[118] with direct resonances with local Indian tradition.

However, the most insightful project presented at CIAM 8, which better resumed the synergy between symbol, monument and heart, was Kenzo Tange's Hiroshima Peace memorial park. Remarkably, one the most intense, transcendental[119] and emblematic symbolic hearts was presented by a non-Western architect. Tange admitted in his lecture "The Core. Its Social and Historical Background"[120] that he noticed only "germs of the Core"[121] in Japan, temporary examples which could not be shaped into physical form like the Western medieval Piazza. In contrast with this historical absence of the Core within the "closed society" of Japan, Tange's project appeared as a tragic and

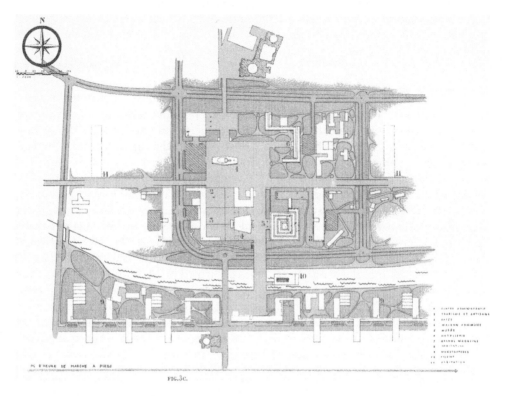

Figure 1.10 Le Corbusier, Plan of St Dié, 1945.

Source: © FLC, by SIAE 2017. In *The Heart of the City: Towards the Humanisation of Urban Life*, ed. Jaqueline Tyrwhitt, Josep Lluís Sert, Ernesto N. Rogers (London: Lund Humphries, 1952), 124.

dramatic attempt to rethink the "fundamental attitudes towards existence" within the nihilism left by the War: "how many bodies had been burnt to a cinder by the intense heat?" – Tange asked himself – "Losing the war meant the re-thinking of fundamental attitudes towards existence . . . It was almost as if one of nature's basic laws had been shown to be false."[122]

Hiroshima, one of the two cities devastated by the atomic bomb, was a major symbol of the horrible destruction of the War. Tange presented a fifteen-year reconstruction program which mirrored the decision of the people of Hiroshima "to stand for peace and . . . to demonstrate it to the world by moulding their ruined community into a monument of permanent peace."[123]

The master plan thus provided a Peace Hall, a Peace Park, a Peace Boulevard and international hotels and dormitories, which were arranged with an axial composition centred around the memorial cenotaph, in order "to create a unique ethos that would inspire the city's reconstruction."[124] The entire city, rather than a single monument, became a symbol of peace: the new plan for Hiroshima was indeed called the "Peace City."[125] This project became a relevant case study. Indeed, it helped to raise "the issue of symbolism at CIAM 8."[126] Rather than a symbolic monument as in the case of Chandigarh, the heart remained an abstract symbolical expression of Peace which had

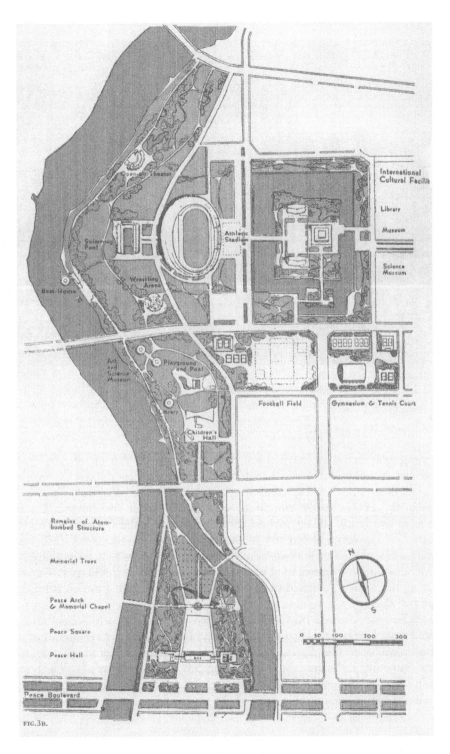

Figure 1.11 Tange Associates, Map Peace Park, Hiroshima, Japan, 1950.

Source: *The Heart of the City* (1952), 136. Courtesy of Tange Associates.

Figure 1.12 The Dome Building, Hiroshima, Japan.

Source: Photo by Alice Covatta, 2017.

to be translated into socio-spatial form by the architect. The topic of reconstruction was not merely a physical, urban structural issue; it concerned an abstract symbolical value of memory, social and cultural progress rather than mechanical value.

Later in the 1960s, Tange himself stressed the relevance for the architect to ask "what is the symbol of the day, where the symbol reveals itself, and how the symbol is created."[127] However, differently from Giedion, Tange considered the symbol as the melting element of technology and humanity. "Can modern technology restore humanity?" – Tange wondered – "'yes' only when modern technology has succeeded in creating in a space a symbol of the spirit of the time. And I am convinced of its possibility."[128]

The dichotomy stressed by Giedion between machines and humans, which had been functionally translated by many projects into the split between car and pedestrian flows, was overtaken by Tange who, on the contrary, pondered the right synergy between humanity and technology. Tange stripped the heart of its post-war humanist values in contrast to those of the machine, keeping its role as a symbol for the design of the city, based on the mutable spirit of the time.

Constellation and classification of the cores

At CIAM 8, each project was presented using a grid suggested by the MARS Group. The grid ("*la grille*") was an analytical system for presenting CIAM projects, which was defined by the ASCORAL group under the leadership of Le Corbusier and adopted at CIAM 7 in Bergamo in 1949.

The grid was considered a useful tool, "a first class work instrument"[129] as Echochard later asserted, for comparing different projects presented by CIAM members by using the same rules, guidelines and dimensions, under the terms of the Athens Charter.

At CIAM 8, the grid proposed by MARS Group was a simplification of the original one.[130] Information on the heart was divided into six columns: the first three were different scales in the progression from the starting point (village, city or neighbourhood) towards the Heart; the fourth column contained the images of the heart and the last two columns described the time linked to the heart, both the daily one and the historical one. Each scale had a specific environment explained with a strong emphasis on the sense of community.

In the official publication of CIAM 8, edited by Tyrwhitt, Sert and Rogers, a more complex index was instead adopted, which tried to express the several issues proposed by the CIAM 8 projects: the Core from the Village to the Small Town, the Urban Neighbourhood, the Urban Sector and the City. Moreover, the projects were listed also as the Core of a New Town, the Search for the Core of a City and the Core of a Government Centre.[131]

The presentation of the projects somehow mirrored the five different scale levels of community that the MARS Group had identified, beyond the basic unit of the family, for analysing the Core and the presence of its "sense of community."

As described by Tyrwhitt, the first scale concerned the Village (rural) or Primary Housing Group (urban) with 500 residents. The second was the Small Market Centre (rural) or Residential Neighbourhood (urban) with 1,500–3,000 people. The

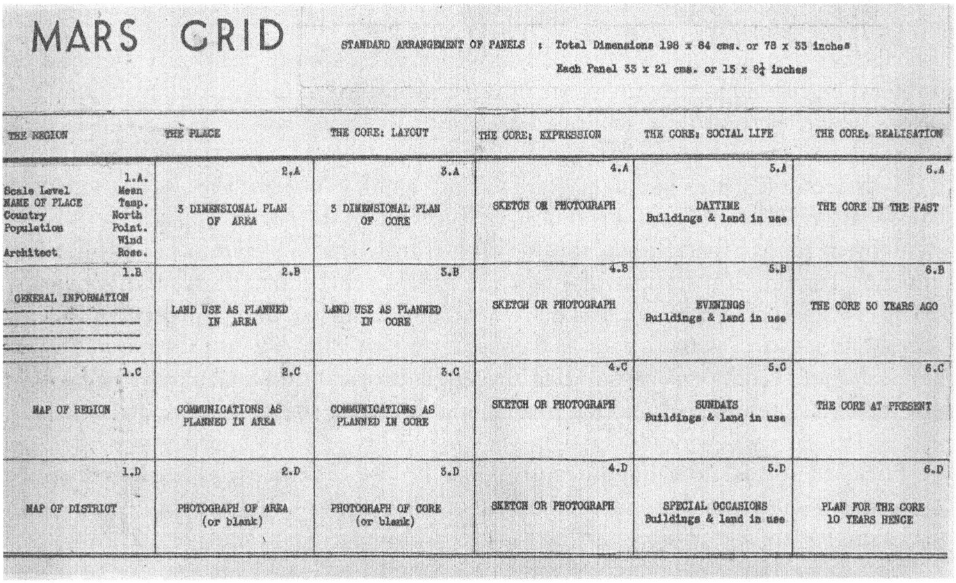

MARS GRID

STANDARD ARRANGEMENT OF PANELS : Total Dimensions 198 x 84 cms. or 78 x 33 inches
Each Panel 33 x 21 cms. or 15 x 8¼ inches

THE REGION		THE PLACE	THE CORE: LAYOUT	THE CORE: EXPRESSION	THE CORE: SOCIAL LIFE	THE CORE: REALISATION
1.A Scale Level NAME OF PLACE Country Population Architect	Mean Temp. North Point. Wind Rose.	2.A 3 DIMENSIONAL PLAN OF AREA	3.A 3 DIMENSIONAL PLAN OF CORE	4.A SKETCH OR PHOTOGRAPH	5.A DAYTIME Buildings & land in use	6.A THE CORE IN THE PAST
1.B GENERAL INFORMATION		2.B LAND USE AS PLANNED IN AREA	3.B LAND USE AS PLANNED IN CORE	4.B SKETCH OR PHOTOGRAPH	5.B EVENINGS Buildings & land in use	6.B THE CORE 50 YEARS AGO
1.C MAP OF REGION		2.C COMMUNICATIONS AS PLANNED IN AREA	3.C COMMUNICATIONS AS PLANNED IN CORE	4.C SKETCH OR PHOTOGRAPH	5.C SUNDAYS Buildings & land in use	6.C THE CORE AT PRESENT
1.D MAP OF DISTRICT		2.D PHOTOGRAPH OF AREA (or blank)	3.D PHOTOGRAPH OF CORE (or blank)	4.D SKETCH OR PHOTOGRAPH	5.D SPECIAL OCCASIONS Buildings & land in use	6.D PLAN FOR THE CORE 10 YEARS HENCE

Figure 1.13 MARS, CIAM 8's Grid.

Source: gta/ETH Archive, 42_CG_12 in *The Heart of the City* (1952), 102.

third regarded the Town (rural) or City Sector (urban) with 25,000–100,000 inhabitants. The fourth represented the City itself or Large Town with a population of 250,000–1,000,000 people. Finally, the fifth and last scale regarded the Metropolis or "International Centre"[132] with millions of people where the Core could no longer be concentrated in one single area.

Remarkably, the first four scale levels of the Core were considered by Jaqueline Tyrwhitt as the essential ones for the constitution of the "urban constellation."[133] Her idea of "urban constellation" stemmed from an urban interpretation of the scientific images of both macro-astronomic and microscopic-nuclear entities, animal tissues and inorganic crystals, which György Kepes showed in the exhibition "The New Landscape" at MIT the same year in 1951. Tyrwhitt remarked that at all scales, in all kind of systems, the same general phenomena could be observed and analysed: "there is everywhere a freely disposed arrangement of differentiated but related elements, each to some extent complete in itself, but all oriented in an informal but organized manner toward a more important body of matter – the nucleus of the constellation."[134] Within this "order within disorder – or disorder within order,"[135] the structure of urban constellation mirrored the "staggering relationship"[136] which is embedded in the general pattern of life of everything.

Interestingly, the main purpose of this scientific-urban interpretation was to both contrast the civic disease and chaos of the urban sprawl and provide the best pattern for civic defence against the bomb,[137] as proposed by Tyrwhitt. Moreover, the urban constellation was an evolution, a new proposal in parallel to the "neighbourhood unit"[138] idea which somehow influenced the Heart debate[139] and which was broadly developed in the USA since the 1930s, grouping dwellings sufficiently close to the central elementary school, in its first concept. According to Tyrwhitt, this was no longer "really in tune with our twentieth century way of life."[140] Indeed, she denounced that sometimes the neighbourhood unit had even turned into ghettos and segregating enclaves enclosing either very rich people or very poor ones.

The urban constellation was instead supposed to be a more positive reorganisation of the urban region, a "free grouping of different units," differentiated functions and sectors which were orderly separated by major highways and which could enclose either "re-invigorated cores of the older cities"[141] or brand new "hollow core[s]."[142] In this system, the Cores had to operate as both a link between the parts of the Urban Constellation and nucleus of attraction, of "unifying influence."[143]

Finally, as far as other classifications different from the constellation are concerned, Jaqueline Tyrwhitt also proposed a morpho-typological schematisation of the CIAM 8 projects. This categorisation was more related to the urban design process of the city rather than its size. It was a pivotal classification that went beyond the mere division into scales and functions surrounding the single projects. In particular, it referred to four possible combinations among formal and informal, open and enclosed:

A   Enclosed formal: the buildings are visually tied together and the open public space is considered as an extension of the internal, private one. The main examples are the projects for Lausanne, Chimbote, Oslo and Bogota.

B   Enclosed informal: the architectural buildings are still tied but the design of the public space is more informal, as in the medieval cities of Coventry and Kolsdal.

C   Open informal: the relation between buildings is not so direct and the public space is usually not limited by them. The open space dominates the plan, merging sometimes with landscaping elements. Examples are Hiroshima and Gustavsberg.

D Open formal: still the open space dominates the plan, but the buildings are distributed in a more formal pattern. Examples are Medellin and Chandigarh.

Tyrwhitt's proposed schematisation can be considered as a first alternative to the rational grid and, more generally, to the "universalist and exclusive"[144] approach of

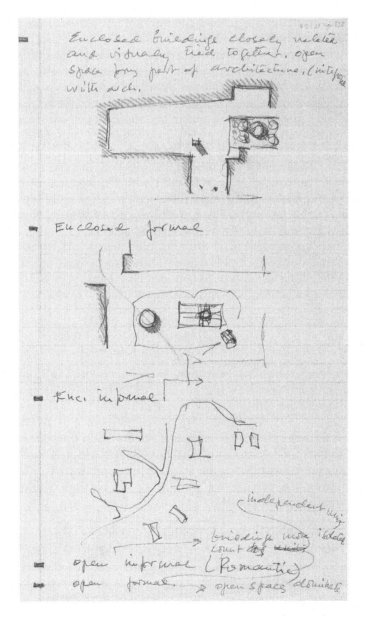

Figure 1.14 Jaqueline Tyrwhitt, CIAM 8, Sketches Formal-Informal.

Source: gta/ETH Archive, 42_JT_9_325.

CIAM, which was aiming to explain the city in pre-established categories and analytical divisions of the city. These variations, deformations and alternatives to the grid mirrored the epistemological shift[145] that occurred since the CIAM 8. In this perspective, the introduction of "informal" as a category seems relevant and was an anticipator of a rising interest in the different types and natures of human settlements from Western modern ones. Only a couple of years later, the "Scale of Association" proposed by Team 10 would completely overtake the functional categories, proposing other relational complexities within the city, similarly to Tyrwhitt's proposal.[146] The "*grille*" became even more "a structure, and one moreover, that allows for contradiction,"[147] as highlighted by Rosalind Krauss.

Finally, Tyrwhitt drew some sketches concerning these formal/informal groups, which were omitted in the final publication. This classification was exemplified with drawings of *Piazza San Marco* in Venice as a paradigm of the "enclosed formal" and *Pisa*'s *Campo dei Miracoli* as the "enclosed informal." The third sketch represented a cluster of buildings unified by an informal public space ("open informal").

The three sketches can be read as a shift from formal to informal, from closed to open, from Western history to a broader global tradition which is evident in the discourse of the late CIAMs and is mirrored in the following chapters as well.

Indeed, if we try to overlap these references with the structure of this book, we notice that the two piazzas are the main references in St Dié and Fort Worth which are analysed in the chapter on the First Urban Design and Victor Gruen (first actor), and in the CIAM Summer School in Venice (second actor).

While the cluster becomes the main topic in Gruen (first actor), it does so more particularly in Bakema and Team 10 (third actor). Therefore, the formal space division with regards to the Heart of the City, as considered by Tyrwhitt in her three sketches, coherently and methodologically overlaps with the "actors" which are analysed further later.

Out of CIAM: *Mensch + Raum* (*Darmstädter Gespräch*, 1951)

At CIAM 8, J.L. Sert opened his exposition about the "Centres of Community Life" with a long quote from "The Revolt of the Masses" written by the Spanish philosopher José Ortega y Gasset (1883–1955):

> For in truth the most accurate definition of the *urbis* and the *polis* is very like the comic definition of a cannon. You take a hole, wrap some steel wire tightly round it, and that's your cannon. So, the *urbis* or the *polis* starts by being an empty space, the forum, the agora, and all the rest are just a means of fixing that empty space, of limiting its outlines.[148]

This quote from "Revolt of the Masses" within CIAM is interesting and arguable. On the one hand, the negative critique of the masses, the agglomeration, the plenitude labelled by the Spanish philosopher in his book seems somehow in contradiction with the social interest in gathering and community which was embedded in the CIAM members' discourses and projects about the Heart of the City and later about the "habitat of the greatest number."

On the other hand, Mumford[149] already underlined that the elitist role of CIAM could share resonances or even match with the natural intellectual elites praised by

Ortega y Gasset, which should have guided society, in order avoid the decaying influence of the masses.

As far as the quote about the *Urbis* is concerned, another split was radically claimed. Besides the separation between elite and masses, both the Spanish thinkers, Ortega y Gasset and Sert, sought for a neat physical division between civic space and landscape, between the internal hole of the "cannon" and the external "Geo-Botanic cosmos." Sert adopted the metaphor of the "cannon" in order to highlight the necessary recentralisation of the city facing the depravity and chaos of the urban sprawl,

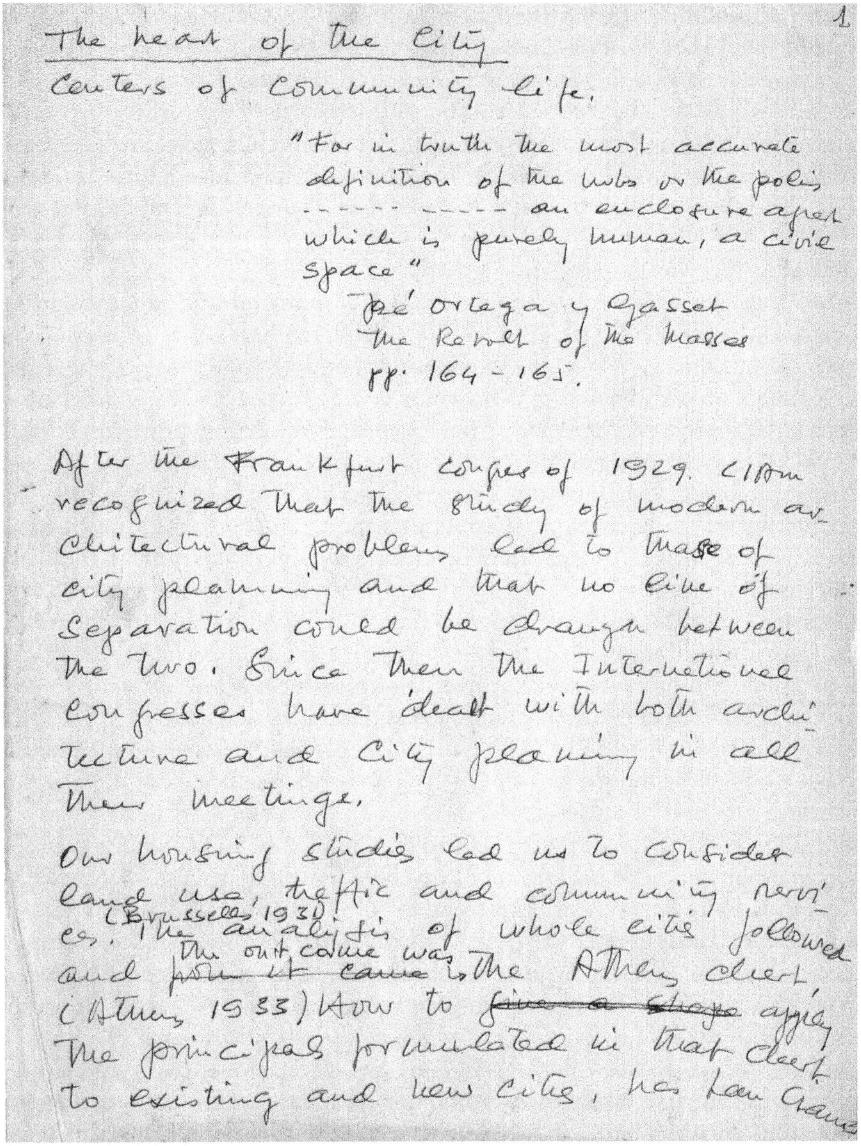

1

The heart of the City
Centers of Community life.

"For in truth the most accurate definition of the urbs or the polis ------ ----- an enclosure apart which is purely human, a civic space"

José Ortega y Gasset
The Revolt of the masses
pp. 164 - 165.

After the Frankfurt congress of 1929. CIAM recognized that the study of modern architectural problems lead to those of city planning and that no line of separation could be drawn between the two. Since then the International congresses have dealt with both architecture and City planning in all their meetings.

Our housing studies lead us to consider land use, traffic and community services. (Brussels 1930) The analysis of whole cities followed and ~~from it came~~ the outcome was the Athens chart, (Athens 1933) How to ~~give a shape~~ apply the principals formulated in that chart to existing and new cities, has been

Figure 1.15 Sert, Manuscript, "The Heart of the City, Centers of Community Life," 1951.

Source: Sert Collection D14. Courtesy of the Frances Loeb Library, Harvard Graduate School of Design.

as described later in the following chapters. On the other hand, the philosopher reiterated this rift even after "The Revolt of the Masses" in order to theoretically claim the essence of the human being as an intruder of Nature, without any proper Habitat (unlike other animals), unsuited to any *milieu*. According to Ortega y Gasset, only the act of building and the technique as "a giant orthopaedic device"[150] could assimilate and humanise the space.

Interestingly, these complementary urban and philosophical interpretations were expounded almost coevally in the summer of 1951. While Sert chaired the CIAM 8 in July 1951, Ortega y Gasset discussed his ideas in "The myth of man over the technique"[151] during the Darmstadt Congress[152] in Germany, as part of the Exhibition "*Mensch und Raum*" ("Man and Space"), organised from August 4–6, 1951. In post-war Germany, the German architects[153] organised an alternative to CIAM where they could exhibit infrastructure and urban projects and discuss architecture and philosophy as well. "It seems that the ruins have been for them like an injection of hormones in their body which caused a frantic desire to build . . . The ruin as an aphrodisiac"[154] – Ortega y Gasset interpreted the spirit of the meeting, as a new propulsion towards a new era, a new Germany to be reconstructed after the War.[155]

Remarkably, during these Colloquia in 1951, another outstanding philosopher, the German Martin Heidegger (1889–1976), delivered his lecture proposing one of his most famous theories: "*Bauen, Wohnen, Denken*" ("Build, Dwell, Think"). Heidegger's lecture was addressed to all architects who, after the War, had the task of rebuilding the destroyed cities. However, his proposed idea of "dwelling" was destined to echo in many other architectural and philosophical debates until today.

Heidegger's idea of dwelling was different from the beliefs of the Spanish philosopher. "Building is really dwelling. Dwelling is the manner in which mortals are on the earth"[156] (Heidegger) – was a counterforce, a conflict in front of the need for an intermediary, auxiliary tool for dwelling on earth, as supported by the Spanish philosopher. If Heidegger considered that we can build only if we are able to dwell, only if "poetically, Man dwells,"[157] then Ortega y Gasset stated on the contrary that we need to build in order to seek to dwell and transform Man's original illness into a wellness. If for Heidegger the technique was described as the Greek "*techne*," as a creative revealing of the truth belonging to "*poiesis*" (making), then in the philosophy of Ortega y Gasset, technique was simply "a giant orthopaedic device"[158] which helps us to survive on earth.

Finally, it is possible to conclude that similar complexity and conflicts, between the poetical and phenomenological vision of dwelling and the ravages of technology and functionalism, were palpable at both meetings of Hoddesdon and Darmstadt, facing the new urban condition after the tragedy of the War. "The formulation of questions and issues are similar" – as Werner Oechslin indeed affirms – "the rediscovery of urban space, respectively the highlighting of the city and its duties against the government's one-way reconstruction policy, and the same for the answers."[159]

Moreover, in many cases, both the congresses were imbued with ambiguity and contradictions, lacking concrete and immediate solutions for their contemporary urban condition, *hic et nunc*. If CIAM 8 remained a "light background sketch for a future painting,"[160] then Lefebvre in the 1960s concretely criticised Heidegger's "*Bauen, Wohnen, Denken*" for warning us about dwelling but "he does not tell us how to construct, 'here and now', buildings and cities."[161]

Lastly, both congresses clearly referred to the human being as the central issue of the debate: on one side, the Heart was a symbol of a brand new social interest within the public realm, and on the other side, "Man and Space" became the frame for one of the most outstanding philosophical expositions of the last century on the human existence. "You said to me something of an unspoken unanimity between your creating and my attempting,"[162] the architect Hans Scharoun wrote to Heidegger a few years after Darmstadt, disclosing the interference and interdependency between architecture and philosophy, between the tangible and intangible discourse on human beings and their habitat.

Notes

1 Le Corbusier, "Preliminary," in *The Heart of the City: Towards the Humanisation of Urban Life*, ed. Jaqueline Tyrwhitt, Josep Lluís Sert, Ernesto N. Rogers (London: L. Humphries, 1952), xi.
2 CIAM 6 was held in 1947 in Bridgewater in England while CIAM 7 was organised in Bergamo, Italy, in 1949.
3 "The theme itself and all the rest that happened in that lonely Victorian mansion in Hoddesdon, not far from London though without rail connection to it, can only be considered as a light background sketch for a future painting, in which we and others will bring to conscious life that which slumbers unfulfilled in the hearts of all." Sigfried Giedion, "The Heart of the City: A Summing-Up," in *The Heart of the City*, 160.
4 Other tours were organised to the prefabricated Hertfordshire schools by Charles H. Aslin and the new town of Harlow, designed by Gibberd. Ibid.
5 Bevis Hillier, Mary Banham, ed., *Tonic to the Nation: Festival of Britain, 1951* (London: Thames & Hudson Ltd, 1976). Quoted in Nicholas Bullock, *Building the Post-War World, Modern Architecture and Reconstruction in Britain* (London: Routledge, 2002), 69. The central theme celebrated was the "innate curiosity" thanks to which British people made important discoveries in all fields.
    This spirit was transmitted by the pavilions such as the Dome of Discovery by Ralph Tubbs, which was considered by critics in the 1950s as "the largest dome in the world." Another interesting building was the Sea and Ships pavilion, designed by the Scottish architect Basil Spence, which was later described by Reyner Banham as "a megastructure of sorts before the time had come." Reiner Banham, *Megastructure: Urban Futures of the Recent Past* (London: Thames and Hudson, 1976), 34.
6 The English MARS Group was founded by Wells Coats before the Fourth Congress. Other members: Edwin Maxwell Fry, F.R.S. Yorke, Godfrey Samuel, Serge Chermayeff, John Gloag, Berthold Lubetkin, Erno Goldfinger, Raymond McGrath, Amyas Connell, Basil Ward, Colin Lucas and the architectural journalists Shand, J.M. Richards, Hubert de Cronin Hastings and John Betjeman. See Mumford, *The CIAM Discourse on Urbanism, 1928–1960* (Cambridge: MIT Press, 2000), 91.
7 Josep Lluís Sert, letter to Sigfried Giedion, December 21, 1949, CIAM 42-SG-34-52, gta/ ETH. Quoted in Mumford, *The CIAM Discourse on Urbanism, 1928–1960*, 201.
8 "I was interested on the Civic Center and I approved it when the Dutch architects have presented it at our last reunion in Bergamo." (in Italian: "*Ho parlato a lungo con Corbusier sul tema del CIAM 8. Ero interessato al Centro Civico e l'ho sostenuto quando gli olandesi l'hanno presentato alla nostra ultima riunione di Bergamo.*") Josep Lluís Sert, Letter to Godfrey Samuel, 5 March 1950. Quoted in Italian in Jos Bosman, "I CIAM del dopoguerra: un bilancio del Movimento Moderno," *Rassegna*, anno XIV, 52/4 (1992): 11.
9 In the same letter of March 5, 1950, Sert wrote to Godfrey Samuel that he spoke a lot with Le Corbusier, about the topic of the eighth CIAM. He said the civic centre is a more interesting theme than the "*Charte de l'Habitat*": "Now he is sure about it and he agrees with us and with the majority of the Meeting. He also thinks that the 8th CIAM should take place in London, and that the MARS group should organize it." (in Italian: "*Ora è convinto e concorda con noi e con la maggioranza del Congresso. Pensa anche che il CIAM 8*

dovrebbe rivolgersi a Londra e che il gruppo MARS dovrebbe curarne l'organizzazione."), Ibid.

10 Nevertheless, Le Corbusier's plea was fulfilled at the following CIAM 9 in 1953, transforming CIAM 8 into a *de facto* threshold meeting for the prolific ambiguous research and struggle about the topic of Habitat throughout the 1950s.

11 Walter Gropius, "Letter to Mr. Wells Coates, cc. Giedion and Sert, December 22, 1949," 42/SG/34/54, gta/ETH.

12 SG-34-32, gta/ETH. It is presented, with some differences, also in CIAM 8, *Report of Hoddesdon Conference*, 1951, BIB 200583, CCA Library, Montreal.

13 MARS, "Text of Mars Group Invitation. The Core," in CIAM 8, *Report of Hoddesdon Conference*. In the letter written in French in November 1949 we read a more poetical and passionate explanation of the Core as an expression of the collective emotion: "*Elle est l'expression tantôt a demi consciente, tantôt passionnément voulus, de la vie collective même . . . Les paroles volent de bouche en bouche, elles soulèvent les émotions, on abandonne la tache individuelle ou les intérêts sectionnelles et on sort dans la rue; des groupes plains d'animation se forment, ils s'unissent a' d'autres, et bientôt une vaste foule est en marche vers quoi? La Place Marche'? La Place de La Cathédrale? Les monceaux de scories derrière l'Usine a' Gaz? Il-y-a toujours quelque part un cadre physique approprie' a' l'expression de l' émotion collective, c'est le cœur de l'Organisme.*" MARS, November 1949, SG-34-32, gta/ETH.

14 Jaqueline Tyrwhitt, "CIAM and Delos," *Ekistics*, 52, no. 314/315 (November/December 1985): 471.

15 See Volker M. Welter, "In-between Space and Society. On Some British Roots of Team 10's Urban Thought in the 1950s," in *TEAM 10 1953–81: In Search of a Utopia of the Present*, ed. Max Risselada, Dirk van den Heuvel (Rotterdam: Nai Publishers, 2006), 259. However, for instance, Bakema will reconsider "the humane Core of St. Louis" at the end of the 1950s, as we will discuss later and Woods will consider the Core in relation with the cluster: "First the core is determined, then the cluster is formed. [. . .] The idea of clustering the cells proceeds from the core. The core is usually expressed in the master plan as a fixed point in the general scheme, out of contact with the greater part of homes." Shadrach Woods, Team 10, "The role of the Architect in Community Building," in *Human Identity in the Urban Environment*, ed. Jaqueline Tyrwhitt, Gwen Bell (London: Penguin Books, 1972), 386.

16 Lewis Mumford, Letter to Sert, December 28, 1940 (folder E1, JLS). Quoted in Mumford, *The CIAM Discourse on Urbanism*, 133.

17 Josep Lluís Sert, *Can Our Cities Survive? An ABC of Urban Problems, their Analysis, their Solutions* (Cambridge: The Harvard University Press; London: Humphrey Milford Oxford University Press, 1944).

18 Ibid. As far as the relation between the refusal of Mumford and the decision of the Heart theme is concerned, see also Welter, "In-between space and society," 259. The Heart idea might be considered therefore as an afterthought of the previous CIAM statements as suggested by the American critic ten years before CIAM 8.

19 Grahame Shane, "The Street in the Twentieth Century," 36.

20 An "aggregation of individuals" (Giedion), an "element which makes a community a community" (MARS), a "natural expression of contemplation . . . of Italian dolce far niente" (Rogers), a "background of spontaneity" (Johnson), a "meeting place of the arts" (Le Corbusier), an "abstract Core" (Opbouw Group), and so on. This variety of definitions is already listed by Welter. See Welter, "From Locus Genii to Heart of the City," 52.

21 For instance, Welter highlighted the continuity of the CIAM 8 with Mumford's social core, Reclus' communal city centre, Geddes' cultural Acropolis and Taut's city crown. Ibid., 52.

    Moreover, the American contributions seem very important since some historians have identified the origins of the CIAM 8 theme as early as the 1930s, in the American neighbourhood theory and in a constant transatlantic exchange of ideas between the US and Europe. See Konstanze Domhardt, "From the 'Functional City' to the 'Heart of the City.' Green Space and Public Space in the CIAM Debates of 1942–1952," in *Greening the City: Urban Landscapes in the Twentieth Century*, ed. Dorothee Brantz, Sonja Dümpelmann (Charlottesville: University of Virginia Press, 2011), 133–156. See also Eric Mumford, "CIAM Urbanism After the Athens Charter," *Planning Perspectives*, 7 (1992): 413. Bosman, "I CIAM del dopoguerra," 8.

22 Of course, we can be critical with this summary because our historical distance allows us to consider the Heart theme in a more complex and complete way than it has been considered by our more illustrious predecessors.

23 "Summary of needs at the Core:

    1 That there should be only one main Core in each City.

    2 That the Core is an artefact – a man-made thing.

    3 That the Core should be a place secure from traffic – where the pedestrian can move about freely.

    4 That cars should arrive and park on the periphery of the Core, but not cross it.

    5 That uncontrolled commercial advertising – such as appears in the Cores of many cities today – should be ornized and controlled.

    6 That varying (mobile) elements can make an important contribution to animation at the Core, and that the architectural setting should be planned to allow for the inclusion of such elements.

    7 That in planning the Core the architect should employ contemporary means of expression and – whenever possible – should work in co-operation with painters and sculptors." CIAM, "A Short Outline of the Core," in *The Heart of the City: Towards the Humanisation of Urban Life*, 164.

24 "The core was viewed largely as an image, a place where the 'sense of community' is physically expressed, and not as a place that could be scientifically described." Marina Lathouri, "CIAM Meetings 1947–59 and the 'Core' of the City: Transformations of an Idea," in *La Città Nouva: The New City*, ed. Katrina Deines, Kay Bea Jones (Washington: ACSA International Conference Press, 2000), 404.

25 Le Corbusier, "fig.101, Philadelphia: The Business Quarter Is to Be Seen in the Heart of the City," in *Aircraft* (London: The Studio, 1935; New York: The Studio Publications (collection The New Vision), 1935), fig.101.

26 CIAM, "A Short Outline of the Core," 165.

27 Le Corbusier, "Preliminary," in *The Heart of the City*, xi.

28 Henri Lefebvre, *The Production of Space*, trans. Donald Nicholson-Smith (Malden, MA: Blackwell Publishing, 2010), 138.

29 Walter Gropius, "Letter to Mr. Wells Coates, cc. Giedion and Sert, December 22, 1949," 42/SG/34/54, gta/ETH.

30 Christian Norberg-Schulz, "Commission 3A (Young Architects), Report on Architectural Education," In CIAM 8, *Report of Hoddesdon Conference*, 113.

31 See Mumford, *The CIAM Discourse on Urbanism*, 205.

32 See also Domhardt, "From the 'Functional City' to the 'Heart of the City'," 147.

33 Originally in French: "*chaque langue organise le monde urbain d'une façon, par hypothèse, spécifique.*" Christian Topalov, Laurent Coudroy De Lille, Jean-Charles Depaule, Brigitte Marin, ed., *L'aventure des mots de la ville à travers le temps, les langues, les sociétés* (Paris: Robert Laffont, 2010), XVIII.

34 "*On m'a reproché, même Giedion qui aurait du être le premier d'accord, d'avoir fait à Sigtuna une querelle linguistique à propos du mot Habitat.*" André Wogenscky, "Letter from to Sert, Paris, April 9, 1953," BAKE0153, g21, Bakema Archive, Het Nieuwe Instituut, Rotterdam.

35 Josep Lluís Sert, "The Heart of the City," transcript from the CIAM Archive at ETH Zurich, in *The Writings of Josep Lluís Sert*, ed. Eric Mumford (New Haven and London: Yale University Press; Cambridge: Harvard GSD, 2015), 2.

36 CIAM, "Notes on CIAM Meeting Held on June 5, 1950, at 9 East 59th St. New York. Present: S. Giedion, L. Holm, A. Iriarte, J.L. Sert, J. Tyrwhitt, P.L. Wiener," 42 JLS-25-1, gta/ETH.

37 Ernesto Nathan Rogers, "The Heart: Human Problem of Cities," in *The Heart of the City*, 69.

38 Giedion, "The Heart of the City: A Summing-Up," 159.

39 CIAM, "Conversation at CIAM 8," in *The Heart of the City*, 38.

40 "Batista: Is the Core different from the Neighbourhood Unit? Sert: It is quite different. There could be no neighbourhood unit, without its own small core, but this is only a small reflection of the Core of the City, and the whole subject of Cores." The Theme of the Congress. Resume of the open session of 8th July. Chairman J.L. Sert. In CIAM 8, 1951, *Report of Hoddesdon Conference*, 44.

41 "Core/Civic Core" appears in 106 pages, "Heart" appears in twenty-two pages, "Hearth" appears in three pages, "Centre" appears in fifty-eight pages. in *The Heart of the City*. In the Italian edition, "*Cuore/Cuore della Città*" appears in 106 pages, "Centro/Centro della Città" in sixty-seven pages. In Jaqueline Tyrwhitt, Josep Lluís Sert, Ernesto N. Rogers, ed., *Il Cuore della Città: per una vita più umana delle comunità*, transl. Julia Banfi Bertolotti (Milano: Hoepli editore, 1954).

42 Josep Lluís Sert letter to Jaqueline Tyrwhitt, September 7, 1951, CIAM Collection_Correspondence 1951 July–September, GSD/Harvard Special Archive, C9. The insistence of Sert regarding the title "The Heart of the City," is manifested in several letters to Jaqueline Tyrwhitt.

43 "Dear Jacky, [. . .] In reference to the title of the book, I do not think it matters if it is called THE HEART OF THE CITY and would refer to the 'CORE' in the different articles. This is defined in my introduction and there is no doubt that the term HEART will have more popular appeal regardless of [what] Peter Gregory may say about it." Josep Lluís Sert letter to Jaqueline Tyrwhitt, October 1, 1951, CIAM Collection, GSD/Harvard Special Archive, C10.

44 Interestingly, Sert's fears about the unpopularity and the misunderstanding of the use of the Core found confirmation in John Rannells's book "The Core of the City," published in 1956, the year of CIAM's demise. Rannells' book regards "a pilot study of changing land uses in central business districts." Here the Core has almost nothing to do with the cultural, symbolical, humanising process argued and exhibited through projects by the CIAM members only five years before. Rannells' "Core" is indeed merely associated with the CBD, the central business district, a term coined in the 1920s to describe the American downtown, the inner economic centre, the business centre of North American cities. The human values expressed within the public sphere of CIAM 8 are indirectly reconducted to an urban technical, functional discourse by Rannells. John Rannells, *The Core of the City: A Pilot Study of Changing Land Uses in Central Business Districts* (New York: Columbia University Press, 1956).

45 "I have no feelings on the matter and suggest that the decision is made on the title that will sell best. I don't think we should change the word 'core' throughout the book in any case."
    Jaqueline Tyrwhitt letter to Sert, September 22, 1951, CIAM Collection, GSD/Harvard Special Archive, C9.

46 A second edition was published in 1979, Nendeln [Liechtenstein]: Kraus Reprint. NA682. I52 H4 1979, CCA Library, Montreal.

47 See Giorgio Ciucci: "Without pretending to reconstruct a 'true' and 'complete' history, which in any case is impossible, I should like only to underline several points, examine a few facts, make comparisons and suggest relationships, discuss traditional hypotheses, and try to find connections that are not already taken for granted." Giorgio Ciucci, "The Invention of the Modern Movement," in *Oppositions Reader*, ed. K. Michael Hays (New York: Princeton Architectural Press, 1998), 554. Originally published in *Oppositions*, 24 (1981), 68–69.
    Also Jaqueline Tyrwhitt wanted to write a history of the CIAM movement. However, this remained "an unfulfilled project." Jaqueline Tyrwhitt, "History of the CIAM Movement. An unfulfilled Project," *Ekistics*, 52, no. 314/315 (1985): 486–487.

48 "This may have been the underlying reason for the selection of the 'Core of the City' as the theme for CIAM 8 (Hoddesdon, England, July 1951)." Giedion, *Architecture You and Me*, 126.

49 Sigfried Giedion, "Man in Equipoise," in *Human Identity in the Urban Environment*, ed. Jaqueline Tyrwhitt, Gwen Bell (London: Penguin Books, 1972), 225.

50 "Corbusier has said that in every private house there is a Core: in the early days around the hearth; in our days, or in the coming days, perhaps round the television screen? Or around the mechanized kitchen?" Bakema, "Relationship Between Men and Things," 67.

51 An example was the "H House," published in "Mechanization Takes Command" by Sigfried Giedion, designed by J. and N. Fletcher, who in 1945 won a competition for a small-medium size family apartment with a central mechanical core which worked as a link between the living and sleeping areas. Bosman, "I CIAM del dopoguerra," 14.

52 "In a Coreless community . . . the orbits of men are from their house to the places where they work and back again, the orbits of the house-wives will consist of the homes, a few

shops, and the doorsteps where they chat with their neighbours." Gregor Paulsson, "The Past and the Present," in *The Heart of the City*, 29.
53 Ibid., 28.
54 André Wogenscky Letter to Sert, Paris, April 9, 1953, BAKE0153, g21, Bakema Archive, Het Nieuwe Instituut, Rotterdam.
55 Giedion, *Architecture You and Me*, 128.
56 Walter Gropius letter to Forbat, March 20, 1952, Am 1970–18, Forbat Archive, Arkdes Stockholm.
57 Elizabeth Darling wrote that in Great Britain the health of society became an important issue during the World Wars because of the limited number of people with access to public health insurance. Many debates were focused on the so-called "health of the race," especially after the loss of 700,000 productive young men during the last War. Elizabeth Darling, *Re-forming Britain, Narratives of Modernity Before Reconstruction* (London and New York: Routledge, 2006), 52.
58 James M. Richards, "The Idea Behind the Idea," *Architectural Review*, 77 (1935): 209.
59 George Scott Williamson, "The Individual and the Community," in *The Heart of the City*, 30–35.
60 Ibid., 30–31.
61 Ibid.
62 CIAM 8, "Conversation about the Core, The Human Aspect of the Core, Resume of open Session, Tuesday, July 10th CIAM 8, 1951," in *Report of Hoddesdon Conference*, 68.
63 Scott Williamson, "The Individual and the Community," 31.
64 "Each family brought its home with it into the Centre – or such parts of its home as it was prepared to exhibited to public gaze." Ibid. This openness is of course requested, on one hand, as a sort of healing method, and on the other, in order to allow doctors to make all analyses in the best and easiest way.
65 Richards, "The Idea Behind the Idea," 203–216.
66 The whole building is planned on a grid 18ft square, varied at either wing to give a 24ft span for gymnasium and theatre. Cruciform pillars carrying the concrete floor spaces, and affording conduits for power, waterand so forth allow flexibility of internal planning.
67 Richards, "The Idea Behind the Idea," 209.
68 Innes Pearse, Lucy Crocker, *The Peckham Experiment: A Study of the Living Structure of Society* (London: George Allen and Unwin, 1943) and Darling, *Re-forming Britain, Narratives of Modernity Before Reconstruction*, 65.
69 Richards, "The Idea Behind the Idea," 203–216.
70 Giedion, *Architecture You and Me*, 123.
71 Sigfried Giedion, "Art[,] a Fundamental Experience," 1950, Giedion Vortrag gta Archives, ETh Zurich. quoted in Sarah Deyong, An Architctural Theory of Relations: Sigfried Giedion and Team X, *JSAH*, 73, no. 2 (June 2014): 243.
72 In particular, as far as the symbol in Giedion's theory is concerned, Christopher Hight has compared Giedion's and Cassirer's writings, affirming that both of them consider "the symbolic and its associated matters of scale and proportion" as the starting point for the distinction between "Man" and the rest of Nature. Christopher Hight, *Architectural Principles in the Age of Cybernetics* (New York and London: Routledge, 2007), 131.
73 Giedion, *Architecture You and Me*.
74 See Strauven, *Aldo van Eyck: The Shape of Relativity*.
75 Giedion, *Architecture You and Me*, 124.
76 Aporia (Ancient Greek: ἀπορία: *impasse, lack of resources, puzzlement, doubt, confusion*). Mid-sixteenth century: via late Latin from Greek, from aporos "impassable," from a- "without" + *poros* "passage." *Oxford English Dictionary*.
77 See Giedion, "Historical Background to the Core," 17. The same discourse is present in *Space, Time and Architecture*, 1941 and in *Architecture You and Me*, 1958.
78 Built in a society which did not know yet what freedom is, it is a "symbol of the vanished liberties of the medieval city-republic that he held in his heart." Giedion, "Historical Background to the Core," in *The Heart of the City*, 25.
79 Ibid.

80 Only in the fifth century BC did the Agora become the place for the exchange of trade as well, mutating its essence.
81 Giedion, "Historical Background to the Core," 17.
82 "The understanding of the core as a human heart emerged from an architectural debate in which function seemed to have yielded to passion." Ignasi de Solà-Morales, "Architecture and Existentialism," in *Differences: Topographies of Contemporary Architecture* (Cambridge: MIT Press, 1997), 49.
83 The image of the pendulum is used by Denise Scott Brown to explain the rise of young movements against old ones. "A young movement, while its future is insecure, will often, because it must to survive and grow, try to destroy its past. This is easy to do when the pendulum has swung too far in one direction." Denise Scott Brown, "Team 10, Perspecta 10, and the Present State of the Architectural Theory," *Journal of the American Institute of Planners*, 1 (1967): 49.
84 "Humanism was an organizing principle in architectural thinking in the post-war period, both in terms of reconfiguring traditions and seeking lost or exotic alternatives. But humanism also implied a new mode of sensitivity to values which responded to recent experiences of totalitarianism and scientifically planned mass destruction." Curtis, "The Heart of the City," 52. Barry Curtis reminds also that "Man" was part of the discourse in the statements of UNESCO on race and difference in 1950–1951. Ibid.
85 "The Heart of the City could be brought into being for the City of Man, which concretely stands midway between the transcendent City of God and the totalitarian City of the Sun." Rogers, "The Heart: Human Problem of Cities," 73.
86 Ibid.
87 Jaqueline Tyrwhitt, "Ideal Cities and Utopias, January 1952," TJJ/16/3, RIBA, London.
88 Giedion, *Architecture You and Me*, 37.
89 "Symbols, on this view, always imply an emotional investment, an effective charge (fear, attraction, etc.) which is so to speak deposited at a particular place and thereafter 'represented' for the benefit of everyone elsewhere." Lefebvre, *The Production of Space*, 141.
90 "Today the immediate impact of aesthetic or emotional values has become of the utmost importance.[. . .] This is the revolt of the humiliated human instincts." Giedion, *Architecture You and Me*, 69.
91 "Without this inner connection between methods of thinking and methods of feeling it is impossible to have a positive way of life or genuine culture." Giedion, *Architecure You and Me*, 13.
92 "*La cultura nasce quando l'uomo, consapevolmente o inconsapevolmente, pone gli oggetti della conoscenza in rapporto con a struttura emotiva.*" (translated: "The culture is born when man, consciously or unconsciously, positioned the objects of knowledge in relation to emotional structure.") Giedion, *Breviario di Architettura*, 109.
93 Rogers, "The Heart: Human Problem of Cities," 69.
94 *Homage à Giedion* (Basel and Stutgart: Birkhäuser Verlag, 1971), 121–122; quoted in Jos Bosman, "My Association With CIAM Gave Me New Perspective," *Ekistics*, 52, no. 314/315 (September–December 1985): 478.
95 Jaqueline Tyrwhitt, "The Core of the City, December 15, 1952," Toronto University, for the Commerce Journal, TjJ/38/9/3, RIBA Archive, London.
96 Jaqueline Tyrwhitt, "Slides for the Public Lecture on 'The CORE', March 1953," University of Toronto, TjJ/18/4, RIBA Archive, London.
97 "This is the primary need of the core: space where the pedestrian can move about freely unobstructed by traffic. Indeed it can be said that the most important thing about the core is no-thing – is emptiness – a space that can be filled by human emotion. But this emptiness must be to the human scale; it must be a gathering place not a civic desert; it must be an urban space not a landscape garden; it must be at the heart of the city's life which is not necessary the same place as the Civic Centre; it must be easily accessible to the pedestrian not circled by an endless belt of moving vehicles . . . It is the urban open space – the no-thing – that can act as a unifying influence; that can create the opportunity to pause after some experience by which one has been moved or stimulated . . . to integrate it with one's total personality – before plunging back into the swiftly obliterating current of one's daily life." Jaqueline Tyrwhitt, "The Core of the City," TjJ/38/9/3, RIBA. See also Ellen Shoshkes, *Jaqueline Tyrwhitt: A Transnational Life in Urban Planning and Design* (New York: Routledge, 2013), 142.

98 Patrick Geddes, *Cities in Evolution: An Introduction to the Town Planning Movement and to the Study of Cities* (London: Williams and Norgate, 1915), 71. In Bosman, "My Association With CIAM Gave Me New Perspective," 483.

99 The Core even became the ultimate expression, "the most symbolical element of Geddes's theory" (Welter) described in "Cities in Evolution," edited by Tyrwhitt herself in 1949. "This idea was strongly influenced by Geddes's claim that a highly visible physical concentration in the urban fabric of cultural and civic institutions was indispensable for any city that wished to be a community of citizens." Welter, *In-between Space and Society*, 258.

100 Ellen Shoshkes, "Jaqueline Tyrwhitt and Transnational Discourse on Modern Planning and Design, 1941–1951," *Urban History*, 36, no. 2 (2009): 263.

101 Jaqueline Tyrwhitt, "Principles of Town Planning, Lecture 10: The Urban Constellation and the Core of the City," University of Toronto, 1951, TjJ/16/1, RIBA Archive, London.

102 "Its emphasis was on creation, or rehabilitation, of urban places of anonymous friendliness where – as was repeatedly stated – men and women can meet with their fellow citizens 'to see and be seen.'" Jaqueline Tyrwhitt, September 1974, Tyrwhitt TjJ/38/1, RIBA Archive, London.

103 The symbolic interpretation of the Core shared many resonances within coeval discourses proposed by other theorists: for instance, Kevin Lynch in "*The Image of the City*" (1959) affirmed that the Core is "*the focus and symbol of an important region*" with some echoes of Giedion's discourse. However, the symbol of the heart lost its post-war humanist value in opposition to the tyranny of the machines. For Lynch, it became the *node*, which is one of the elements that forms the public image of the city as a result of a "*constant interacting process*" between the observer and the environment. Moreover, Lynch's node kept its symbolical value omitting any organic references; indeed "these concentration nodes are the focus and epitome of a district, over which their influence radiates and of which they stand as symbol. They may be called cores." Kevin Lynch, *The Image of the City* (Cambridge: MIT Press, 1959), 48–76. It is interesting to note that Lynch taught at MIT and Giedion at Harvard in the same period. Interestingly, in the late 1950s, Kepes also helped the representation of the "The Image of the City" (Lynch).

104 "*Uomo in quanto tale, il nudo, scoperto uomo, non definito dalla classe sociale, dalla religione o dalla razza, si esprime direttamente in forme o simboliche sono eco del suo sentimento interiore.*" (translated: "Man as such, bare naked man, not defined by any social class, religion or race, he is expressed directly in symbolic forms or he's echoes of his inner feeling.") Giedion, *Breviario di Architettura*, 137.

105 Giedion, *Architecture You and Me*, 128. Giedion, "Historical Background to the Core," 17.

106 The school of Würzburg is mentioned in the Italian edition (Breviario di Architettura, 1961) and not in the American one (*Architecture You and Me*, 1958).

107 "*En réalité, le mot humanisme a deux sens très différents: Par humanisme on peut entendre une théorie qui prend l'homme comme fin et comme valeur supérieure . . . Cet humanisme est absurde, car seule le chien ou le cheval pourraient porter un jugement d' ensemble sur l' homme . . . Mais il y a un autre sens de l' humanisme, qui signifie au fond ceci: l' homme est constamment hors de lui-même, c'est en se projetant et en se perdant hors de lui qu'il fait exister l' homme et, d' autre part, c' est en poursuivant des buts transcendants qu'il peut exister; l' homme étant ce dépassement et ne saisissant les objets que par rapport à ce dépassement, est au coeur, au centre de ce dépassement.*" in Jean-Paul Sartre, *L' existentialisme est un humanisme* (Paris: Les Editions Nagel, 1946), 90–93.

108 Avermaete, *Another Modern*, 142, 384.

109 Giedion, *Architecture You and Me*, 28.

110 Lewis Mumford, "Monumentalism, Symbolism and Style," *Architecture Review* 105/628, (April 1949): 179. Quoted in Giedion, *Architecture You and Me*, 23.

111 Ibid., 162.

112 Lewis Mumford, "The Death of the Monument," in *Circle; An International Survey of Constructive Art*, ed. James L. Martin, Ben Nicholson, N. Gabo (London: Faber and Faber, 1937), 263–270.

113 Sigfried Giedion, "The Need for a New Monumentality," in *New Architecture and City Planning*, ed. Paul Zucker (New York: Philosophical Library, 1944).

114 Giedion, "The Heart of the City: A Summing-Up," 161.
115 But was two storeys high by the river's edge beside the highway. Thanks to Grahame Shane for the description.
    See the redrawn section of St Dié in David Grahame Shane, *Urban Design Since 1945: A Global Perspective* (New York: John Wiley & Sons Inc, 2011), 76.
116 The master plan of Chandigarh was designed by Le Corbusier with Jeannert, Drew and Frey, who were part of the MARS Group, organiser of the CIAM 8. Curtis affirms that "Thapar and Varma set out to find a new chief architect. They continued to feel that there was no one in India remotely capable of handling such a thing . . . They went to London and spoke to Jane Drew and Maxwell Fry, who had experience designing in the tropics but who hesitated to take the whole job on and recommended Le Corbusier." See William J. Curtis, "The Symbolism of Chandigarh," in William J. Curtis, *Le Corbusier: Ideas and Forms* (New York: Rizzoli, 1986), 188.
117 Ibid., 188–201.
118 Ibid., 194.
119 "Monumentality is the transcendental, most inspired expression of the essence, the will, the greatness of an epoch." Alfred Roth, during a symposium for architects held at the Museum of Modern Art, New York, February 1948, quoted in Christiane C. Collins, George R. Collins, "Monumentality. A Critical Matter in Modern Architecture," *Harvard Architectural Review*, 4 (Spring 1984): 29.
120 Kenzo Tange, "The Core. Its Social and Historical Background, June 1951," 42-JLS-17-60, gta/ETH.
121 Ibid.
122 Paolo Riani, *Kenzo Tange (20th Century Masters)* (New York: Hamlyn, 1971), 8.
123 Kenzo Tange, "Hiroshima," in *The Heart of the City: Towards the Humanisation of Urban Life*, ed. Jaqueline Tyrwhitt, Josep Lluís Sert, Ernesto N. Rogers (London: L. Humphries, 1952), 137.
124 Zhongjie Lin, *Kenzo Tange and the Metabolist Movement: Urban Utopias of Modern Japan* (London and New York: Routledge, 2010), 178.
125 Kenzo Tange, "Hiroshima," 136.
126 Lin, *Kenzo Tange and the Metabolist Movement*, 177.
127 Tange, "Function, Structure, Symbol," 243.
128 Kenzo Tange, "Technology and Humanity," *Japan Architect* (October 1960): 11–12, quote in Lin, *Kenzo Tange and the Metabolist Movement*, 178.
129 "*C'est un instrument de travail de premier ordre*," CIAM, "Le Documents de Sigtuna, June 1952, p. 11, A0612," Forbat Archive Am 1970–18, Arkdes Stockholm.
130 The MARS Group itself seemed to be somehow critical with this proposal by Le Corbusier. One year later, the British members fostered an easier and more immediate approach than the CIAM grid, "a kind of logistical tour-de-force": it was no "good trying to force all material into an arbitrary grid where each (horizontal) subject is treated from the same number of (vertical) angles." CIAM, *Le Documents de Sigtuna*. Quoted also in Pedret, "Representing History or Describing Historical Reality?: The Universal and the Individual in the 1950s."
131 CIAM, *The Heart of the City: Towards the Humanisation of Urban Life*, 102.
132 Jaqueline Tyrwhitt, "Principles of Town Planning. Lecture 10: The Urban Constellation and the Core of the City," TjJ/16/1, RIBA Archive, London.
133 "City plus countryside. . . , that area within which a full life can be lived with freedom of opportunity for the development of the potentialities of each individual." Jaqueline Tyrwhitt, "Cores Within the Urban Constellation," in *The Heart of the City: Towards the Humanisation of Urban Life*, ed. Jaqueline Tyrwhitt, Josep Lluís Sert, Ernesto N. Rogers (London: L. Humphries, 1952), 105.
134 Jaqueline Tyrwhitt, Manuscript to Progressive Architecture: "Civil Defence 'Do New Towns Provide Safety? NO' by Jaqueline Tyrwhitt, September 1951," TjJ/38/7/2, RIBA Archive, London.
135 This idea of order in disorder and vice versa was metaphorically described in the act of throwing: "this order within disorder – or disorder within order – is entirely different from a rigid geometrical relationship of satellites to a central sphere. It is the difference between

daffodil bulbs planted in a woodside glade by a tidy-minded gardener, who places them all exactly inches apart; and the same bulb thrown in handfuls and planted where they fall. The sight of the first mechanical grouping in a natural woodland setting offends us, while the second type of planting (which is in the fact no less 'grouped') charms us by its 'naturalness'. By the very act of throwing, a constellation has been created, through (in this case) with in invisible nucleus – the moment of throwing."

Jaqueline Tyrwhitt, "New Towns for Defence – The Urban Constellation," Progressive Architecture, June 1951 (Part of an address given to the AIA at Chicago, may, 1951), TjJ/38/7/2/1, RIBA Archive, London.

136 Ibid.
137 "It seems that the best pattern for living may also prove the best pattern for defence." Jaqueline Tyrwhitt, "Progressive Architecture, September 1951," TjJ/38/7/1, RIBA Archive, London. "Whether as a defence against the bomb or as a plan for living, the urban constellation seems to offer the most hopeful framework for planning . . . The only defence against death is life." Jaqueline Tyrwhitt, "New Towns for Defence – The Urban Constellation," TjJ/38/7/2/1, RIBA Archive, London.
138 "The 'neighbourhood unit', which started out with the ideal of creating integrated neighbourhoods, has too often only succeeded in creating segregated neighbourhoods, not very distinct from well built ghettos." Jaqueline Tyrwhitt, TjJ/38/9/10, RIBA Archive, London.
139 For a transatlantic influence between "neighbourhood unit" and "the heart of the city" see Domhardt, "From the 'Functional City' to the 'Heart of the City.' Green Space and Public Space in the CIAM Debates of 1942–1952," 133–156.
140 Jaqueline Tyrwhitt, TjJ/38/9/10, RIBA Archive, London.
141 Ibid.
142 Jaqueline Tyrwhitt, "The CORE, March 1953," TjJ/18/4, RIBA Archive, London.
143 Jaqueline Tyrwhitt, "The Core of the City, December 15, 1952," TjJ/38/9/3, RIBA Archive, London.
144 See Pedret, "Representing History or Describing Historical Reality?: The Universal and the Individual in the 1950s."
145 See Avermaete, Another Modern, 142.
146 "Their [Team 10] understanding of the 'Valley Section' was based on reading Tyrwhitt's translations of Geddes' texts and conversations with Tyrwhitt, who advised them." Shoshkes, "Jaqueline Tyrwhitt: From Town Planning to Urban Design," 13. Accessed on June 1, 2017, www.academia.edu/10315770/Jaqueline_Tyrwhitt_From_Town_Planning_to_Urban_Design

At CIAM 9 in 1953, significant alterations and additions to the classic grid were proposed, in particular, in Smithson's "Urban Re-identification Grid" and in the "Habitat du plus grand nombre Grid" proposed by the GAMMA group, Candilis and Woods.

The former was an attempt to introduce the topic of everyday life into the grid, adopting new categories – "house," "street," "relationship" – and photographs of children playing in the street. The latter revealed for the first time the realm of the everyday life of bidonville, shifting interest from formal modern projects to informal settlements.
147 Rosalind E. Krauss, The Originality of the Avant-Garde and Other Modernist Myths (Cambridge: MIT Press, 1986), 13. quoted in Avermaete, Another Modern, 151 and note 13, 397.
148 José Ortega y Gasset, The Revolt of the Masses (New York: W.W. Norton and Company Inc., 1932), 164–165. Quoted in Josep Lluís Sert, "Centres on Community Life," in The Heart of the City: Towards the Humanisation of Urban Life, ed. Jaqueline Tyrwhitt, Josep Lluís Sert, Ernesto N. Rogers (London: L. Humphries, 1952), 3.
149 Mumford, The CIAM Discourse on Urbanism, 1928–1960, 207.
150 "Un dispositivo ortopédico gigante." JoséOrtega y Gasset, Meditación de la técnica (Madrid: Alianza Editoriale, 2002), 108, quoted in Costruire, Abitare, Pensare, ed. Fabio Filippuzzi, Luca Taddio (Milan-Udine: Mimesis/Estetica e Architettura, 2010), 58.
151 José Ortegay Gasset, Meditación de la técnica (Madrid: Alianza Editoriale, 2002), quoted in José Ortega y Gasset, "Intorno al Colloquio di Darmstadt, 1951," in Costruire, Abitare, Pensare, 67.
152 Darmstadt Congress, August 4–6, 1951. CIAM 8 in Hoddesdon was held between July 7–14, 1951.

153 Among others: Bartning, Gerhard Weber, Franz Schuster, P. F. Schneider, Peter Grund, Ernst Neufert, Aloys Giefer and Hermann Mäckler, Rudolf Scwarz and Sep Ruf, Scharoun. The only non-German architect presenting a project was Willem Marius Dudok. The main reference of the exhibition was the "Artistic Colony of Darmstadt" held in 1901 and mostly all eleven exhibited projects are kindergartens and schools.

154 José Ortega y Gasset, *Meditación de la técnica*, 109 quoted in *Costruire, Abitare, Pensare*, 62 (In Italian: "*La rovina come afrodisiaco*").

155 This spirit was totally different in comparison for instance with the behaviour of Japanese Metabolists in front of Tokyo's ruins.

156 "we learn three things:

Building is really dwelling.
Dwelling is the manner in which mortals are on the earth.
Building as dwelling unfolds into the building that cultivates growing things and the building that erects buildings . . . The fundamental feature of living is that of taking care."
Martin Heidegger, "Bauen, Wohnen, Danken," in *Vorträge und Aufsätze* (Pfullingen: Günther Neske Verlag, 1954), 145–162. In English "Building, Dwelling, Thinking," in *Poetry, Language, Thought*, trans. Albert Hofstadter (New York: Harper Colophon Books, 1971), 145–161.

157 Lecture at Bühler Hohe spa in the mountains above Baden Baden, October 6, 1951. Adam Sharr, *Heidegger for Architects* (London and New York: Routledge, 2007), 75.

158 In German: "*Diese neue Welt der Technik also ist wie ein riesiger orthopädischer Apparat*" José Ortega y Gasset, "Der Mythus des menschen hinter der technic," in *Mensch und Raum*, Das Darmstädter Gespräch, 1951 (Braunschweig: Vieweg, 1991).

159 Originally in Italian: "*A Hoddesdon nel 1951 come a Darmstadt la formulazione delle domande e le tematiche si assomigliano: la 'riscoperta' dello spazio urbano, rispettivamente la messa in rilievo della città e dei suoi compiti contro la politica di ricostruzione a senso unico del governo – e così anche le riposte.*" Werner Oechslin, I Darmstädter Gespräche, *Rassegna*, 52, no. 4 (1992): 80.

160 Quoted in Mumford, *The CIAM Discourse on Urbanism, 1928–1960*, 215.

161 Henri Lefebvre, "Preface to the Study of the Habitat of the Pavillon," in *Henri Lefebvre: Key Writings*, ed. Stuart Elden, Elizabeth Lebas, Elenore Kofman (New York: Bloomsbury Academic, Continuum, 2003), 122. Originally published in French: Henri Lefebvre, "Preface," in *L'Habitat pavillonnaire*, ed. Henri Raymond et al. (Paris: CRU, 1966), 3–23.

Neither the pre-war functionalist "dwelling" of Le Corbusier nor the poetical dwelling depicted by Heidegger were positive, correct references for Lefebvre, as already highlighted by Stanek. See Łukasz Stanek, *Henri Lefebvre on Space: Architecture, Urban Research, and the Production of Theory* (Minneapolis: University of Minnesota Press, 2011), 88.

162 "*Denn Sie Sagte mir etwas von einer unausgesprochenen Einstimmigkeit zwischen Ihrem Schaffen und meinem Versuchen*," Heidegger in Scharoun-Archiv (23 Juni 1952, 13) quoted in Gerd de Bruyn, *Fisch und Frosch oder die Selbstkritik der Moderne* (Basel: Birkhäuser, 2001), 100. Quoted also in Marcello Barison, "Eterotopie-Gropius-Heidegger-Scharoun," in *Costruire, Abitare, Pensare*, 126–127.

Part II

Anatomy of the Heart of the City

2 First UD Conference and Victor Gruen

The Heart of the City as Urban Design and invention of the city

The man of the fields is still a sort of vegetable.[1]

Josep Lluís Sert, "Centres of Community Life," 1952

All human identity and human scale seems lost
in the sprawl of the contemporary urban region.
Man has become a faceless insect.[2]

Jaqueline Tyrwhitt, Josep Lluís Sert,
"The Shape of American Cities," 1958

The First Urban Design Conference

The need for recentralisation[3]

At CIAM 8, the president, Josep Lluís Sert, introduced the issue of the dangerous negation of urban centrality due to urban sprawl and the constant enlargement of city boundaries.

This negation of centrality was approached by Sert as another form of destruction, but a kind which represented "a real menace to all our cities and to the stability of civic values,"[4] rather than the bombed centre. This perspective, in Sert's opinion, led to the heart of the city principally becoming an important ethical issue of recentralisation. From his point of view, the typicality of the metaphor of the heart with its organic characteristics of limitation, specific size and dimension, requiring translation into a correct, human-scale urban form, remained of paramount importance.

This need to recentralise the city was not, however, a new concept within CIAM, as it had already been stressed in previous congresses. For instance, Le Corbusier's "biological development" of the *Ville Radieuse* was already an example of increasing densities within the city in the 1930s, since "extreme manifestations of vitality are to be found in places of great concentration."[5]

Regarding the use of the organic image in Sert, as early as 1944, in his essay entitled "The Human Scale in City Planning,"[6] the Spanish architect compared one of his plans to Leonardo da Vinci's Vitruvian Man, in order to highlight the human dimension of the city itself and to enhance the "centralization and concentration"[7] of the urban structure. In his diagram, Sert emphasised the humanisation of the city through the strict connections between eight units or organs, using the organic metaphor as counterforce to the decentralised patterns, of the "neither-city-nor-country-complex."[8] The proximity, the well-defined dimensions, the limited size and the defined relations

THE HUMAN SCALE IN CITY PLANNING

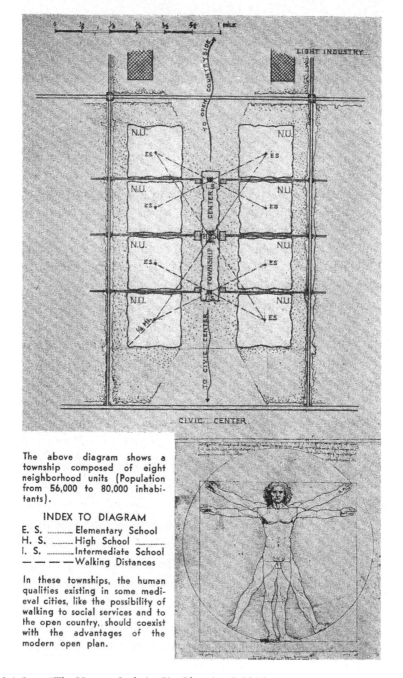

The above diagram shows a township composed of eight neighborhood units (Population from 56,000 to 80,000 inhabitants).

INDEX TO DIAGRAM

E. S. .... Elementary School
H. S. .... High School
I. S. ....Intermediate School
— — — —Walking Distances

In these townships, the human qualities existing in some medieval cities, like the possibility of walking to social services and to the open country, should coexist with the advantages of the modern open plan.

Figure 2.1 Sert, "The Human Scale in City Planning," 1944.

The main aim of the diagram and of the organic metaphor, was the rescue of "civic values" inside an urban structure which, for the first time in history, was going to be profoundly deformed.

Source: Courtesy of the Philosophical Library. Sert Collection D16, Courtesy of the Frances Loeb Library, Harvard Graduate School of Design. In Zucker ed., *New Architecture and City Planning*.

and functions of the organs aimed to re-create the human qualities existing in some medieval cities, which were threatened in the political and economic conditions of the post-war world. Hence, the human scale was not a symbolical concept, but a physical module where each organ had a "specific function to perform" and "the function of one part should not hinder that of another,"[9] exactly like the organic living body. Not surprisingly, the basic unit of Sert's plan was the functional and self-contained "neighbourhood unit," considered as an "expression of family group organization"[10] structured around the elementary school as Clarence Perry conceived it the 1920s.[11]

Similarly to Sert, in 1953 his collaborator Paul Lester Wiener also published in "*Nuestra Architectura*," the "Diagram of the Human Environment"[12] where Man is centrally inscribed within a system of squares symbolising the home, the neighbourhood, the city, the region and a final circle representing the world and the cosmos.[13] This inscribing within squares and circles resonates with the Vitruvian Man which was exhumed by Sert. The latter, however, presumed the perfect, ideal, canonical Renaissance proportions mirrored in the city while the Man drawn by Wiener highlighted both its spiritual-conceptual and physical centrality inside hierarchical levels of habitat. In any case, for both architects, the physical urban recentralisation and the metaphorical centrality of Man became important ethical and civic topics, the predestined cure for the city's survival. This belief of recentralisation also reverberated in the already mentioned "comic" metaphor of Ortega y Gasset's "cannon," which opened Sert's discourse at CIAM 8 and theoretically linked the coeval congresses of Hoddesdon and Darmstadt in 1951.

A few years later, in 1954, the Italian Philosopher Enzo Paci focused his attention on the contradictions resulting from the exaggeration and insistence on Man's centralisation as discussed by some of the architects present at CIAM 8.

In particular, in his article "*Il Cuore della Città*" (The Heart of the City) published in *Casabella Continuità*, the Italian philosopher foresaw Sert's conservative, anachronistic metaphor of the cannon as the cause of the isolation of the city itself, "even though perfect like the stellar city of the *Filarete*."[14] Paci underlined how the "Heart of the City" theme, as conceived by Sert, was influenced both by the philosopher Gianbattista Vico (1668–1744) and Max Weber (1864–1920), who considered the founding of a city as the configuration of human space carved into the *ingens sylva* of savagery, with its own time of *societas*, "as opposed to that of [the] farmer."[15] The cannon, similarly to the Vitruvian Man, was only partially acceptable. It was too fixed an image of the city and no longer corresponded to the social, cultural or even philosophical contemporary context. With regard to decentralisation and recentralisation, Paci conversely reckoned that the city should be considered as a point of junction between the closed and the open, "with a centripetal diastolic movement, but, at the same time, a systolic centrifugal one."[16] This specific reference to the movement of Heart, to both its diastolic and systolic movement, was not a mere functionalist reference to the blood-pumping system. The heart's movement instead concerned the necessity of life, the active and continuous relationship between *urbia* and geo-botanic cosmos, between civic space and landscape, between culture and nature, and so on. It was a sophisticated interpretation of the organic metaphor which invested both the physical and cultural aspects of the city. Moreover, similar critiques would be developed within Team 10's debate. In the latter, the Vitruvian Man inscribed within the limited and absolute boundaries of the circle, similar to the cannon, could be no longer in the totalising centre; in his place, the complexity, contradictions and relationships of the entire open social-urban structure became the most intensive point of the scale of association in Geddes' Valley section, as reinterpreted by the Team 10 youngsters.

Finally, a few years after the meeting at Hoddesdon, in contrast to Paci and Team 10's assumptions, Sert reiterated his ideas on centrality, centralisation and concentration, remarkably relying on the younger generations as his main urban-minded supporters:

> The younger generation in this country . . . has become aware that the uncontrolled sprawl of our communities only aggravates their problems, and that the solution lies in the re-shaping the city as a whole. The necessary process is not one of decentralization, but one of re-centralization . . . We must be urban minded.[17]

This was April 9, 1956, and Sert was talking at the First Urban Design Conference held at Harvard University in the US, where he was appointed Dean in 1953.

Although 1956 saw the death of CIAM and the disposal of the old avant-garde by the young Team 10,[18] overseas the continuity of CIAM's discussion on the heart as a metaphor of a necessary container or cannon of civic centrality was resilient,[19] and it gave rise to the birth of the Urban Design discipline within the American context. If the roots of CIAM 8 can also be traced in American neighbourhood theory and in a constant transatlantic exchange of ideas between the US and Europe since the 1930s (Domhardt),[20] in the 1950s, the Heart of the City certainly became "the precursor of Urban Design" (Mumford)[21] in the US, relying on the metaphoric heart, recentralisation, densification and the organic connections of the urban structure as the main concerns of departure.

Three-dimensional design

Another issue discussed during the First Urban Design Conference, which had already been highlighted at Hoddesdon as well as in the Athens Charter,[22] was the design of the city in three dimensions. As Sert affirmed in his introduction to the Urban Design Conference in 1956, "Urban Design is the part of city planning that deals with the physical form of the city. It is by nature three or four dimensional (four if we include the time factor)."[23]

However, the interest in three-dimensional design did not concern only the physical complexity and overlapping flows inside the urban structure. It was also imbedded with theoretical, social, historical and functional connotations and interpretations. Moreover, it incorporated other outstanding issues such as the need for both synthesis and synergy between all the professional figures working on the city. As Sert stated during the conclusion of the meeting:

> There is certain misgiving among architects, as someone has said here, that city planners do not know anything about the three-dimensional world we want to help shape. And the city planners think the architects know nothing about city planning . . . It is terribly tragic that while people know how to read and write, they have no way of reading things in three dimensions and, as a result, we are talking completely different languages.[24]

Hence, the capability to design and understand the project in three dimensions was compared to the skill of reading a common vocabulary or language that all urban actors, in particular, architects and urban planners, should know in order to communicate and to understand an idea, a project or a plan. The lack of this common spatial language, as a common professional design tool, could turn professional practice and the city itself into a Babelic experience.

Remarkably the urgency of cooperation among different urban actors was already emphasised during CIAM 8. "We invited a doctor, a sociologist, an economist, a government official and an historian to give us the benefit of their experiences,"[25] summarised Giedion. In *Architecture You and Me*, the Swiss historian even reiterated this idea of a necessary collaboration among different practitioners tackling the human complexity of the urban structure. Since "the problem of the core is a human problem . . . Architects and planners know that they cannot solve this problem alone and they need the cooperation of sociologists, doctors and historians."[26] The Health centre of Dr Williamson, which has been previously described, was certainly one of the emblematic examples of this praised professional teamwork and transdisciplinary presence within CIAM. Moreover, within this multidisciplinary synergy, Le Corbusier particularly underscored the cooperation between the architect and the artist, rather than with the planners, in his text "The Core as a Meeting Place of the Arts."[27] Le Corbusier referred to the core as "a meeting place of arts," the stage of a popular theatre in a similar way as a *piazzetta* in Venice where *The Merchant of Venice* could be enacted. "Le Corbusier's intuition reintegrates the functional requirement of the aesthetic creation in the human community,"[28] as Paci already stated in 1954. It reintegrated the artistic and spiritual values of the human life through the overlapping of different disciplines and beyond the mere functionalist purpose of Architecture. In the final "A Short Outline of the Core," the Heart was indeed recalled as "a centre of the Arts" where "the synthesis of effort contributed by architects, painters, and sculptors working in cooperation in the true communion of a single team"[29] should be most effectively accomplished.

Finally, from painters to architects and from architects to planners, at Hoddesdon in 1951 as well as at Harvard in 1956, the cooperation between professional figures operating in the city was proposed as a main necessity for a proper socio-spatial definition of the humane core as a three-dimensional humanised "artefact: a man-made essential element of the city planning."[30] From this perspective, three-dimensional design's insistence within Urban Design and the Heart of the City Idea somehow confuted any criticism which merely considered the Heart as a fifth element in addition to the previous ones (dwelling, work, recreation and transport). It was instead a counterforce to a planar zoning method of planning, of a bi-dimensional lack of complexity of functions, synergy and human needs.

Giedion and the three space conceptions

Almost forty years after the *Charte d'Athènes*, the complex role and the importance of three-dimensional space in contemporary architecture was subjected to in-depth analysis by one of the main exponents of CIAM.

In "Architecture and the Phenomena of Transition, the Three Space Conceptions in Architecture,"[31] published posthumously in 1971, Giedion presented three different conceptions of space, relating them to three different and significant stages of Western architecture. The First space concerned architecture as space-radiating volumes, as in Greek architecture, embodying the new European democracy with its emphasis upon the individual. The Second space conception was formulated in Roman architecture, based on the evolution of interior space. The Third space conception "has only just begun. Where it will lead no one can tell" – Giedion stated,

> its preliminary stage was occupied with reuniting thinking and feeling, which had been reft asunder in the nineteenth century. The next stage was to bring about a necessary distinction between the collective and private spheres within human society, with an acute awareness of the changes occurring in contemporary life.[32]

If three-dimensional design was conceived as a common vocabulary for practitioners' synergy according to Sert, Giedion's third space conception had a more abstract and social aim reuniting thinking and feeling, collective and private spheres. The latter binomial spheres of the latter certainly coincided with the search for an equipoise between the public heart and private hearth at CIAM 8, as previously discussed. Moreover, for Giedion, the revolution of the third space conception was expressed for the first time in sculpture. In 1916, the sculptor Alexander Archipenko translated the synergy between the interior and exterior space in his artwork "Seated Figure." It represented a seated person whose body is moulded in a continuous "fluctuation of volume and void, interior and exterior,"[33] convex and concave.

This continual interpenetration of space was then translated in Architecture as well. Unsurprisingly, the first architectural project of third space conception presented by Giedion was the St Dié Civic Center, designed by Le Corbusier in 1945, presented at CIAM 8 and already praised by Giedion in *Architecture You and Me* for its monumentality, as previously discussed. According to the Swiss historian, Le Corbusier achieved a freedom of sculptural interrelations between the buildings similarly to Piazza Duomo in Pisa, which is also entirely organised for the pedestrian. Similarly to the sculptures of Giacometti,[34] "each building is so placed that it radiates its own space, while simultaneously it is subordinated to the unity of the whole center,"[35] described Giedion.

However, a few years later, the same sculptural interrelation celebrated by Giedion was vehemently criticised by Rowe and Koetter: in *Collage City*[36] the revolutionary and pioneering three-dimensional concept of Le Corbusier's St Dié was doomed because the quality of public space had been "shrunk to an apologetic ghost." Interestingly, the St Dié plan was compared this time with the ground plan of another Italian city, Parma, underlining the contrast between the prevalence of the "object" in the French master plan and the richness of "space" in the Italian texture: as a result, the "solid and continuous matrix or texture giving energy to its reciprocal condition, the specific space,"[37] typical of the traditional city, was lost together with its sociological values and identity. *Vis-à-vis* this somehow contradictory comparison of Le Corbusier's project with the plans of both Pisa and Parma, it is important to stress the rise of interest in the context and history since the 1950s as the key reference for contemporary urban design. This topic was already massively present at CIAM 8, in particular during the discussion about Italian piazzas, deeply influencing the idea of the Heart and at the CIAM Summer School in Venice, which is later described.

Finally, St Dié became a very important project also for Sert who, during the First Urban Design Conference, described it as "the first physical expression of the emerging

Figure 2.2 Alexander Archipenko, "Seated Figure," 1916.

Source: © Archipenko, by SIAE 2017.

idea of the core."[38] The French plan clearly influenced Sert's projects such as Motor City or Chimbote,[39] which were also discussed in Hoddesdon. The latter project was a new, small, industrial seaport city in Peru, composed of ten neighbourhoods, four of which were grouped around the Core. The residences were designed as one- and two-storey houses, stressing the theme of the patio as the key aspect throughout the entire urban structure. The Core of Chimbote was proposed as "an attempt to provide a modern extension of an old tradition," as Sert explained, with a small stream passing through it and with branches in all directions, "following the Arab tradition and that of the Incas."[40] Sert's Latin America master plans appeared to show intriguing

synergies between contextualised urban local presences and modern space composition, bringing to the fore the interest in "tradition" at Hoddesdon in 1951. The
three-dimensional design and plastic expression were aimed at reconquering the civic
values of a traditionalist image of the organic city. They were conditioned by interest
in social values, local identities combined with modern "space conceptions," in a new
synergy which remain pivotal for our contemporary urban design as well.[41]

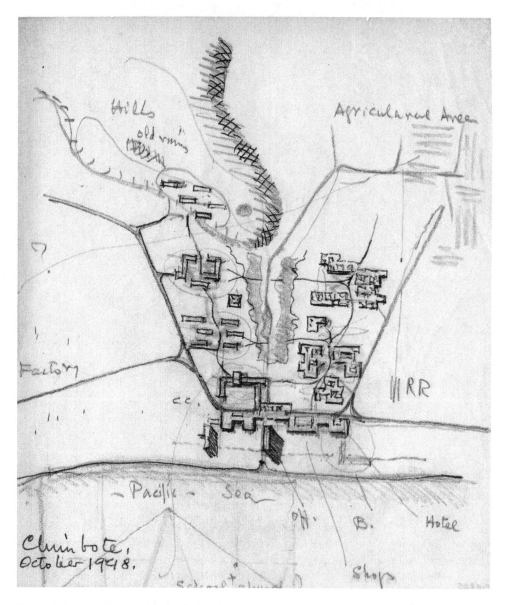

Figure 2.3 Sert, Wiener, Sketch of Chimbote Plan, 1946–48.

Source: Chimbote, Sert collection B75 A. Courtesy of the Frances Loeb Library, Harvard Graduate School
of Design.

The necessity for the pedestrian realm

The importance of the right of the pedestrian, *"la royauté du piéton"* as it was called by Le Corbusier, was an outstanding characteristic of the Core claimed during CIAM 8 as well as at Harvard.[42] It was one of the main features which led Eric Mumford to proclaim CIAM's "Heart of the City" as precursor of Urban Design.[43]

Indeed, in the final "Summary of Needs at The Core," it was already stated "that the Core should be a place secure from traffic – where the pedestrian can move about freely . . . That cars should arrive and park on the periphery of the Core, but not Cross it."[44]

Hence, CIAM 8 brought to the fore the need for separation of flows in order to dam the problem of the prolific rise in the use of private cars. This had radically transformed the urban structure itself as, for instance, later ratified by the Buchanan Report[45] (1963), a milestone for the urban traffic issue, which studied the political tools used to remedy congestion of central areas.

Furthermore, this transformation radically occurred in the 1950s when, according to Frampton, "the traditional city form, capable of combining many different uses within its continuous, densely woven urban fabric, has found itself superseded by an economically optimizing 'motopia'."[46] The city's dependence on the car was very evident, especially in the US, where the topic of the heart was transferred as a germinating idea to the Urban Design discourse. Victoria de Grazia reminds us that as early as the end of the 1930s, while in France and England one-twentieth of the population had a car (in Germany one-fortieth, in Italy one-hundredth), in the US, the proportion was already one-fourth. This was the result of the radical revolution of the Ford standardisation which was imbedded in that American "Irresistible Empire"[47] which peacefully invaded the whole world through consumerism from the beginning of the last century.

Moreover, according to David Grahame Shane,[48] the increasing number of automobiles, alongside the reconstruction of cities after the war, was the main cause of the origin of Urban Design, which can be traced back to 1943, before CIAM 8, in the plans by Patrick Abercrombie and John Henry Forshaw. Interestingly, both issues, automobiles and reconstruction, were central in the debate at CIAM 8, as already mentioned. Thus, Urban Design and the Heart of the City can be considered as coeval and consonant discourses after the war which influenced each other.

Faced with the rise of the automobile, at CIAM 8, the split between car and pedestrian flows was first of all a symbolical rift between the Heart as the most explicit expression of human values within the public realm and the tyranny of the mechanical tools, as described by Giedion. This abstract split between Man and machine easily turned into the functionalist scission of pedestrian and mechanical flows at the level of concrete urban structure. Even though the issue of pedestrian rights seemed to have been rationally solved, the entire road system became a radical functional compromise and compartmentalised solution of the original humanist values. An emblematic example was Le Corbusier's "seven roads-V7,"[49] a system of classification according to the uses and purposes of the roads which was used in the Chandigarh project[50] and presented in Hoddesdon in 1951. "At a very crude level of thought this is obviously a good idea," Christopher Alexander confessed in the 1960s when discussing the separation of pedestrians from moving vehicles as proposed by Le Corbusier and later by Luis Kahn, "but it is not always a good idea." What was missing in general was the overlapping of functions, necessities and desires which characterises society, which is not a strict functionalist structure. From our practical everyday life, we can use "the urban taxi only because pedestrians and vehicles are not strictly separated. . . . Thank God for taxis,"[51] Alexander concluded.

This socio-spatial complexity was somehow more evident in the Bogotá master plan, also presented at Hoddesdon and prepared by the French architect with Sert and Wiener as consultants. The project followed the "V7" system, as Eric Mumford describes it.[52] However, as in all his South America projects, Sert's interest was focused on the integration of the local urban presences, in "a modern extension of an old tradition."[53] The functional division of streets therefore found a more sophisticated vernacular relationship with the pre-existing context and with the history of the place as well.[54]

Finally, the split of flows, and the consequent pedestrianisation as the "hallmark of modern architecture"[55] as depicted by Smiley, was such a relevant topic that it even became an academic assignment to be developed further by students. In 1954, Sert led the Urban Design course at the GSD together with Carlhian and Roland Gourley, assisted by Costantino Nivola, a Sardinian artist and sculptor. The main theme was the requalification of Times Square in New York, along Broadway and 7th Avenue between West 42nd and 47th Streets. The main purpose was the transformation of the New York crossroad into a real square. As we can read in the "preliminary study" assignment given at the course, all the issues discussed earlier were presented to the students: for instance, "the continuity between the new Times Square and the existing one," the improvement of the pedestrian space and the separation from automobile traffic, the location of the right amount of car parking spaces and the attention to the three-dimensional elements. Personal psychological sensibility was also proposed as an important element for analysis:

> Any elements susceptible of creating an impact on the individual's senses should be considered an essential part of the designer's palette – odours, noises as well as all the known (or unknown) visual elements. Psychological behaviour of crowds cannot and should not be ignored.[56]

One of the most interesting projects proposed by students was published in Architectural Forum in August 1955 in the article "Could This Be Times Square Tomorrow?" The project proposed an elevated system for pedestrian circulation. This was based on a three-dimensional structure, partly stretched out across a horizontal plane for the pedestrian route and occasionally broken down vertically in order to lodge billboards and shops. Five buildings were considered obsolete and were eliminated, and the spectacular neon signs were stripped from the façades and replaced with new technological ones. Finally, new car parking towers were added in order to relieve the city centre of car traffic and create new sights to observe the city. This intriguing double ground level in Times Square, which once again highlighted the topic of three-dimensional design in Urban Design, surprisingly anticipated some of the American pedestrian walkways in the 1960s according to Mumford.[57] Therefore, the theories and investigations of CIAM somehow influenced or foresaw the formation and transformation of urban structure in the US through the academic interpretations and design experimentations of the younger generations.[58]

Figure 2.4 GSD Students, Redevelopment Times Square Arch 2–4a fall 1954.

Source: GSD Students, CA005. Courtesy of the Frances Loeb Library, Harvard Graduate School of Design.

Figure 2.5 GSD Students with Nivola, Model Times Square, 1954.

Source: GSD Students, CA005. Courtesy of the Frances Loeb Library, Harvard Graduate School of Design.

From the summary of the core to the Synthesis of Urban Design

In the 1950s as well as nowadays, both the Heart of the City and Urban Design did not and do not have a sufficiently clear frame of significance in urban theory and practice. If in 1951 CIAM members tried to trace a summary of the Core, in 1957 Jaqueline Tyrwhitt wrote a letter to different professional figures related to city design – such as architects, planners, sociologists, lawyers, . . . – to ask them for a short definition of Urban Design. The intriguing inquiry, proposed for the architectural journal *Synthesis*,[59] published by the GSD students, resulted in a total of 32 answers.[60] Twenty reactions were positive and explained different points of view regarding the profession, education, the three-dimensional aspect (Le Corbusier), the social issue of "giving space to a community" (R. Neutra), the efforts to create "the living spaces of our urban surrounding" (W. Gropius), the resolution of chaos in the City (Breger and Tunnard), the modulation of the environment and of our attitude towards it (Gaus, Haar, etc.), and so on.

Similar to the discussion about the Heart of City, held a few years before in Hoddesdon, interpretations of the theme were therefore multiple and not always consistent. Among the CIAM members who answered to Tyrwhitt's proposal, Giedion replied with a very significant definition: "Urban Design has to give visual form to the relationship between You and Me."[61] Almost in the same period, the Austrian historian published the book *Architecture You and Me*, with the original title *Architektur und Gemeinschaft*. Interestingly, this latter book, to which Giedion's definition of Urban Design clearly referred, dealt directly with the Heart of the City theme. Hence, the continuity of theoretical fluxes from the Heart of the City towards Urban Design in the US was again reiterated. While Urban Design was described in *Synthesis* as the correct physical and visual translation of the social collective "relationship between You and Me,"[62] then the Heart of the City was depicted in the book as the symbolic representation of this relationship.[63] Therefore, the Heart somehow might be considered as the final aim of Urban Design.

Furthermore, alongside the various theoretical definitions of Urban Design, the expressive sketches of the Italian artist Costantino Nivola (1911–1988) were released. All the drawings appeared as a comparison between old and new, multiple and singular, vernacular and modern, low and high: many topics of what had been described in words by other architects seemed to be summarised and envisaged in these hand-made drawings, which might also be interpreted as a visual *Synthesis* of all the positions described.

Another insightful sketch which raised the interpretative complexity of the Urban Design topic was proposed by Sidney L. Katz who explained, "The field of urban

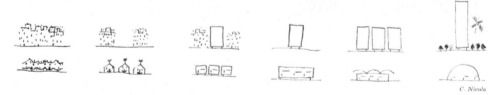

Figure 2.6 Nivola, "Sketches about Urban Design."

Source: In Tyrwhitt, "Definitions of Urban Design," *Synthesis* (April 1957): 30–31. Courtesy of the Frances Loeb Library, Harvard Graduate School of Design.

design deals with integrated concrete solutions to the specialized social needs and inter-relationships of individuals, family, neighbourhoods, communities, cities, regions, states, nations and the world."[64] The related scheme, called "Urban Design reference frame," presented two diagonal lines, where different scales of agglomerations are listed, from the individual on the left to the world on the right, passing through the intersection centre, which defines the City. The four areas, formed by the intersection, are symmetrically divided into "forms" and "information, needs, means."

Interestingly, contrary to the diagrams of Wiener and Sert, in Katz's Urban Design frame, the centrality of Man was undermined by the importance of the City, where the urban form meets the architectural one. Urban Design therefore assumed the role of the discipline which controls the design of these two kinds of forms or structures, with many reverberations in later discussions and books, such as the *Architecture of the City* (1966) by Aldo Rossi.

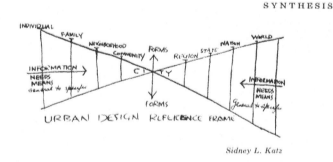

Figure 2.7 Katz, "Urban Design Reference Frame."

Source: In Tyrwhitt, "Definitions of Urban Design," *Synthesis* (April 1957): 29. Courtesy of the Frances Loeb Library, Harvard Graduate School of Design.

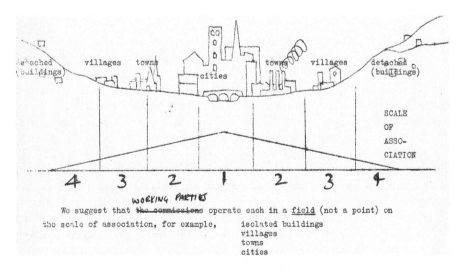

Figure 2.8 Team 10, CIAM, "Scale of Association," 1954.

Source: TTEN_8–1, Naverslag/circulaire "Statement on Habitat," 1954–03–01; A. en P. Smithson. Archiefdeel Team 10/Archivalia, Het Nieuwe Instituut, Rotterdam.

Moreover, Katz's scheme echoed the rising interest on the "human association" of Patrick Geddes' Valley Section interpreted by Team 10 in the Doorn Manifesto in 1954.

Similarly to Katz's scheme, the city was positioned in the central part: although there is still a dimensional distinction as in the five levels of the Heart, attention was focused on the importance of the complex relationships within the city instead of the anthropocentric individual of an "absurd humanism."[65]

The City is the place where human relations are higher than in the other levels, where the design's strengths will be more complex than in other places. This "comparative and synchronic scale that establishes a conceptual relation that binds the smaller communities into a hierarchically structured, larger whole"[66] – as Volker M. Welter defines it – should definitely substitute the functional hierarchy described in the *Charte d'Athènes* as dwelling, work, recreation and transport.

This similarity with the Urban Design scheme was important in order to underline the discontinuity with functional planar zoning, with the four functions of the city, within the Urban Design discourse, and thus in the Heart of the City too. Team 10's scale of association, Katz's interpretation of Urban Design and CIAM's Heart of the City therefore found similar roots, in a continual flux of ideas between Europe and America.

Victor Gruen

At the First Urban Design Conference at Harvard in 1956, among the urban projects discussed as case studies under the title "Urban Design of Today," there was also the urban renewal of the Centre of Fort Worth, designed by one of the most important commercial and urban designers of the last century, both in the US and Europe: Victor Gruen (Vienna, 1903–1980). Victor Gruen was an Austrian-born architect who studied at the *Akademie der Bildenden Künste* of Vienna, where he continued to practise in an architecture firm and in cabaret shows until he emigrated. His training was entirely imbued with European culture. His city of origin, Vienna, Europe's "center of intellectual and cultural life,"[67] represented Gruen's professional and personal link with both the European historical city and European modern architecture, in particular with the works of Loos. The mix of European architectural schooling and traditionalist urban origins of Gruen, the "thoughtful American,"[68] remained as the main reference to be translated, reinterpreted and grounded in the American context where he prepared the rise of a brand new architectural-urban archetype: the shopping centre.

In the USA, Gruen's unexampled work was developed combining both theoretical and design interests for the shopping centre which culminated with the publication of "Shopping Towns USA," written with the economist Larry Smith in 1958–1959. Under this title, Gruen highlighted the necessity to stress "that the role of the new planning concept could expand beyond the goal of creating merely machines for selling, and could satisfy the demand for urban crystallisation points, and thus offer to the suburban population significant life experiences."[69] Therefore, the commercial centre was conceived, or at least propagandised, by the Austrian-born architect neither as a mere consumerist machine for a throwaway society which relied ever more on new values of instantaneity and eliminability[70] within the "*Trente glorieuses*" (Jean Fourastiè), nor as a subdued political-economic weapon of the brand new American "Irresistible Empire"[71] which was engaged in "the struggle for the peaceful [commercial] conquest of the world,"[72] as president Woodrow Wilson claimed as early as 1916. Rather than a paradigm of "*Surmodernitè*,"[73] the Regional Shopping Centre was instead proposed as a new type of gathering place which could structure and polarise the suburban society as "urban crystallization points," contrasting with the sprawl of the city. This idealist purpose certainly echoed the intentions of both CIAM 8 and the First UD.

Regarding Gruen's connection with CIAM, the hidden references and connections between the more institutional, high-cultural, elitist, architectural-urban avant-garde of the Modern Movement and the new archetypical shopping profane avant-garde of the "mall maker,"[74] Victor Gruen, were certainly a biunique correspondence. On the one hand, Gruen – the pioneer of the regional shopping centre – often relied on CIAM either as a reference or as direct theoretical support, even though Smiley underlined that Gruen "tended to distance himself from the debates of architectural circles."[75] On the other, some of CIAM's members were attracted by the potentialities of the shopping centre, the new consumption "Phalanstery,"[76] whose architects had in turn a significant role in "normalizing modernism."[77]

Moreover, the encounters and influences between CIAM's members and Gruen were certainly the effect of a transatlantic flow of ideas and emigration from Europe to the US. Gruen was absorbed and forced to be part of a tragic architectural "diaspora,"[78] as it was called by Sibyl Moholy-Nagy, when Nazism forced him and his wife to emigrate from his beloved Vienna to the US in 1938, before the outbreak of World War II. While many important European members of CIAM decided to continue their debate and career in the American context, the "country of timid people,"[79] as levelled by Le Corbusier, became eager to bet on the commercial experiments of a Viennese cabaret artist-architect and to absorb the mastery of well-known European Masters of the Modern Movement, such as Sert at Harvard.

Remarkably, the biunique influences and fascination between commercial culture and modernism, one of the main issues in post-war Europe according to Mattson,[80] were stressed by several CIAM members themselves. For instance, the shift of Gruen's projects from pure commercial machines to "a centre of social activity"[81] was highlighted and supported by CIAM member Sigfried Giedion, who counted Gruen's Southdale shopping centre among the pioneering ventures of the last hundred years in his book *Architecture You and Me*. In particular, the Southdale Centre, which opened in 1956, became one the first examples of the "enclosed," introverted, "supermodern"[82] shopping centre where the use of air conditioning systems ensured an internal "atmosphere of eternal spring." The warm, surrogate climate inside this "pleasure dome with parking,"[83] favoured social and commercial gathering throughout the year, in contrast with the real chill of the Cold War, as noted by Mennel.[84]

Figure 2.9 Gruen Associates, Southdale Center: Exterior view, 1956.

Source: Courtesy of Gruen Associates. In Gruen, *Centers for the Urban Environment: Survival of the Cities*, 36.

Figure 2.10 Gruen Associates, Southdale Center: Interior, General View of the Garden Court.

Source: Courtesy of Gruen Associates. In Gruen, *Centers for the Urban Environment: Survival of the Cities*, 37.

Furthermore, Mardges Bacon highlighted both the importance of the shopping centre in the neighbourhood community[85] recognised by Sert in "Can Our Cities Survive?"
and the relevance of the new North American shopping centre models on his Latin
American projects. This resonance was already disclosed by Morris Ketchum, one of
Victor Gruen's first partners, who praised the project *Cidade dos Motores* (1944–47),
designed by Sert and Wiener, as a model for the proper integration of shopping facilities in other urban functions, in his book *Shops and Stores*[86] (1948). Sert himself
stressed the importance of the first shopping centre experiments as attempts to design
new centres of community. At CIAM 8, he disclosed that it was "encouraging that
some of the new shopping centres in the USA represent a trend in the right direction"
since they provided solutions "to protect pedestrian circulation from traffic and rain"
and offered "landscaped areas that can make shopping more pleasant."[87] Coherently
with these assumptions, the cover of the CIAM 8's publication shows a project of Cali,
in Colombia, which includes a commercial centre.[88] Furthermore, also at the Urban
Design Seminar on the human scale held at Harvard in 1957, the Spanish architect
stated that shopping centres were the first "notable attempt in the United States to give
the pedestrian a meeting place."[89] Then in 1958, together with Tyrwhitt, Sert again
endorsed the shopping centre as a "hopeful new trend" for the civic preservation and
human life, where "the pedestrian – the citizen standing on his own two feet – had been

able to reassert his age-old and long-lost right to move about freely without fearing for his life."[90]

Therefore, Sert seemed to perfectly agree with Gruen, who defined the shopping centre in "Shopping Towns USA" (1960) as a new contemporary archetype, "one of the few new building types created in our time"; its aim was to satisfy new contemporary human needs and activities, becoming a new "urban organism," a "shopping town."[91]

It is not surprising that the shopping centre also became an urban project theme proposed to students at GSD Harvard, before and during Sert's tenure as Dean. However, in 1945–1946, students' final proposals for a commercial centre in Hingham still seemed a little primordial, more similar to small theatres with some annexed shops and facilities than a shopping centre, and no car parking![92] More interesting still were the projects, for instance, during the autumn term 1957–1958, when the course theme of "shopping centers" introduced more complexity of functions and the study of pedestrian and vehicular movement, which would also become an important aspect in the design of urban civic centres.[93]

Finally, this integration of different urban functions within the shopping centre even became the main theme of the Seventh Urban Design Conference, held in 1963: "the Shopping Center as Nucleus of Inner-City Activity," underlying the overlap of the architectural shopping centre and the urban "heart" of the city. This intriguing

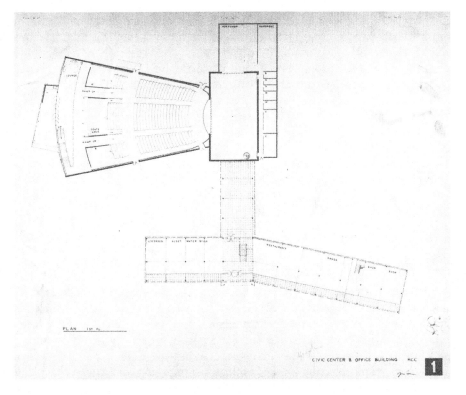

Figure 2.11 GSD Students, Shopping Center Project, Harvard, Academic Year 1945–46.

Source: GSD student CA 182_commercial 45–46 a. Courtesy of the Frances Loeb Library, Harvard Graduate School of Design.

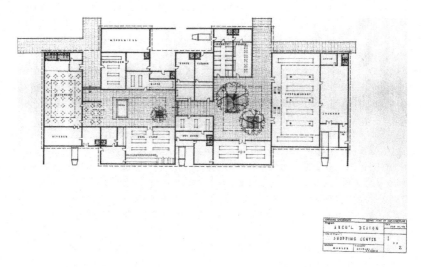

Figure 2.12 GSD Students, Shopping Center Project, Harvard, Academic Year 1957–58.

Source: GSD student CA 184. Courtesy of the Frances Loeb Library, Harvard Graduate School of Design.

social-spatial stratification and appreciation for the shopping model was already high-lighted in 1961 when Sert and Tyrwhitt considered these shopping centres as "an idea of what these new urban cores might be like. Many of these shopping centers, though built purely for private profit, have found it worthwhile to provide a wide mall or plaza, well separated from car parking areas." Ultimately, they even considered them as "our open expression of the new humanizing trend in the urban scene."[94]

Therefore, rather than a purely consumerist machine, the shopping centre was assumed to be a bundle of intriguing devices which perfectly mirrored and responded to the needs of a humanising process, the symbolical and functional split between humans and machines, pedestrian and vehicular flows. Between the 1950s and 1960s, the shopping centre was recognised with the same humanising purpose as the Heart of the City, the ambiguous humanistic symbol of CIAM 8.

From the heart of the city to the heart of (our) cities

Within the productive ambiguity and complexity of the heart, the commercial function was analysed by several participants during the CIAM 8. From the fifth century BC, when the Agora became more intermingled with commerce, to the "decay" of the Roman Empire, when the public space definitely turned into a market, Giedion recon-structed some historical references to commerce and public space in order to stress the sacrosanct right of the pedestrian and her separation from traffic. The commercial aspect of the Core was also taken into consideration by W. J. Holford, who dealt with the issue of the reconstruction of the commercial inner area of London,[95] which had been totally destroyed by the Second World War. Therefore, since the 1940s, commer-cial and shopping design was not only an American discourse for a new and increasingly consumerist society. It was also strictly connected to the reconstruction of the historical structure of European cities that had been devastated by the Second World War.

However, reconstruction was only one of the aspects the Heart discourse should have addressed. CIAM's president Sert juxtaposed the issue of the disappearance of city centres with the dangerous negation of the urban centrality. From obliterated bombed centres to the infinite urban structure, the topic of "recentralisation," mirrored in the boundaries of the metaphorical "cannon,"[96] gained pivotal relevance in Sert's discourse about the urban core, and for Gruen himself about the shopping design. Unsurprisingly, Victor Gruen praised Sert's words on "recentralization," referring directly to the CIAM 8:

> José Luis Sert, . . . sees the problem as one of "recentralization" – reversing the trend of unplanned decentralization. He would create new urban cores, with planned land usage and separated foot and vehicular traffic, to replace the old unplanned districts which have deteriorated. . . . [he] has lamented the tendency of architects to "go suburban," [and he] is right when he says, "It is in the heart of our cities that architecture can achieve its higher expression."[97]

Hence, the *"urbs"* as a "cannon" and the compact recentralised heart became images that were coherent with the purposes of the shopping centres as urban crystallisation points within suburban areas. As highlighted by Mumford, "CIAM 8 can be seen as a reference point for the new forms of public space, including Shopping malls,"[98] influencing the works concerned with public gathering places by Victor Gruen as well. The humanising process of the Heart of the City of CIAM 8 apparently became a main reference for Gruen's theoretical and design work. In fact, he hybridised it with his own personal research on commercial design and with the mounting interest in the environmental issue.

Then it is no coincidence that in the "Megayear 1964," as Banham called it,[99] Gruen published "The Heart of Our Cities – The Urban Crisis Diagnosis and Cure."[100] Banham himself described the book as a "fairly irresistible . . . apparent combination of commercial success and sound cultural preferences,"[101] underlying the mix of commercial and modernist cultural references which were always present in Gruen's theoretical and professional activity. The Austrian-born architect did not refer directly to the CIAM 8 in the text, although the resonance with CIAM 8 was clear and he did list the CIAM 8 published proceedings in the bibliography under "Some Books of Special Interest."

As far as the significance of the Heart was concerned, Gruen's interpretation was totally centred on the core, on the physical inner city, on the "spot of origin" of European cities or on the CBD (central business district) in the US, partially losing the complexity of significance of the heart as an "element of urban culture"[102] (Avermaete), which characterised the CIAM 8. Gruen's discourse on the Heart mainly mirrored only Sert's idea of the segregative recentralisation of "tightly-knit cores . . . , no matter how a city grows outwardly."[103]

Similarly to Sert, Gruen also explained the Core, physically distinguishing the interior "Cityscape" as "a setting where man-made structures are predominant," and "Landscape," as "an environment in which nature is predominant . . . ; the successful marriage of nature and human endeavour." The disease of cities which transformed them into "anti-cities," was then caused, in Gruen's words, by "Cityscape [which] has spilled over the walls, has spread out in the form of sub-cityscape."[104] Meanwhile, the freeway and the automobiles despotically conquered the world.

Figure 2.13 Gruen Associates, "Freeways Conquer the World!"

Source: Courtesy of Gruen Associates. In Gruen, *Centers for the Urban Environment: Survival of the Cities*, 89.

However, if Sert was more concerned with the survey of civic values, Gruen's compact heart dealt with rescuing the environment from soil consumption and air pollution: the Heart itself was a metaphor used to denounce the bad health of city centres, focusing attention on the environmental issue. The main aim therefore was "to create environmental qualities that will help fulfill the human heart's desire in the city's heart"[105]as the author affirmed.

The convergence between Sert's urban "cannon" and Gruen's compact *urbia*, the essence of urbanity, "the Core of the city, which I shall call its 'heart',"[106] appeared more evident at the First Urban Design Conference at Harvard, in 1956. Gruen's unbuilt proposal of Fort Worth was among the projects shown, "A Greater Fort Worth Tomorrow,"[107] a mix or resonances and echoes between Howard's "Garden Cities of To-Morrow"[108] (1902) and the later Disney's "Experimental Prototype Community of Tomorrow (EPCOT)"[109] (1965). Bruno Zevi later suggested that Gruen's proposal represented a new "Downtown like San Marco," dealing with the same functional and symbolic issue which was recurrent both at Hoddesdon in 1951 and at Harvard in 1956: the need for a pedestrian realm, "*la royauté du piéton*," through the humanising separation of cars and pedestrians, in order to preserve the Heart as the "drama in time"[110] of human relationships:

> *Piazza San Marco* in the downtown is not a cold formula of urban calculation, which is useful only to solve an economic American equation. It has a magical appeal, a mythical force undoubtedly superior to that of the garden city or the greenbelt: it is a formula that attacks the city in his heart, and owns all the arcane attractions of the city.[111]

Figure 2.14 Gruen Associates, Fort Worth: Bird's-Eye View of the Proposed Revitalization Project. The Heart Area of Fort Worth.

Source: Courtesy of Gruen Associates. In Gruen, *Centers for the Urban Environment: Survival of the Cities*, 195.

Coherently with the reference of Piazza San Marco, interestingly Fort Worth was the "first of the business-district-on-a-podium projects that inspired megastructuralists,"[112] according to Reyner Banham, where a new artificial pedestrian ground level was separated from the underground goods delivery space, the above cluster of new buildings and the external parking garages.

This new example of a pedestrian podium area became a contradictory issue in later projects, in the USA as well as in Europe. Indeed, on the one hand, the platform defined the separation between cars and pedestrians, as suggested by CIAM members in order to regain the human scale of the city. The Smithsons themselves praised the "cluster . . . the civic scale" and "appropriate relation to motor traffic" of Gruen's Fort Worth in their research on "Cluster City."[113]

On the other, the platform, called in France "*la dalle*,"[114] became an over-scaled element representing the total artificiality of both the natural level and the "*milieu humain* [which] led to catastrophe."[115]

It was a "cold and dreary platform . . . an abstract pedestrian traffic"[116] as criticised by Jane Jacobs, which again stressed the contradictory, and segregative, effect of the functionalist split between pedestrians and traffic.

Regarding the main reference of Gruen's megastructure, the Austrian-born architect relied on his beloved home city, Vienna, in order to safeguard the pedestrian centre from the tyranny of mechanical vehicles. Gruen used its limited size and its enclosed medieval structure as a metaphor for contemporary inner cities, under attack from automobiles. Indeed, Gruen declared that a similar defensive system used in Vienna against attacks by the Turks in the seventeenth century[117] was metaphorically reused for the first time by his firm, in Fort Worth, in order "to repel the invasion of mechanical hordes."[118] Thus, the historical conservative reference became a real source of inspiration for the functional separation between car and pedestrian flows: in Fort Worth, the historical defensive walls of Vienna were reinterpreted as a system of concentric rings of highways – outer, intermediate and inner ones – preserving the central pedestrian nucleus. The inner ring was the impenetrable wall, inside which only pedestrian or public vehicles were allowed to enter. Motorists, coming from the metropolitan region, had to leave their vehicles inside the parking garages. These multi-level parking terminals were thought to have space for 60,000 cars in total; they were organised over several levels and they extend from the ring-road towards the inside, "penetrating like fingers" the central zones. Gruen's team estimated that it would take two to four minutes on foot to reach the pedestrian areas from the garages. Inside the internal ring, the core of Fort Worth was entirely designed with a new framework for public life, with "the creation of human activity nuclei or clusters, based on the scale of acceptable walking distance within each unit."[119]

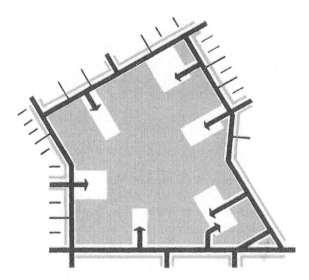

Figure 2.15 Gruen Associates, Fort Worth: Scheme of Parking Garage Like Fingers.

Source: Courtesy of Gruen Associates. In *A Greater Fort Worth Tomorrow* (1956), 19.

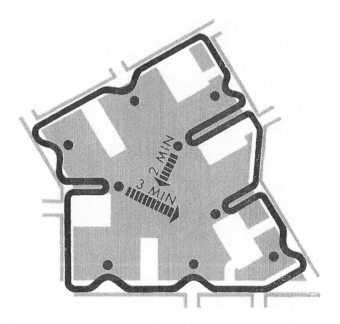

Figure 2.16 Gruen Associates, Fort Worth: Scheme of Walking Distance.

Source: Courtesy of Gruen Associates. In *A Greater Fort Worth Tomorrow* (1956), 19.

Figure 2.17 Gruen Associates, Fort Worth: Diagram of the Defensive Ring.

Source: Courtesy of Gruen Associates. In *A Greater Fort Worth Tomorrow* (1956), 18–19.

1. Widen and improve the surface delivery system.

2. Construct new elevated delivery facilities.

3. Construct new underground delivery facilities.

Figure 2.18 Gruen Associates, Fort Worth: Elements of the Plan: Service.

Three possibilities in section for delivery facilities.

Source: Courtesy of Gruen Associates. In *A Greater Fort Worth Tomorrow*, 20.

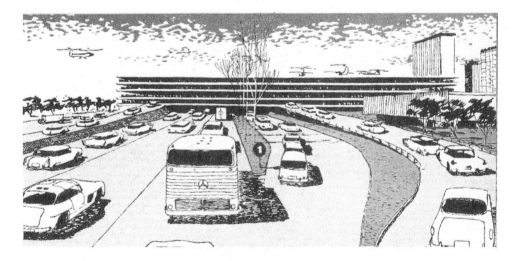

Figure 2.19 Gruen Associates, Fort Worth: View of Large Parking Garage.

Source: Courtesy of Gruen Associates. In *A Greater Fort Worth Tomorrow* (1956), 6.

Interestingly, the same defensive rings in Fort Worth, recalling Vienna's walls, were then proposed by Gruen for Vienna itself. Between November 1969 and December 1971, he conducted a study to "delineate measures to increase the dynamism of the city Core with respect to all urban functions."[120] The final scheme was very similar to the Fort Worth one, with an external viability ring and fingers

Figure 2.20 Gruen Associates, Fort Worth: Street View of Fort Worth.

Source: Courtesy of Gruen Associates. In *A Greater Fort Worth Tomorrow* (1956), 26.

of parking garages, hosting approximately 20,000 cars, inserted in the pedestrian Core. The scheme was proposed as the only way to save his beloved city from the traffic problem.

Hence, Gruen provocatively displayed a dystopian view of the Core of Vienna, with high sarcasm, probably typical of his past profession as an entertainer at cabaret theatres and Socialist idealist. In *Centers for the Urban Environment: Survival of the Cities*, he drew a vignette with a highway passing through St Stephan Cathedral, the city's main monument, and a huge car park which substituted the entire City: "If the automobile were to be given freedom of the city of Vienna, a freeway through Saint Stephan's Cathedral might be required." He then continued in this cabaret-like vein: "To Provide sufficient parking space in the city of Vienna, demolition of all structures might be required (For sentimental reasons, Saint Stephan's Cathedral might be spared)."[121]

Figure 2.21 Gruen, Sketch of Saint Stephan's Cathedral. Ironical Proposal.

Source: Gruen, *Centers for the Urban Environment: Survival of the Cities* (1973), 179.

Figure 2.22 Gruen, Sketch of Vienna. Ironical Proposal.

Source: Gruen, *Centers for the Urban Environment: Survival of the Cities* (1973), 179.

Finally, from the Turkish invasion of Austria which was eradicated and interpreted metaphorically in American territory, to the dystopian vision of the plague of cars in Vienna, the ideal model of the Austrian capital was also transformed into a concrete, ambitious and precursor drafting of a manifesto for the environment: "Die Charta von Wien" (The Vienna Charter).

If Gruen's most successful building in the USA, the Southdale Center, mirrored an innovative consumerist machine for Utopian control of society (Skinner, 1948) by artificially manipulating the climate, as underlined by Mennel,[122] then the European Vienna became an urban symbol for safeguarding society through defence of the environment.

From the Athens Charter to the Vienna Charter

The Charter of Vienna was a final declared attempt to appropriate and update the legacy of CIAM, at the very moment when Gruen decided to retire from his firm in Los Angeles, Victor Gruen Associates, and to move back to his old central district of the Austrian capital. The charter represented a continuity with CIAM's statements, in particular with the Heart of the City; the new element introduced by Gruen was the emphasis on the ecological environment, as a rising and necessary theme, in the early 1970s, in addition to the preservation of human values.

The Athens Charter, written by the CIAM founders in 1933, was conceived not only as a reference, but also as an integrated part of the new charter, because of the importance of some of its outstanding, always valid, principles. Indeed, Gruen affirmed that CIAM's Charter was very powerful in its foresight. In particular, he was interested in the seventy-sixth paragraph concerning the right shape of the human environment: "The dimensions of all elements within the urban system can only be governed by human proportions."[123] The humanising process, as deeply stressed with the Heart of the City at CIAM 8, therefore became the main theme, which should be highlighted again for a new manifesto of environmental planning, in the face of the new contemporary conditions and needs, which had changed profoundly over the last forty years.

These new conditions and issues were also described in his book *Centers for the Urban Environment: Survival of the Cities*, published in the same period as the Charter, in 1973. As we can read from the Foreword, the book

> represents an expression of the effort of the Foundation to bring about a greater public understanding of the decisive role which "Environmental Planning" should and must play if the ecological and biological balance of our planet, which is essential for the continuous existence of the human species, is to be assured.[124]

Similarly to the Charter, the "Center of Urban Environment" was centred on both the human and environmental issue of the city, which had already been drafted in the book on *The Heart of Our Cities*.

The environmental aspect was already subtly present in some of the discourses at CIAM 8 too, such as Gregor Paulsson's connections between Habitat, Ecology and Heart of the City during his speech "The Past and the Present."[125] Moreover, the struggle between CIAM and Team 10 for the ideological content of a charter of Habitat already highlighted concern about a more complex and realistic debate about the built environment, for a definition of Habitat which should be defined as an ecological, socio-biological issue with the help of a praxeological analysis.

But the 1950s were too soon for CIAM members to recognise environmental sustainability as a key topic for planning. It was difficult even for Gruen himself to introduce it as the basis of planning twenty years later, as Alex Wall stated, "when the threat to the environment was neither widely accepted nor understood."[126] Indeed, the UN's first major conference on international environmental issues (United Nations Conference on the Human Environment) was held in Stockholm in 1972, coevally with the Vienna Charter.

As far as this latter is specifically concerned, the principle theses were listed and summarised into four points in the first part of the Charter:

"A. Man stays at the medium point of each urban planning and architecture.
 B. The first aim of both urban planning and architecture must be therefore the satisfaction of both human needs and human hopes.
 C. The conquests of Science and Technology must be used in order to satisfy the main aim: the greater satisfaction of Human life.
 D. It is necessary not to allow Science and Technology to become mere purposes. Indeed they can neither tyrannize nor liquidate the Humanity."[127]

These statements definitely echoed or even coincided with the humanising process over the tyranny of mechanical progress, which was praised at CIAM 8 as early as 1951 by Giedion and Sert. The Charter of Vienna then continues with a further six short chapters, where the previous principles are explained: "the global environmental crisis," "The needs and hopes of Man," "The essence of urbanity," "Bureaucracy of the Project," "The essence of the Architecture" and "New opportunities, ways and paths."

As far as the fundamental conditions of the Charter are concerned, Gruen listed compactness, maximum integration of human functions and maximum separation between mechanical/service functions and human functions. These three conditions were also the same presented by both CIAM 8 and Sert's discourse at the First Urban Design Conference at Harvard. In particular, the aim of centralisation, compactness of the urban structure passed from the survey of civic values (Sert) to the rescue of the environment (Gruen), as already stated.

Furthermore, the integration of human functions was achieved through a correct three-dimensional design which was praised both at CIAM and by Gruen himself. This was adopted also in new urban developments, where the principles described within the Vienna Charter were grounded and where both the commercial design devices and the environmental-humanistic values were reinterpreted and elaborated at the urban scale. When Gruen somehow recognised both the social-urban failure[128] and bastardisation[129] into parasitical commercial evolutions of his architectural-social archetype of shopping centre, he started to test his ideas through the design of newly founded cities. Finally, the Regional Shopping Centre became an integrated and focal part of Gruen's urban model, the "Cellular Metropolis,"[130] rather than being an attempt at social crystallisation inside the existing suburban context. The model of the metropolis should be structured as a cluster of cells, "the basic unit of life,"[131] consisting of a nucleus and protoplasm, which were combined in a specialised organ which forms a town. Referring to Howard's *Garden Cities of To-Morrow*,[132] and sharing hidden resonances with various urban models,[133] the new urban pattern was a hierarchical scheme, rather than a master plan, which Gruen reinterpreted and grounded in several real contexts in both the USA and Europe, with the aim to melt "the new technological apparatus" with "human and urban needs."[134] It was the final and largest reading and translation of the organic metaphor where the compactness and the boundary of the cell/heart was reinterpreted at different scales from the enclosed architecture of the shopping centre, to the morphosis of the existing city into a new Vienna, to the new idealist Metropolis or Utopia.[135]

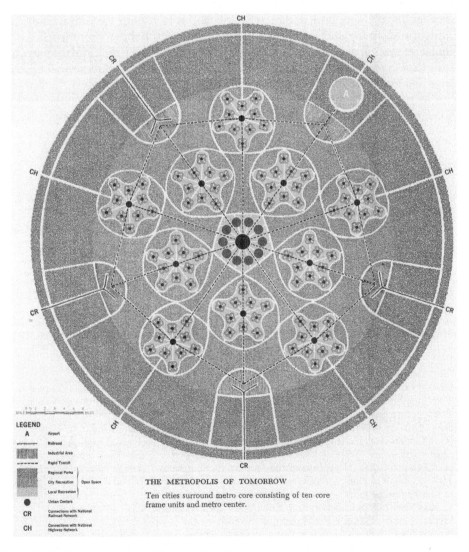

Figure 2.23 Gruen Associates, Metropolis of Tomorrow.

Source: Courtesy of Gruen Associates. In Gruen, *The Heart of Our Cities* (1964), 273.

In conclusion, if in the 1960s Gruen reinterpreted the CIAM 8 theme in the book *The Heart of Our Cities*, referring it to his shopping design experience in the North American context, then in the early 1970s he used the Heart issues to revision CIAM itself. The environmental reading of the Heart of the City allowed Gruen to reinterpret all of CIAM's principles many years after its decline, detecting a possible continuity of the Modern Movement. In contrast to the "unwillingness of the younger members of CIAM to rework the *Charte d' Athènes . . .* in a period of great skepticism of the value of didactic statements,"[136] as Jaqueline Tyrwhitt confirmed, Gruen surprisingly took charge of it. CIAM's fundamentals were updated coherently with the mutable urban-social conditions in order to reaffirm their validity. Finally, the transatlantic encounters between Gruen and CIAM had erased any hierarchy between the Modern Movement and the shopping design avant-gardes; in fact, both their legacies are still radically transforming and influencing our contemporary built environment.

Similar interests in the gathering relationship between the individual and the mass, and on the urban crystallisation portrayed by the heart metaphor, with its several different nuances and interpretations, has allowed the architecture of the consumer, "a character often relegated to the margins of most theories of modernism,"[137] (Mattsson) to become an outstanding Modern experiment for the shape of a new society and discipline.

Notes

1 Sert, "Centres of Community Life," 3.
2 Jaqueline Tyrwhitt, Josep Lluís Sert, "The Shape of American Cities, June 1958," p. 6, TjJ/38/9/10, RIBA.
3 This subchapter has been partially translated from Leonardo Zuccaro Marchi, "Cuore della Città e Urban Design: contraddizioni e ibridazioni nel Dopoguerra," *Territorio*, 72 (2015): 131–141.
4 Sert, "Centres on Community Life," 4.
5 Le Corbusier, "Response to Moscow," translated and quoted in Jean Louis Cohen, *Le Corbusier and the Mystique of the USSR* (Princeton: Princeton University Press, 1992), 139. Quoted in Mumford, *The CIAM Discourse on Urbanism*, 46.
6 Josep Lluís Sert, "The Human Scale in City Planning," in *New Architecture and City Planning*, ed. Paul Zucker (New York: Philosophical Library, 1944), 392–412.
7 Ibid., 402.
8 Ibid., 393.
9 Ibid., 398.
10 Ibid., 399.
11 The "neighbourhood unit" was later revised by CIAM members themselves "as a tool to shape postwar urban visions." Gaia Caremellino, *Reassessing the Discourse on Neighbourhood During WWII: The Contribution of American Architects.* Conference Paper. 17th IPHS Conference, Delft History Urbanism Resilience, 2016. See also Domhardt, *The Heart of the City.*
12 Paul Lester Wiener, "Diagram of the Human Environment," *Nuestra Architectura* (1953). Timothy Hyde, "Planos, Planes y Planificación. Josep Lluís Sert and the Idea of Planning," in *Josep Lluís Sert: The Architect of Urban Design, 1953–1969*, ed. Eric Mumford, Hashim Sarkis (New Haven and London: Yale University Press, 2008), 57.
13 Hyde, "Planos, Planes y Planificación," 56–57.
14 (Originally in Italian: "*una non cauta insistenza sulla centralità dell'uomo può associarsi ad una valutazione troppo intellettualistica del 'soggetto:' la città risulterebbe allora isolate come una città stellare di Filarete.*") Enzo Paci, "Il cuore della città," *Casabella Continuità* 202 (1954): vii.
15 (Originally in Italian: "*la città e il concetto di cittadino, in antitesi a quello del contadino.*") Paci, "Il cuore della città," vii, quoted also from Max Weber, *La città* (Milano: Bompiani, 1950), 34.

16 (Originally in Italian: "*la città è di fatto un punto di incontro tra il chiuso e l'aperto, tra la delimitazione e la relazione. Il suo cuore, come ogni cuore, non ha soltanto un movimento centripeto di diastole, ma, contemporaneamente, un movimento centrifugo di sistole. Ha un movimento di aspirazione dall'esterno verso il centro ma ha anche un movimento di espansione dal centro verso l'esterno.*") Paci, "Il cuore della città," vii.

17 Josep Lluís Sert, "Introduction to the Urban Design Conference, April 9, 1956," Rare NAC 46 Harv 1956, GSD/Harvard. And in "Urban Design," *Progressive Architecture*, 37, no. 8 (August 1956): 97–112.

18 See Mumford, "The Emergence of Urban Design in the Breakup of CIAM," 15. Mumford, *Defining Urban Design*, 113.

19 At Harvard, many of the old members are involved: during the UD Conference six members of CIAM were among the participants, namely Sert, Tyrwhitt, Chermayeff, Neutra, Muschenheim, and Coats (member of the British MARS Group and organiser of the CIAM 8). These continue their research by developing many issues about the Core that had already been presented at Hoddesdon. The Core is also the main theme during the Eighth Urban Design Conference but, as Richard Marshall affirms, "by 1964, in a reflection of much of what was happening in the United States, social, political, and economic concerns outweighed any emphasis on form or aesthetics." Marshall, "The Elusiveness of Urban Design: The Perpetual Problem of Definition and Role," 50–51.

20 Domhardt, *The Heart of the City: Die Stadt in den transatlantischen Debatten der CIAM 1933–1951*.

21 "Sert and the CIAM 'Heart of the City': Precursor to Urban Design, 1947–52," in Eric Mumford, *Defining Urban Design: CIAM Architects and the Formation of a Discipline, 1937–69*, (New Haven and London: Yale University Press, 2009), 80.

22 Le Corbusier, *La Charte d'Athènes* (Paris: Plon, 1943). Translated by Anthony Eardley, *The Athens Charter* (New York: Grossman, 1973).
At CIAM 8, the importance of three dimensions is still considered: "three dimensional space at all scale levels is the base of the architectural disciplines." Commission 3, Architectural Education (Gropius, Rogers, van Eesteren, Giedion, Chermayeff, Tyrwhitt), CIAM 8, "Report of Hoddesdon Conference, 1951," p. 110. BIB 200583, CCA Library, Montreal.

23 Josep Lluís Sert, "Introduction to the Urban Design Conference, April 9, 1956."

24 Josep Lluís Sert, "Conclusion of the First Urban Design Conference," Rare NAC 46 Harv 1956, GSD/Harvard. Also in "Urban Design," *Progressive Architecture* (August 1956): 112. In 1967, Denise Scott Brown attacked planners who did not recognise "that architecture has its own socially-minded critics," whose books should be read by them as well. The social interest was common to both the professions and should be recognised by both sides. "Such communication might spell hope for a better collaboration between planners and architects one day, and real hope for an urban architecture," she considered. Scott Brown, "Team 10, Perspecta 10, and the Present State of the Architectural Theory," 49.

25 Giedion, "The Heart of the City: A Summing-Up," 160.

26 Giedion, *Architecture You and Me*, 128.

27 Le Corbusier, "The Core as a Meeting Place of the Arts," in *The Heart of the City: Towards the Humanisation of Urban Life*, ed. Jaqueline Tyrwhitt, Josep Lluís Sert, Ernesto N. Rogers (London: L. Humphries, 1952), 41–52.

28 (Originally in Italian: "*l'intuizione di Le Corbusier reinserisce nella comunità umana l'esigenza funzionale della creazione estetica.*") Paci, "Il cuore della città," ix.

29 CIAM, "A Short Outline of the Core," in *The Heart of the City*, 168.

30 Ibid.

31 Sigfried Giedion, *Architecture and the Phenomena of Transition, the Three Space Conceptions in Architecture* (Cambridge, MA: Harvard University Press, 1971). The reasons for transition to the new space conception are to be found first on the progress of technological development, first interpreted by engineers, not by architects, with the development of anonymous iron construction in the nineteenth century. In the twentieth century, it is the artists who first introduced the new conception, basing it on the plane surface, analysed and interpreted first by Cubists.

32 Ibid., Preface. More recently, in the 1990s, Edward Soja reused the term "third space," based on Lefebvre's theory of "thirding-as-Othering." In particular, Soja reconsidered the

fundamental necessity, stressed by the French philosopher, to always consider an alternative, an-Other alternative between two terms, avoiding any "binary logic in thinking about space and their complexity of the modern world."
Edward W. Soja, *Thirdspace* (Malden, MA: Blackwell, 1996), 53–57.

33 "In Archipenko's 'Seated Figures', 1916, we can follow the contours of the back without interruption, but the front of the figure is partly solid and partly hollowed out. This fluctuation of volume and void, interior and exterior, was followed up in architecture, where interior and exterior space continually interpenetrated one another, establishing new interrelationships. In an enclosed architectural space one is still made aware of the exterior." Sigfried Giedion, *Architecture and the Phenomena of Transition, the Three Space Conceptions in Architecture* (Cambridge, MA: Harvard University Press, 1971), 268.

34 For Giedion, this sculptural interrelation presented in St Dié was even similar to the artwork of Alberto Giacometti, "*Project pour une place*" (1930–31): free objects are disposed around a free-standing vertical form while a base unifies the entire composition of group forms, similarly to Le Corbusier's proposal of a parking platform.

35 Giedion, *Architecture and the Phenomena of Transition, the Three Space Conceptions in Architecture*, 270.
Giedion also mentioned two references to this notion of group form: "Group Design in Greek Architecture" (1949) by American archaeologist, Robert Scranton; "Investigations in Collective Form" (1964) by Japanese architect, Fumihiko Maki.

36 Colin Rowe, Fred Koetter, *Collage City* (Cambridge, MA and London, UK: MIT Press, 1983), 65.

37 Ibid., 65.

38 "Urban Design. Condensed report of an invitation conference sponsored by Faculty and Alumni Association of Graduate School of Design, Harvard University, April 9–10 1956," *Progressive Architecture*, 37 (August 1956): 100–101; see also Bacon, "Josep Lluís Sert's Evolving Concept of the Urban Core," 94.

39 See Bacon, "Josep Lluís Sert's Evolving Concept of the Urban Core," 105.

40 Josep Lluís Sert, Paul Lester Wiener, "Chimbote," in *The Heart of the City*, 130.

41 "Although the aesthetic and functional significance of Sert's own work remains controversial, his effort to synthesize the historic and the new, the technological and the artistic, in a context of strengthening urban pedestrian activity during a time of rapid urban decentralization remains of considerable contemporary importance." Mumford, "The Emergence of Urban Design in the Breakup of CIAM," in *Urban Design*, 31–32.

42 Eric Mumford affirms that the attention to pedestrian streets was new in CIAM in 1951. But already in 1947, Le Corbusier had published *Propos d'urbanisme*, where post-war Paris was evoked without car traffic. Mumford, *Defining Urban Design*, 85–88.

43 Mumford, "Sert and the CIAM 'Heart of the City': Precursor to Urban Design, 1947–52" in *Defining Urban Design*, 80.

44 CIAM 8, "A Short Outline of the Core," in *The Heart of the City*, 164.

45 Constant criticised the Buchanan report, in *New Babylon Bulletin*, 1 (1963), saying that it only aimed to "advocate the development of machines for joyriding." Simon Sadler, *The Situationist City* (Cambridge, MA: MIT Press, 1998), 25.

46 "What were still essentially nineteenth-century cities in the early Fifties have since become surrounded and partially penetrated be megalopolitan development." Kenneth Frampton, *Labour, Work and Architecture: Collected Essays on Architecture and Design* (London: Phaidon Press, 2002), 11.

47 Victoria de Grazia affirms that Henry Ford should be considered as one of the founders of United Europe, since he had been the first to consider the whole of Europe as a single unique selling area. See Victoria de Grazia, *Irresistible Empire: America's Advance Through Twentieth-Century Europe* (Cambridge, MA: Harvard University Press, 2005).

48 Grahame Shane, *Urban Design Since 1945*, 9–11.

49 Each of these roads has a proper function: V1 is for express highways, V2 for monumental avenues, V3 for fast traffic roads without pedestrian accessibility, V4 for shopping streets, V5 for distributor streets from shopping areas to neighbourhoods, V6 for service streets to houses and finally V7 is only for footpaths and green ways. Le Corbusier, Pierre Jeanneret, Jane B. Drew, E. Maxwell Fry, "Chandigarh," in *The Heart of the City*, 153–155.

50 See Tom Avermaete, Maristella Casciato, *Casablanca Chandigarh: A Report on Modernization* (Montreal: Canadian Center for Architecture; Zürich: Park Books, 2014).

51 "Imagine yourself coming out of a Fifth Avenue store; you have been shopping all the afternoon; your arms are full of parcels; you need a drink; your wife is limping. Thank God for taxis." Alexander, "A City Is Not a Tree," in *Human Identity in the Urban Environment*, 416.

52 See Mumford, *Defining Urban Design*, 89–91.

53 Sert, Wiener, "Chimbote," in *The Heart of the City*, 130.

54 For example, in Chimbote, the stream recalls the Inca tradition; in Motor City, Sert maintains the local "*praça*" and "*corso*"; finally, in Bogotá, the old Plaza Bolívar becomes a porticoed promenade for pedestrians, recalling the old Latin American tradition. Ibid.

55 Smiley, *Pedestrian Modern*, 249.

56 Dean Sert, Prof Carlhian, "Problem VII: Preliminary Study for the Redevelopment of Times Square,- Studio #1 Urban Design, Fall Term, 1954–55, Arch, 2–4a," p. 2, GSD Students, CC098, GSD/Harvard.

57 Eric Mumford already mentions this anticipation in the footnotes to the project, published in *Defining Urban Design*: "Student studio work that anticipated many of the urbanistic ideas of the 1960s." Mumford, *Defining Urban Design*, 127.

58 An example is Vincent Ponte's project for the Heart of Montreal, where the pedestrian is instead designed underground. See Zuccaro Marchi, "Cuore della Città e Urban Design: contraddizioni e ibridazioni nel Dopoguerra," *Territorio*, 72 (2015): 141.

59 *Synthesis* is an architectural journal published by the GSD students at Harvard University. First number appears in April 1957.

60 "Replies were received from 12 architects, 1 landscape architect, 8 planners and 11 others who encompassed the field of art, history, law, geography, government, administration, economics and promotion." Jaqueline Tyrwhitt, ed., "Definitions of Urban Design," in *Synthesis – GSD Harvard* 1 (April 1957): 27. Some of them were negative such as that of Frank Lloyd Wright, who rapidly answered:

"My Dear Radoslav L. Sutnar:
Sorry – I am not interested.
Sincerely Yours.
Frank Lloyd Wright." Ibid., 28.

61 Tyrwhitt, "Definitions of Urban Design," 29.

62 Ibid., 29.

63 Giedion, *Architecture You and Me*, 124, 126–127.

64 Tyrwhitt, "Definitions of Urban Design," 29.

65 Sartre, *L'existentialisme est un humanisme*, 90–93.

66 Welter, "In-Between Space and Society," 260.

67 Victor Gruen, *Centers for the Urban Environment: Survival of the Cities* (New York: Van Nostrand Reinhold Company, 1973), 173.

68 Bruno Zevi, "Downtown come San Marco, una nuova Philosophy urbanistica nell'economia americana," *Urbanistica*, 20 (1956): 116. His European background became an exceptional "tool in order to not surrender to an [American] society which is happy only in the propaganda of the magazines," according to Zevi.

69 Gruen, *Centers for the Urban Environment*, IX.

70 See David Harvey, *The Condition of Postmodernity: An Enquiry into the Origins of Cultural Change* (Malden, MA: Blackwell Publisher, 1989).

71 de Grazia, *Irresistible Empire*.

72 President Woodrow Wilson, Detroit, July 10, 1916 in de Grazia, *Irresistible Empire*, 1.

73 The "*Surmodernitè*" is described by the sociologist Marc Augé as a combination of historical acceleration – shrinkage of the space and in relation with the negative proliferation of non-places. Shopping malls, invented by Victor Gruen, are listed by Augé in these non-places as creators of "a solitary contracts," in contrast with the "anthropological places which make the social organism." Marc Augé Non-Lieux, *Introduction a une anthroplogie de la supermodernitè* (Paris: Le Seuil, 1992).

74 Hardwick, *Mall Maker: Victor Gruen, Architect of an American Dream.*

75 Smiley, *Pedestrian Modern*, 204.

76 "The unified world of premodern times might be reconstituted through the medium of consumption, an ironic reversal of the redemptive design projects imagined by nineteenth-century utopians such as Fourier and Owen, who sought unity through collective productive activity and social reorganisation. Although Fourier's Phalanstery merged the arcade and the palace into a prefigurative mall form, its glass-roofed corridors were intended to encourage social intercourse and foster communal emotions, rather than stimulate consumption." Crawford, "The World in a Shopping Mall," 6.

77 Smiley, *Pedestrian Modern*, 12–15.

78 Sibyl Moholy-Nagy, "The Diaspora," *Journal of the Society of Architectural Historians*, 24 (March 1965): 24.

79 Le Corbusier, *When the Cathedrals Were White: A Journey to the Country of Timid People* (New York: Reynal and Hitchcock, 1947). Originally published as *Quand les cathedrals etaient blanches* (Paris: Plon, 1937).

80 Helena Mattsson, "Designing the Reasonable Consumer," in *Swedish Modernism. Architecture, Consumption and the Welfare State*, ed. Helena Mattsson, Sven Olov Wallenstein (London: Black Dog Publishing, 2010), 74.

81 "Southdale Shopping Center, Minneapolis, Minnesota – Victor Gruen
    The out-of-town shopping center, developed for purely commercial reasons, here begins to take on some attributes of a center of social activity." Other projects listed together with the Southdale Center in 1956 are Lafayette Park, Detroit, Michigan by Mies van der Rohe and Alexander Polder, Holland by Bakema and Opbouw Group. Giedion, *Architecture You and Me*, 212.

82 Gruen always designed introspected, closed-box buildings where all the technological tools were hidden: the external façade did not reveal the internal program, stressing "the neutrality, the 'undefined', the implicit qualities that are not only confined to the architectural substance but are also a powerful expression in a new spatial sensitivity." Hans Ibelings considered Gruen's buildings as one of the main references for 1990s Supermodernism Architecture, characterised by introversion and neutrality. Hans Ibelings, *Supermodernism* (Rotterdam: Nai Uitgevers Publishing, 1998), 62.

83 Malcolm Gladwell, "The Terrazzo Jungle," *The New Yorker* (March 15, 2004). Accessed on February 3, 2015, www.newyorker.com/magazine/2004/03/15/the-terrazzo-jungle.

84 "Enclosure would keep out both cold war worries and actual cold." Mennel, "Victor Gruen and the Construction of Cold War Utopias," 129.

85 Bacon affirms that Sert agreed with Stein and Bauer, who state that "the economic success of a neighbourhood community and the well-being of its inhabitants depend to a great extent on the planning of the neighbourhood shopping center." Mardges Bacon, "Josep Lluís Sert's Evolving Concept of the Urban Core, Between Corbusian Form and Mumfordian Social Practice," 97.

86 Ketchum stated that if the right conditions exist, "regional shopping facilities should be planned as a part of a larger group of civic and institutional buildings also serving the same geographical area. The tremendous possibilities of this approach to regional planning are proved by the layout of the proposed Cidade dos Motores." The layout of the Latin American project was therefore considered a model for the proper integration of shopping facilities in other urban functions. Morris Ketchum, *Shops and Stores* (New York: Progressive Architecture Library, Reinhold Publishing Corporation, Knickerbocker Printing Corp., 1948), 281.

87 Josep Lluís Sert, "Centres on Community Life," *The Heart of the City*, 11.

88 See Mumford, ed., *The Writings of Josep Lluís Sert*, 3.

89 Josep Lluís Sert, *Urban Design Seminar: The Human Scale*, GSD Harvard, Cambridge, 1957, Twelfth Meeting, 1–3, and Thirteenth Meeting, 1–2 (HU sc Loeb) quoted in Mumford, *Defining Urban Design*, 135.

90 Sert, Tyrwhitt, "The Shape of American Cities, June 1958," TjJ/38/9/10, RIBA, London.

91 Victor Gruen, Larry Smith, *Shopping Town USA: The Planning of Shopping Centers* (New York: Reinhold Publishing Corporation, 1960), 11.

92 GSD, W. F. Bogner, C. H. Burchard, "Arch. 2b. Problem II, A Commercial Center for Hingham, Mass. 1945–46," GSD Student CA 182, GSD/Harvard.

93 GSD, Prof. Gourley, Mr. Goodwin, "Problem L2. SHOPPING CENTER. Arch. 2–2ab. Fall Term 1957–58," GSD Student CA 184–185, GSD/Harvard.

94 Josep Lluís Sert, Jaqueline Tyrwhitt, "The Shape of *the* American City," in *Contemporary Architecture of the World 1961* (Tokyo: Shokokusha, 1961), p. 106 quoted in Eric Mumford, *Defining Urban Design*, 144.

95 William J. Holford, "The Commercial Core of London," in *The Heart of the City*, 97.

96 Sert, "Centres on Community Life," in *The Heart of the City*, 3. Ortega y Gasset, *The Revolt of the Masses*, 165.

97 Victor Gruen, "Dynamic Planning for Retail Areas," *Harvard Business Review*, 32, no. 6 (November–December 1954): 53.

98 Mumford, *The CIAM Discourse on Urbanism, 1928–1960*, 215.

99 Banham, *Megastructure*, 70.

100 Victor Gruen, *The Heart of Our Cities: The Urban Crisis Diagnosis and Cure* (London: Thames and Hudson, 1964).

101 Banham, *Megastructure*, 76.

102 Avermaete, *Another Modern*, 71.

103 Victor Gruen Associates, *A Greater Fort Worth Tomorrow* (Los Angeles: Victor Gruen Associates, 1956), Fort Worth Public Library, LH 976.45315 G.

104 Victor Gruen, *Cityscape and Landscape: Experts From a Speech Recently Given at the International Conference of Design in Aspen*, Colorado (1955).

105 Gruen, *The Heart of Our Cities*, 299.

106 Ibid., 12.

107 Victor Gruen and Associates, *A Greater Fort Worth Tomorrow*.

108 Ebenezer Howard, *Garden Cities of To-Morrow* (London: Swan Sonnenschein & Co, 1902).

109 "Shopping Utopia? Perhaps a more influential source of Walt's utopian vision is Victor Gruen, the inventor of the American shopping mall. Walt owns several copies of Gruen's Heart of Our Cities, which are kept at his office and in the studio library." Chuihua Judy Chung, "Disney Space," in *Harvard Design School: Guide to Shopping*, eds. Rem Koolhaas, Chuihua Judy Chung, Jeffrey Inaba, Sze Tsung Leong (Los Angeles: Taschen, 2001), 288.

110 "But a city is more than a place in space, it is a drama in time." Jaqueline Tyrwhitt, The Valley Section. Patrick Geddes' World Image, *Journal of the Town Planning Institute*, 37 (1951): 64.

111 "*Piazza San Marco nella downtown non è una formula fredda di calcolo urbanistico, utile soltanto a risolvere un'equazione economica americana. Ha un richiamo magico, una forza mitica indubbiamente superiore a quella della città giardino o della greenbelt: è una formula che aggredisce la città nel suo cuore e possiede della città tutte le arcane attrattive.*" Bruno Zevi, "Downtown come San Marco, una nuova Philosophy urbanistica nell'economia americana," *Urbanistica* 20 (1956), 116.

112 Banham, *Megastructure*, 42.

113 Alison Smithson, Peter Smithson, "Cluster City," *The Architectural Review*, 422, no. 730 (November 1957): 333–336.

114 Surprisingly, Gruen proposed a project for the *Tête de la Défense* at the end of the 1960s. Gruen mentioned only that the plan was in principle accepted in January 1970. Gruen, *Centers for the Urban Environment*, 139.

115 "*De Metropolis de Fritz Lang au Cinquième Élément de Luc Besson, en passant par Blade Runner de Ridley Scott, l'artificialisation du milieu humain conduit a la catastrophe.*" Lefèbvre, *Paris: Ville moderne: Maine-Montparnasse et La Défense 1950–1975*, 17.

116 "The pedestrians, having somewhere along the line morphosed from whole and various human beings into abstract 'pedestrian traffic', become an excuse for a showy but fake, inflexible and limited pretence at city environment." Jane Jacobs, "Do Not Segregate Pedestrians and Automobiles," in *The Pedestrian in the City*, ed. David Lewis (Princeton, NJ: Van Nostrand Company, inc., 1966), 109–110.

117 Gruen's city of birth, Vienna, is a perfect example of concentric fortification. Outside the inner wall there was a deep water-filled ditch and beyond that an open area called *Glacis* with no houses inside it in order to have an uninterrupted view of the enemy. The second ring was called *Linienwall*, surrounded by outer communities, and it was built in a similar way as the first. Finally, an outer ring had the function of slowing down enemy attacks. Gruen, *The Heart of Our Cities*, 214.

118 Gruen, *The Heart of Our Cities*, 214.
119 Victor Gruen, "Modern Architecture," quoted in Alex Wall, *Victor Gruen: From Urban Shop to New City* (Barcelona: Actar, 2005), 190.
120 Gruen, *Centers for the Urban Environment: Survival of the Cities*, 172.
121 Ibid., 179.
122 The alteration of the environmental variables influence the behaviour of organisms, and it can generate a sociocultural system which is close to utopia. Burrhus Skinner, *Walden Two* (New York: Macmillan, 1948). See Mennel, "Victor Gruen and the Construction of Cold War Utopias," 129.
123 Le Corbusier, *The Athens Charter*, 95.
124 Gruen, *Centers for the Urban Environment: Survival of the Cities*, v.
125 Paulsson, "The Past and the Present," *The Heart of the City*, 28.
126 Wall, *Victor Gruen: From Urban Shop to New City*, 231.
127 Victor Gruen Foundation for Environmental Planning, "Die Charta von Wien," in *Das Überleben der Städte: Wege aus der Umweltkrise: Zentren als urbane Brennpunkte*, ed. Victor Gruen (Wien: Molden, 1973) ("The Charter of Vienna," Victor Gruen Papers: Box 48, Folder 5, Library of Congress, Washington).
128 The failure of his architectural invention was partially caused by the lack of social and physical connections with the surrounding context. On the one hand, the vast parking area could not allow any visual, physical relationships; on the other, spare time degenerated into consumerism, within the so called "Gruen Transfer": "The Gruen transfer (named after architect Victor Gruen) designates the moment when a 'destination buyer', with a specific purchase in mind, is transformed into an impulse shopper, a crucial point immediately visible in the shift from a determined stride to an erratic and meandering gait." Crawford, "The World in a Shopping Mall," 14.
129 "In a speech given in London that year (1978), he criticized Americans for perverting his ideas. The very popularity of the shopping mall gave him easy target. He looked at what he had built and despised what he saw. 'I refuse to pay alimony for those bastard developments,' he proclaimed. Gruen said that American in their blind pursuit of profit had corrupted his vision." Hardwick, *Mall Maker*, 216.
130 Gruen, *The Heart of Our Cities*, 283.
131 He quotes the magazine *Guideposts to Knowledge*: "The basic unit of life, whether plant or animal, is the same. Millions of cells enter into the structure of higher plants and animals but the simplest forms of life are one-celled organisms. Cells show great variety of shape, being spherical, disk-shaped, elliptical, oblong, etc. A typical cell consists of a mass of protoplasm, in the center of which is a denser mass called nucleus. . . . (add by G.: Most cells are surrounded by cell walls . . .) In the more highly organized plants and animals the vital processes are carried on by groups of cells that form specialized organs." Gruen, *The Heart of Our Cities: The Urban Crisis Diagnosis and Cure*, 271.
132 "I had arrived at the idea of the cellular organization after a period of many years, and I wrote about it for the first time in an article published by Architectural Forum in September, 1956. When, quite recently, in the process of doing research for this book, I read Ebenezer Howard's Garden Cities of Tomorrow." Gruen, *The Heart of Our Cities: The Urban Crisis Diagnosis and Cure*, 283.
133 Many other urban projects have similar organic references. Some similarities can be traced for instance in the scheme of an industrial City by Unwin (1922), the Central City of suburb – satellites by Robert Whitten (Cleveland, 1923), the scheme of a poly-centric city by de Groer (1936), the cellular reference of Gustav Bardet (1940) which are all published in *"Le nouvel urbanisme"* by Bardet himself. See Gaston Bardet, *Le Nouvel urbanisme* (Paris: Editions Vincent. Freal et Cie 1948). Also Alex Wall mentions the similarities between Gruen's Cellular Metropolis and some of these projects.
    He also mentions Erich Gloeden's Polynuclear Metropolis (1923) while the transportation networks and the use of green belts echoes, in Wall's opinion, more recent urban proposals by Saarinen, Ungers, Duany and Plater-Zyberk. Wall, *Victor Gruen*, 202–205. Other important and clear references are Christaller's Central Place Theory (1930) and Howard's garden City (1908).

134 Gruen, *The Heart of Our Cities: The Urban Crisis Diagnosis and Cure*, 271.
135 See Tafuri about "cell" and "City Organism": Manfredo Tafuri, *Architecture and Utopia* (Cambridge: MIT Press, 1976), 104.
136 Tyrwhitt, "CIAM and Delos," 470.
137 "In Sweden . . . the consumer, a character often relegated to the margins of most theories of modernism, appeared as figure whose desires must become essential for the making of the new society." Mattsson, "Designing the Reasonable Consumer," 74.

3   CIAM Summer School in Venice
The Heart of the City as continuity

*Il faut remettre la roue à sa place, il faut séparer le piéton
de l'automobile et donner la primauté au piéton. Vous, gens
de Venise, vous avec chez vous ce miracle ... Venise reste, au
milieu d'un ordre moderne, un don de Dieu qui est là présent et
qu'il ne faut pas toucher, qu'il ne faut pas détruire.*[1]

Le Corbusier, 1956

Continuity

It was at the Hoddesdon CIAM, also via the "Heart of the City" theme, that the issue started to emerge, an issue that will be of central importance for the next forty years: the idea of listening to the "*contesto*," the project, viewed as a deposited form of the history of a specific place, as a means of dialogue with the "*contesto*" itself. . . . It initiated the question of the value and the defence of the historical city, the preservation of tissues and not just of isolated monuments, the theme of memory and tradition as important materials for the project.[2]

Vittorio Gregotti in an editorial in *Rassegna*, 1992

The Heart of City therefore attained a brand new meaning as proposed by the Italian architect who personally participated in the discussion of CIAM 8, since he was present in Hoddesdon among the young generations. Indeed, the Heart of the City at CIAM 8 is considered as the starting point, the germinating moment of "history as the ground of the project,"[3] the rising importance of the relationship with the "*contesto*" as the main essence of the architectural project. This interpretative artery of the heart articulated and deepened a new relationship with history and tradition tackling the only apparent anti-historical approach[4] of the Modern Movement, adopted by architects as "their revenge on the past"[5] and on the nineteenth century consumption of history. Moreover, this artery opened up and influenced a worldwide debate which is still current today, and one which found its most critical and radical examples in the 1960s and 1970s with different nuances, ambiguities and connotations from its accent on historical processes as in Rogers and Rossi to "critical regionalism"[6] in Tzonis-Lefaivre and Frampton, from Smithsons' "context thinking"[7] and functionalist design in Alexander, to more formal properties of figure/ground-voids/solids relationships as in Rowes' "contextualism,"[8] up to its utmost aggressive denial summarised in the well-known laconic statement "fuck context."[9]

Out of this perspective, it is no coincidence that Gregotti, as opposed to any of his other foreign colleagues at CIAM 8, highlighted the historical value of the Heart. Indeed, the issue of historical continuity was perceived with particular intensity in the Italian *milieu*. "The story begins in Milan in 1950s,"[10] Adrian Forty reminds us when discussing "context" along with Rogers' critiques to some modernist architects in *Casabella Continuità*. Even the title of the magazine was significant, underlying the necessity for Continuity (*Continuità*) with a previous discourse, in a total flowing process. In the article/manifesto "Continuity," in 1954, Rogers indeed argued: "no work is truly modern which is not genuinely rooted in tradition, while no ancient work has significance today unless it can resonate through our voice."[11]

CIAM member Rogers used *"preesistenze ambientali"* or *"ambiente"* to describe and emphasise the deepness and complexity of the existing "context," and later translated it into English with a confusing and different meaning in the Anglo-Saxon discourse.[12] "To consider '*l'ambiente*' means to consider history,"[13] Rogers stated, linking the two entities in an indissoluble necessity for the design of new projects.[14] The presence of history and "continuity" expressed within his theoretical discourse was also coherently translated into physical form by Rogers. For instance, *Torre Velasca*, built in Milan in 1956–1958, was an attempt to give an urban identity with resonances in the historical context surrounding the tower or, as Tafuri asserted, an "homage to a historical centre virtually destroyed by real estate speculators."[15] Furthermore, Rogers' continuity also influenced the theoretical and design production of his pupil Aldo Rossi.[16] This latter affirmed within *"permanenze"* (Poete, Lavedane, Rossi), having a similar meaning to Rogers' *"preesistenze ambientali,"* that "awareness of the past defines the term of comparison and measurement of the future,"[17] describing the city as a human entity *par excellence*, a testimony to values, permanence and memory. Therefore, if the Heart of the City is the origin of the discourse on continuity and the role of history within the project, then indirect influences can be traced from CIAM 8 to Rogers and to Rossi's *"L'Architettura della città,"* which Domhardt already suggested as having strong theoretical similarities with "the system of cores in the CIAM's urban planning."[18]

Remarkably, Rogers' idea of continuity and focus on this conceptual Möbius loop between roots and contemporary voice included different concerns and dimensions, regarding the project of the city as well as role of the architect within CIAM. This was already evident in 1951 at CIAM 8, where Rogers expressed his rejection of a distinction between "eternal and temporary art,"[19] remarking that the moral responsibility was to consider the spatial consequence of the drawing of a line forever. At the same time, he also denied the rift between "the adjectives 'young' and 'old' [which] cannot be applied to us, modern architects."[20] Therefore "continuity" for Rogers did not concern only the relationship with history and *"contesto,"* as expressed and emphasised in the magazine *Casabella Continuità*; it also meant the continuity of CIAM's modern strengths via cooperation between generations, "under the sign of [a] single group"[21] as a "body which renews itself,"[22] as a "Continuing Revolution."[23] Coherently with this necessity, the proposal for the institutionalisation of the "New CIAM of 30"[24] (1956) and of "CICON [which] is derived from CIAM Continuity, *Continuità*, *Continuité*, etc."[25] (1957) were attempts, though abortive ones, to guarantee this generational continuousness within CIAM.

Figure 3.1 BBPR, Torre Velasca, Milano, 1956–58.

Source: Photo by Massimo Giuseppe Castaldo, 2017.

Finally, Rogers' two nuances of continuity, regarding both the relationship of the project with history and the organisation of CIAM, surprisingly collapsed on each other at the last CIAM meeting held in Otterlo in 1959. Indeed, here the historical consistency of the exhibited *Torre Velasca* fomented the already announced generational and cultural rift within CIAM and was the most evident scandal of the meeting.[26] The indigestible functionalism and the Italian efforts to "overcome the abstract schematism of the 'modern' language in order to confer a new grade of modernity to architecture"[27] were instead labelled as mere historical formalism, in particular by Peter Smithson, who disclosed the impossibility to accept anymore the dialectic contradictions within CIAM. As result, at the *Kröller-Müller* museum in Otterlo, the powerful revolutionary thinking of the CIAMs remained exiled "at the Museum"[28] as Rogers impotently proclaimed.

However, Rogers optimistically still confided in the inescapable deep legacy and influence of CIAM within future generations:

> In this sense I talk about continuity. And there will be much to welcome and to actively transform in the coming years because no young person will be indifferent, in all his work, to this fertile reality that was the experience of the CIAMs.[29]

Venice and the discussion on Italian piazzas

In Hoddesdon, the interest in historical continuity and public space was manifested particularly during the "discussion on Italian Piazzas,"[30] involving several CIAM members. Italian piazzas were already considered by Rogers in a previous speech as "spaces open and welcome as vases, . . . wonderful examples of generous Hearts."[31] Interestingly, the discussion on these generous Italian public spaces was, from the very beginning, not focused on all Italian piazzas; indeed, almost all the presentations converged into one single square: Piazza San Marco in Venice.

Furthermore, inasmuch as the discussion at CIAM 8 on the meaning of the Heart was ambiguous, complex and variegated, the interpretations of what was generally considered one if its highest manifestations were also similarly multifaceted. For instance, Gropius talked about one of his best students in the USA who refused to accept the opportunity to design a contemporary core of similar character to Piazza San Marco, but he radically changed his idea after he visited it. Rogers defined the Venetian piazza as "a very high expression of dolce far niente" (translated in English as "to think, without effort"), pointing out the problem of "how the Core can expand."[32] Paulson instead remarked on the contradiction of considering Piazza San Marco as an expression of human life since Venice is almost a dead city. Hence, Sert emphasised again the strict distinction between "civic landscape" and "natural landscape," of which the Venetian square embodied the best example: "consider for a moment how horrible a tree would look on the Piazza San Marco!"[33] He then described the three most important elements of the Core, which were perfectly exemplified in Piazza San Marco: the monumentality, the "feeling of being cuddled" and "the feeling of processional development within the Core."[34] Finally Giedion, in a different conversation at CIAM 8, instead focused attention on the time span of the Heart, on the indispensable slow passage of years before transforming and creating the right space for the human scale, a mature space which resists the transformations of society. "The most beautiful Cores have always taken a long time to grow – the Piazza San Marco took 500 years."[35] – Giedion remarked, *de facto* highlighting one of the main issues of Urban Design which remains of paramount importance even nowadays.

Therefore, Piazza San Marco, on the one hand, became a nostalgic, romantic representation of the memory, the collective, public life and, on the other, it was considered a progressive example for the future design of public space where the human scale is enhanced. It was a principal manifestation of those "places of 'visual acoustic' – places of such perfect proportions that the onlooker is made one with the surroundings,"[36] as portrayed by Le Corbusier at CIAM 8 while he uttered about a *piazzetta* in Venice where *The Merchant of Venice* was staged.

Interestingly, this pivotal and ambivalent role of the Venetian square was also mirrored and stressed in the editing choice of the CIAM's publication about the Heart. Inside the front and back cover of the book, there is a sketch of the inner life of Piazza San Marco drawn by Saul Steinberg in 1951 which introduces and concludes the reading of the book. It is the very first and last image that physically and theoretically compresses and summarises all the complexity of the Heart of the City discourses.

The sketch shows the Piazza from above, from west to east, as it would be seen from a window of *Museo Correr*. Steinberg drew, in detail sometimes, or as a draft, the architectural buildings covered with advertising signs and the public square. However, the most important focus is the ordinary life in the square, the life of the Venetians, the tourists, the waiters, the postcards sellers, the *flaneur* playing with pigeons, drinking coffee, playing music, talking while gesturing widely, recalling an Italian *cliché*. Steinberg's sketch was therefore a representation of the human life in Piazza San Marco rather the physical public space itself. It was also a perfect representation of and introduction to the new humanistic, social and praxeological interest in the ordinariness of everyday life, on the public human practices, *hic et nunc* (here and now), which characterised the CIAM 8 discourses and deeply reverberated in the later research on Habitat.

Finally, this emphasis on Venice and Piazza Marco had effects on the structure of CIAM itself. Not coincidentally, during CIAM 8, the members presented the program of a laboratory in Venice for students and young architects, the CIAM Summer School. The continual presence of Venice in the conversation about the Heart transmuted into a concrete pedagogical experience. In particular, during the "Resume of open session of Architectural Education" held in Hoddesdon in 1951, the Italian architect Franco Albini showed the Plans for a Summer School in Venice to be held in 1952, after the failed attempts of the previous years.[37] The school was open to thirty students, divided into five or six groups, at the final stage of their

Figure 3.2 Saul Steinberg, Piazza San Marco, Venice, 1951.

Ink and coloured inks on paper, 58.4 × 73.7 cm
Private collection

Source: © The Saul Steinberg Foundation/Pictoright 2017.

architectural education or already graduates. The staff should be composed of four Italian members and others from outside.[38]

From Hoddesdon to Venice, the Heart of the City discourse would continue throughout almost all the 1950s, evolving through four editions of the CIAM Summer School (1952, 1953, 1954 and 1956), plus one called V Seminario internazionale di Architettura in 1957. These editions enhanced the confrontation between older and newer generations, but above all they represented the moment in which a common site, Venice, became the ground to test, verify and contradict theories previously exposed in the main congresses.[39]

In Venice, the tensions between technological modernisation and the historical city, between the civic/built and landscape/natural environments, between above and below water level, would deeply involve the Heart as Continuity, according to Gregotti, the unique or most important interpretative artery. In Venice, the summer school tackled the issue of the Modern project in the historical tradition, anticipating the rising polemic regarding the relationship of the unbuilt projects of the Masters with the historical context, starting from Wright's *Masieri* Memorial in 1954.[40] As explained within CIAM after Hoddesdon, Venice was "a particularly suitable background" where the International School "will help to show that when we adhere to the underlying and not to the surface characteristics of a tradition, architectural and town-planning mistakes. . . , and that modern methods need not destroy the historical character of Venice."[41]

About education and young generations

In CIAM, the need to invite young participants emerged right after the War. As Jos Bosman already reminds us, in 1947, Benjamin Merkelbach proposed that each State should send a member of its younger generation: "It is our opinion that the produced themes for the next Congress . . . lack of the presence of the younger generation, which has not taken a responsibility position yet."[42] Giedion, in the introduction of "A Decade of New Architecture," stated that after CIAM VI, "far from dissolving CIAM, it proved necessary to agree to open its doors more widely – especially to youth."[43] During CIAM 8, the Swiss historian continued to mention the new young generation – "twenty-five years of age" – also in order to justify the need to study and analyse a contemporary, evolving process of humanisation of the environment.[44]

The 1951 Congress was indeed the first one where students and younger generation architects met to share opinions and discuss the same topics as well as show their projects, preparing the ground for the rise of autonomous directions out of CIAM.[45] The rising role of the younger generation was mirrored in the project of the students who were present at CIAM 8, which represented "a decisive moment of change,"[46] according to Bosman. These projects were from the main Anglo-American Institutions mirroring the general focus only on Western transatlantic architecture and education: the Chicago Housing Project by students of the Institute of Design, the New York district by students of the Pratt Institute, the Stevenage district by students of the Architectural Association, the project in Providence by students of Harvard University and the New Haven project by students from Yale University.

Figure 3.3 CIAM 8, Van den Brock and Students, Hoddesdon, 1951.

Source: gta/ETH Archive, 42_JT_9_555.

Ten points for the rise of a new education

In parallel with the presentation and debate on proposals by students from elitist universities, education was one of the most important topics discussed in Hoddesdon, by the third commission composed of Gropius (President), Rogers (Vice President), van Eesteren, Giedion, Chermayeff and Tyrwhitt. Similarly to the discussion already held at CIAM 7 in Bergamo,[47] the necessity for an international educational system was stressed yet again. It would ensure the essential integration between the arts and sciences with courses common to Artists, Architects and Engineers. As a result, "Members of CIAM must take the initiative in bringing all schools, wherever these may be located, in sympathy with these principals into the closest possible contact and to provide opportunities for direct interchanges such as CIAM summer schools."[48]

This necessity for Summer Schools was also stressed by the young architects present in the committee. On July 12, 1951, the young Christian Norberg-Schulz, who was there with Giedion, presented a report about education by fifteen young architects present in Hoddesdon, to the CIAM commission. Despite the cultural diversity among the young participants, most of them agreed on the lack of proper education at their respective universities. "I can say that most of us have not been satisfied with our education," he explained. "After finishing our studies, we feel a great lack of understanding of human beings and of the society for which we must work."[49] A total and global reorganisation of architectural schooling was generally felt as necessary and urgent. In order to satisfy this proposal, Norberg-Schulz presented the "Ten Points." It was an ambitious Manifesto for a new concept of worldwide architectural education written by the CIAM younger generation (among whom we find Gregotti,

Tavora, and Candilis). On the one hand, these statements should have been useful in order to cultivate a global consciousness of the importance of education in architecture among CIAM members; on the other, these rules should have been adopted to develop a new young professional figure who might better satisfy the needs of contemporary society.

The first three points state that, since the architect is assumed to be the person who shapes the world, by coordinating different specialists, the architect should "have a broad understanding of man, nature and the social structure of our day." Therefore, students should attend general courses at the first year, whether they consider undertaking a career as an architect, engineer, designer or artist. In the next three points, Norberg-Schulz programmed later specialised courses while architecture statics or construction subjects should be always integrated with the main design problems. All students should collaborate in teams formed by students along with teachers and architects, artists and other specialists as mentioned in the seventh point. The last year of school should collect all the specialists together in order deal with a large-scale planning problem as a team (eighth point), while industrial production should be always included in the teaching program (ninth point).

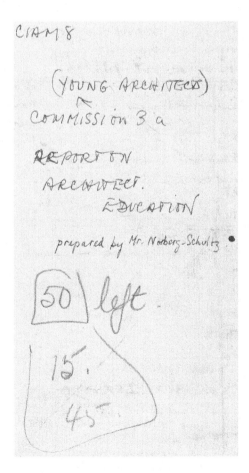

Figure 3.4 CIAM 8, Commission 3a (Young Architects), Report Architect Education, Prepared by Mr Norberg-Schulz, 1951.

Source: gta/ETH Archive, 42_JT_7_400.2.

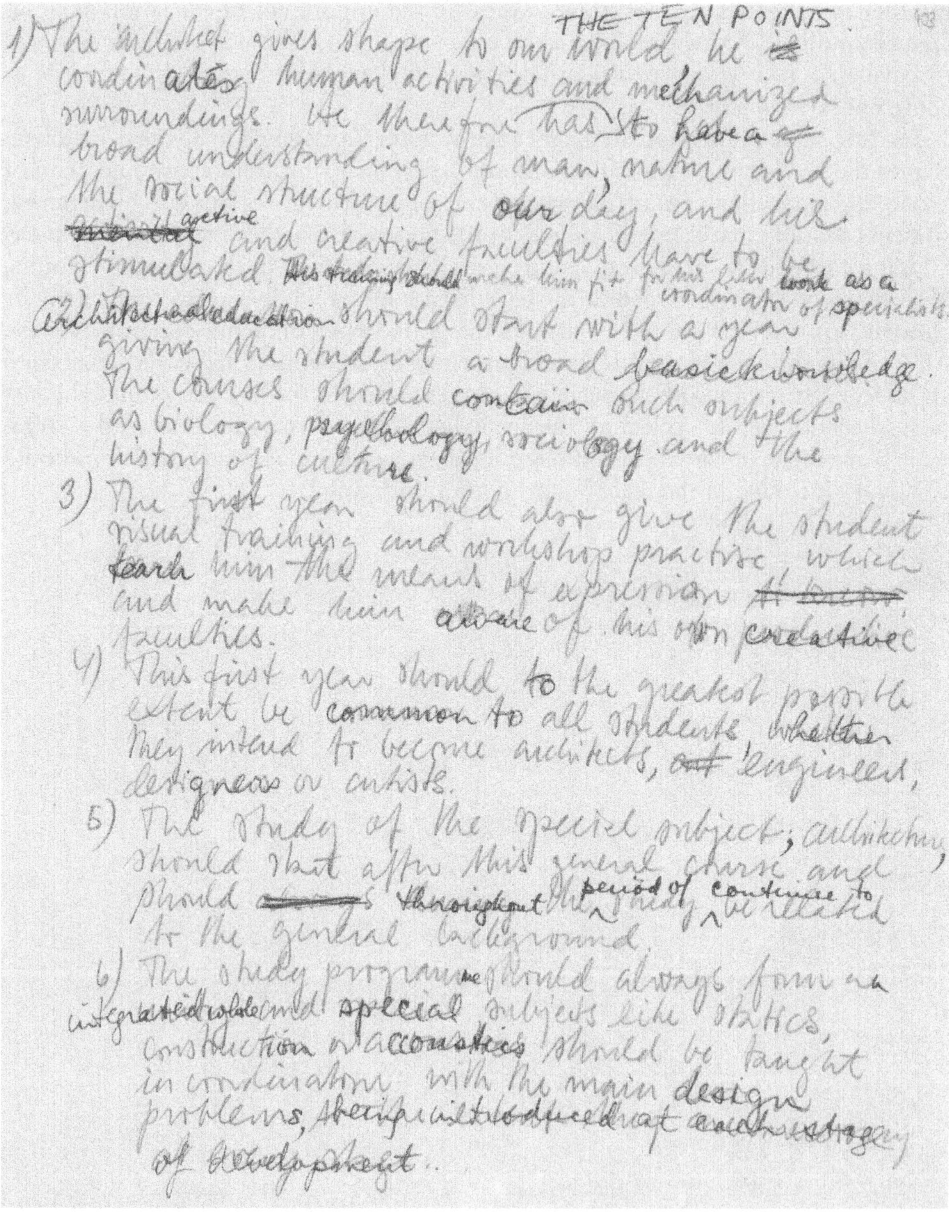

THE TEN POINTS

1) The architect gives shape to our world, he coordinates human activities and mechanized surroundings. He therefore has to have a broad understanding of man, nature and the social structure of our day, and his active and creative faculties have to be stimulated ... as a coordinator of specialists.

2) Architectural education should start with a year giving the student a broad basic knowledge. The courses should contain such subjects as biology, psychology, sociology and the history of culture.

3) The first year should also give the student visual training and workshop practice, which teach him the means of expression and make him aware of his own creative faculties.

4) This first year should to the greatest possible extent be common to all students whether they intend to become architects, engineers, designers or artists.

5) The study of the special subject, architecture, should start after this general course and should ... throughout the study ... period of continue to be related to the general background.

6) The study programme should always form an integrated whole and special subjects like statics, construction or acoustics should be taught in combination with the main design problems ... of development.

Figure 3.5 CIAM 8, The Ten Points (1–6), 1951.

Source: gta/ETH Archive, 42_JT_7_403.

Finally, in the tenth and last point, the young group highlighted the need for exchanges among students and teachers from different universities. This could also be achieved thanks to an international Summer School, which "might supplement the general study program."[50] It is very important to stress that the Summer School was posed as the final part of the ten-point statement by Norberg-Schulz, as probably the

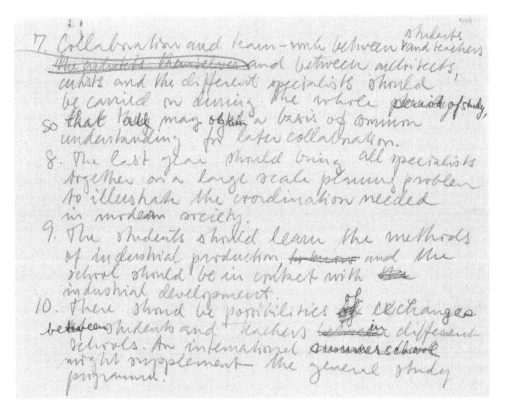

Figure 3.6 CIAM 8, The Ten Points (7–10), 1951.

Source: gta/ETH Archive, 42_JT_7_404.

paramount and more concrete proposal contained in the pedagogical Manifesto, to be realised in the following months. Moreover, the Summer School was not only a course organised and set up by the masters of CIAM, but it was a need that had arisen from the bottom of the organisation, from the younger generation. The latter could benefit from CIAM as a global organisation in order to propose a conversion of the entire system of architectural education throughout the world, within which the Summer School could have been a small experiment for an ideally internationalised school.

Effects of the summer school

The real effect that the CIAM Summer School had in the end on the university system around the world is unclear and probably impossible to determine. On a local level, it had a direct effect on the hosting Institution, IUAV University in Venice. It was during the first CIAM Summer School held in London in 1949 that Samonà, the Dean of IUAV University, collaborated with Albini, Gardella and Rogers.[51] In a few months, the same architects were called by Samonà to become professors in Venice. Then the international character of the CIAM Summer School would remain as a main feature of IUAV University in the next decades, hosting the most outstanding Italian architects and historians as professors and many visitors from all over the world, making IUAV and the "school of Venice" one of the most vibrant and important academies in the world in following decades.

Moreover, the CIAM Summer School in Venice anticipated and prepared the ground for other forms of international educational organisations held in Italy too, such as the ILAUD (or I.L.A. & U.D. International Laboratory of Architecture and Urban Design). The latter was founded in 1976 by Giancarlo De Carlo, one of the assistants and critics of the editions of the summer school in Venice, a member of young Team 10 and a fervent detractor of that "large quantity of inaccurate and worldly nonsense"[52] which characterised CIAM 8. ILAUD was neither an institutional school nor a summer school, but an annual international laboratory with the aim of making the younger generation reflect on urban issues through readings, analysis and design proposals. As De Carlo described it, ILAUD was a "'place' where teachers and students from different countries meet, compare their views and the outcomes of their activity," which regarded issues both "in their country and in such 'place.'"[53] Therefore, it strongly echoed the main pedagogical purposes of the Ten Points presented at CIAM 8.

Interestingly, while the summer schools held in Venice in the 1950s were in direct relationship with and under the umbrella of CIAM, ILAUD was directly influenced by the ideas of Team 10,[54] whose members actively participated in its activities. Moreover, both laboratories were held in Italy. For almost fifty years, Venice and Urbino became concrete sites and paradigms where the legacy of history became an important "place" of learning. They enhanced, within the younger generation, the complex discourse, interaction and tension between modernity and tradition and between physical structure and social expectations.

Besides Venice and the important educational organisms in Italy, on a more international level the CIAM Summer Schools boosted a network of peerships among the young participants which remained pivotal for their entire professional life, as argued by Gregotti himself.[55] This web of peerships and often friendships are impossible to map exhaustively. The following pages will try to reconstruct some of them. However, these contacts can be considered without a doubt as the most important and fruitful result of the CIAM Summer Schools and as one of the most interesting and important legacies of the international organisation (CIAM), without the necessary incidence and formation of either an institutional presence or hard core junior groups which were rising up coevally.

Team (10)

In parallel with the informal condensation of peerships among young students attending the CIAM Summer Schools, many efforts were spent by Norberg-Schulz himself on the formal constitution of young groups within CIAM. The Norwegian architect carried on the idea of the organisation of a Junior-CIAM group, through the publication of "TEAM, Collaboration of Young Architects and Artists," edited by Norberg-Schulz himself and Neuenschwander, and published for the first time on May 1, 1951, before the Heart of the City Congress.

Most of the issues on education and the position of younger generations discussed at both CIAM 7 and CIAM 8 were present in the aims of TEAM. Indeed, as stated in the "Synthesis" of the first issue of TEAM, the authors considered themselves as the "first generation following the pioneers," which was concerned with the situation of young architects and students and which had to deal with "a threefold task: Synthesis of medium, integration of methods, reorganization of architectural schooling."[56]

The second journal issue of TEAM,[57] published in February 1952, referred directly to CIAM 8, with the report of the CIAM 8-Commission 3 on Architectural Education[58] published inside. "CIAM 8 decided to establish Junior Groups in as many countries as possible to get an effective continuity in the work of CIAM,"[59] as the editors stated. These groups were formed by students and young architects with less than two years of practical experience. The first one was organised "in Oslo in autumn 1949 as a result of Dr. Giedion direct appeal and inspiration,"[60] as explained in TEAM 2. It was the PAGON Group (*Progressive Arkitekters Gruppe Oslo Norway*) and it was formed by Norberg-Schulz himself, with Carl Corwin, Robert C. Esdaile, Sverre Fehn, Geir Grung, Arne Korsmo, P.A.M. Mellbye, Håkon Mjelva, Erik Rolfsen, Odd Østbye and Jorn Utzon.[61] The editors also published the project presented at CIAM 8, designed by Norberg-Schulz with Mjelva and Østbye,[62] for the new heart of Tveten, in Oslo (Norway) for about 25,000 people.[63] Norberg-Schulz, in February 1951, explained in a letter to Giedion that the project was so experimental that, "One may speak almost of a Norwegian-Marseille project!"[64] emphasising the resonances and strong influence of Le Corbusier, and more in general of the older principal masters of CIAM on the projects of the younger group.

Then the editors of TEAM 2 mentioned the elections of the CIAM Council members, Howell (London) and Candilis (Rabat), among the young architects present at CIAM 8, and of Norberg-Schulz (Oslo) as the delegate for the junior groups. The election of "the two representatives of the new generation,"[65] was later also confirmed during an "Extraordinary Council Meeting" organised in Paris, on May 10–11, 1952, in order to discuss "particularly on the suggestion, made at CIAM 8 (Hoddesdon) that CIAM should be 'handed over' to the younger architects."[66] In the same meeting

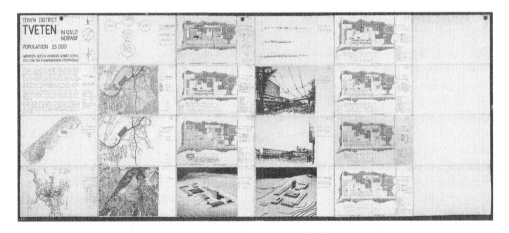

Figure 3.7 Mjelva, Norberg-Schulz, Østbye, Coll.: Rolfsen, Korsmo, Norseng, Corwin, Esdale, "Town District Tveten," 1951.

Source: Courtesy of The National Museum of Art, Architecture and Design, NAMT.ako061.

the Second CIAM Summer School was confirmed, which would be held from September 10 to October 10, in Venice, in the Architectural Institute, *Palazzo Grassi, Fondamenta Nani*.

However, the participation of younger architects was not so active, as reported by the Norwegian architect himself. In a letter dated June 26, 1952, which was read during the preparatory CIAM meeting in Sigtuna, the member of PAGON criticised and complained about this lack of interest: he received only four positive answers, Basel-Zagreb-Paris-Karlsruhe, from among the 40 universities which had been asked to collaborate.

"We may assume that the younger architects and students interested in joining CIAM have rather vague idea about the aims and work of CIAM," affirmed Norberg-Schulz. "We therefore would ask the elder members to make a statement which can give a basis and an answer to the question: "why do we join CIAM?"[67] Interestingly, in Sigtuna only Rogers directly answered this question, emphasising again the continuity and unity of CIAM as an ambitious and progressive way to change society itself. Indeed, only by participating at CIAM and insisting on its international and singular differences it was thinkable "to build a free and democratic society."[68] However, despite Rogers' answer concerning the ethical responsibility of CIAM, Norberg-Schulz's question seemed to agitate the internal, visceral polemical dispute within CIAM. It was destined to question the basis of CIAM itself, to widen the rift between young and old members, rather than accentuating its democratic role in society as stressed by the Italian architect.

Finally, in September of the same year, Norberg-Schulz and Neuenschwander published the third issue of TEAM. The magazine was totally focused on the organisation and support of CIAM junior groups, with an almost revolutionary tone:

> A call. Having been freed from the ties of academism this coming generation will further have to free itself of materialism that architecture may retake its stand among human activities as pure creation of the spirit . . . A new generation must throw a new light on architecture . . . We must realize for ourselves the fundamental new vision of man which lies at the base of new architecture.[69]

This call of a new generation of architects and architecture later reverberated in the young group of Team 10. From TEAM to Team 10,[70] the struggle for the creation of young groups, as stressed by Norberg-Schulz, helped to radically transform CIAM's structure and the discipline of Architecture itself in later decades. The formation of another group, different from CIAM, later Team 10 where remarkably Norberg-Schulz had no significant role, was already felt as a concrete necessity even though it had not yet been structured.

Finally, in the same month as the publication of "TEAM 3," the first CIAM Summer School in Venice was held, becoming the main laboratory for the exchange of ideas and architectural experiences between different generations in a "Revolutionary continuity," as described by Rogers at CIAM 8. The summer school experience would follow the destiny of CIAM itself, closing simultaneously with the last effective CIAM Congress in 1956.[71]

TEAM

COLLABORATION OF |YOUNG ARCHITECTS AND ARTISTS
ZUSAMMENARBEIT JUNGER ARCHITEKTEN UND KÜNSTLER
COLLABORATION DE JEUNES ARCHITECTES ET ARTISTES

Synthesis. We are concerned with the situation of the young trained architect, the practising graduate, the architectural student to-day.

Ours is the first generation following the pioneers, and we inherit an already far advanced and extensive, rich architectural vocabulary. The architecture of our time exists posed in all its essential problems, and their many individual solutions.

Our situation now confronts us with a threefold task.

> synthesis of mediums
> integration of methods
> reorganisation of architectural schooling.

Synthesis of mediums. We call mediums the elements of creation set before us. Functional organization: the sequence and coordination of movements and activities, statics, problems of isolation and acoustics, hygienic and economic necessities or constructive methods, are for us mediums, equally capable of realization as the building materials with their physical nature, their tangible structural qualities and the emotional response they solicit.

For each of these elements holds a double programme. It presents on one hand specific, objectively measurable functions, qualities and necessities; but it simultaneously responds to the changing and fluctuating demands of every age according to its attitude, whose varied interpretation through the sensibility of the architect constitutes it the real instrument of creation.

The projects and buildings of our architectural pioneers show us the responsibilities and potentialities of the architect of our time. As optical expressions, they create the formal language of a new attitude. It is our task to understand the fundamental rules of this language, and instead of piecing together eclectically single formal details, synthetically to translate the views of our age into our own formal equivalences.

But the intensity of our imaginative feeling must no longer tempt us into bolstering up under the pretence of originality an individual achievement by the hasardous formal products of self-expression. Our task lies in the anonymous and the standard, more and more purified of irrelevancies and seeking its greatest accomplishment in clarity and simplicity. We are not here to create fashion but to interpret a new mode of living.

Integration of methods. The indivisible unity of all artistic activities is essential to us, and therefore an intensive study of the arts and heightening of our sensibility for painting, sculpture etc. an absolute condition for critical formal creativeness in our own field. For our development we are de-

Figure 3.8 Norberg-Schulz, Neuenschwander eds., "TEAM," May 1951.

Source: gta/ETH 42-x-150.

TEAM

2

COLLABORATION OF YOUNG ARCHITECTS AND ARTISTS
ZUSAMMENARBEIT JUNGER ARCHITEKTEN UND KÜNSTLER
COLLABORATION DE JEUNES ARCHITECTES ET ARTISTES

Einzel- oder Massenausbildung. Wir haben an einer Schule studiert, welche auf Einzelausbildung des Architekten eingerichtet war. Infolge Überfüllung wurden in den untern Semestern um die 100, im Diplomsemester an die 45 Kandidaten durchgeschleust. Da weder ein numerus clausus eingeführt noch die Anzahl der Lehrkräfte erhöht werden konnte, ergab sich eine zunehmende Spannung zwischen Schulprogramm und den wirklichen Ausbildungsmöglichkeiten.

Wir waren ebensosehr Objekt wie Träger dieser Verhältnisse und möchten die eigene Auseinandersetzung damit von unserem Standpunkt aus schildern.

Von der Hochschule hatten wir erwartet, dass neben der selbstverständlichen Grundschulung die Entwicklung humaner koordinativer Fähigkeiten im Vordergrund stünde. Darin sahen wir den Unterschied zu Bauschulen und die Ergänzung zur Werkpraxis, welche Einzelwissen und Detailerfahrung verschaffen. Das ursprüngliche System unserer Architekturabteilung hatte dieses Programm ermöglicht, weil es auf dem persönlichen Kontakt der Studierenden mit den Lehrkräften beruhte. Diese Einzelausbildung wurde aber von den Verhältnissen überholt. Die Einheit von Lernen und Training in der Zusammenarbeit der Professoren mit wenigen Studierenden ging verloren.

Die Umstellung der Schule auf Massenausbildung vollzog sich in unseren Studienjahren und wir verfolgten mit Unruhe, wie durch scheinbar berechtigte Anlässe zunehmend die Initiative der Studenten gelenkt und beherrscht wurde. Die persönliche Entwicklung des Einzelnen hätte zum Chaos geführt und jeder Sprung aus der Ordnung bedrohte die mühevoll errichtete Disziplin. In unserer Fachbibliothek verbot die entstehende Mittelschul-Mentalität sogar die Auflage wichtiger Fachzeitschriften oder die Anschaffung bedeutender Werke über zeitgenössische Architektur und Kunst, um Information und Kritik zu vermeiden, welche 'in unseren Köpfen nur Verwirrung stiften konnten.'

Die Übungen zu den Vorlesungen mussten strenger durch Termine und organisatorische Regeln geordnet werden und verloren stetig ihre Beziehung zur Entwurfsarbeit. Als losgelöstes Fachwissen war der Stoff oft unverständlich geworden, weil das Verständnis aus der Anwendung am Projekt fehlte. Gleichgültig wurde das Fachpensum durchgegangen und gegenüber der Entwurfsarbeit griff dieselbe Haltung um sich. Nicht selten wurde versucht, durch Anpassung oder durch Nachahmung sich die Aufmerksamkeit und Zufriedenheit des Professors zu verschaffen.

Diese würgende Passivität in der Massenausbildung, wo der eine nicht mehr den Namen des andern kannte, weckte in vielen Unzufriedenheit, aber es war schwer, sich einen Masstab zur Kritik an den Verhältnissen zu schaffen. Selbst wer sich Kenntnisse erwerben und eine eigene Einstellung bilden konnte, fand nicht den Boden, sie im Entwurf zu üben und anzuwenden.

Es war ein grosser Zufall, dass sich in dieser gespannten Atmosphäre eine Gruppe von Studenten zusammenfand, die nicht eigene Interessen ausserhalb der Schule suchten, sondern im Gegenteil mit sehr viel Begeisterung und Ausdauer ihre Kritik und ihre Vorschläge in die Schule hineintrugen.

Es war unser erstes Programm, uns für unser Studium und unseren Lehrgang verantwortlich zu machen.

Figure 3.9 Norberg-Schulz, Neuenschwander eds., "TEAM 2," February 1952.

Source: gta/ETH 42-SG-39–64.

TEAM
3

CIAM JUNIOR GROUPS - GROUPES DES JEUNES - JUNIOR GRUPPEN

CONTENTS: 'A Call' and 'the concrete symbol' by P. KEATINGE CLAY. CIAM Junior-Gruppen, junior groups, Aufbau der Junior-Gruppen. Organization of CIAM Junior-Groups. Original woodcuts from a drawing by LANFRANCO BOMBELLI TIRAVANTI, Paris.

A call. Having been freed from the ties of academicism this coming generation will further have to free itself of materialism that architecture may retake its stand among human activities as pure creation of the spirit.

This does not imply that mechanics, economics and social planning be layed aside but contained and that those who have the calling to architecture differentiate it as a creative art or otherwise chose those alternate professions.

A new generation must throw a new light on architecture which does not mean the presentation of theories nor the manifestation of principles but the outbreaking of a new vision that comes with experience itself in an architecture as clearly defined from planning as music is from sonics.

This is a call to those who have that calling that they may identify eachother wherever they may spring up.

An opportunity is being granted by the generation of the pioneer movement before us that those who are revealing this new trend in their own work can work together despite the barriers of nationality.

CIAM is offering this opportunity which can only be earned by our strength to take the initiative independant of the traditions of the receding generation and in gratitude to the pioneers before us.

This call is now in the time of preparation for those whose creative instinct is listening. The means of communication of these young architects is not the word but the architecture itself.
The synthesis

That this form of communication be made possible an exhibition to witness the new spirit will be necessary. In this way the really creative people will be able to identify eachother and through the similarity of this fresh direction in their work will be able to form a working body in CIAM as in their independant practice.

The value of these young people in CIAM will be according to their creative ability. There is no repetition in creation and what is to unfold in CIAM is unknown.

CIAM will in this way not be a systematised organisation but the meeting point of the outstandig creators of the day. It will be free every time to find its own purpose and meaning freshly through its own work.

This call in its very nature will single out those who have the calling within them.

Figure 3.10 Norberg-Schulz, Neuenschwander eds., "TEAM 3," September 1952.
Source: gta/ETH 42-WM-X-1.

Figure 3.11 Graphics in TEAM 3, Synthesis of Arts.

Source: gta/ETH 42-WM-X-1.

Figure 3.12 Graphics in TEAM 3, Synthesis of Arts.

Source: gta/ETH 42-WM-X-1.

Digression: Norberg-Schulz from the Heart of the City to Genius Loci[72]

Christian Norberg-Schulz wrote again about CIAM 8 almost thirty years later in his well-known book *Genius Loci: Towards a Phenomenology of Architecture*, in the final chapter regarding "Place Today": "and in 1951 a CIAM conference discussed the Core of the City, that is, the problem of introducing in the open tissue of the modern settlement a gathering focus."[73]

At the end of the 1970s, the Norwegian architect reiterated the idea of the Core of the City as the attempt to remediate the lack of quality of the modern settlement, which was too "open," resonating with the critique to prevalence for the "object" as described in *Collage City*.[74] The Core as "a gathering focus," was a process of reidentification "with the natural and man-made things which constitute his environment,"[75] in contrast to social alienation. For the author, "gathering" implied both a physical and symbolic movement of things from one place to another. In particular, the symbolic movement as a creative translation[76] was a compelling idea that echoed the symbolic presence of the Heart as already described. As matter of fact, the author of *Genius Loci* continued quoting his master, Giedion, about the Core as "part of a general humanizing process; of a return to the human scale and the assertion of the rights of the individual."[77]

This humanising process within the Core idea was then intertwined by Norberg-Schulz with the "new regionalism" described by Giedion[78] in 1954, to the undeniable regional connection and its influence on the project and identity. Therefore, this anthropological and humanist entity of the heart was intrinsically linked also to the *genius loci*, the eternal divinity, enduringly present as the identity of a place. According to Norberg-Schulz, only if we recognise the *genius* of the local place, guardian and spirit of the place, and therefore if we are able to dwell[79] there, as Heidegger[80] explained in Darmstadt, at the same time as CIAM 8, we become able to transmute social alienation into "a gathering focus," which has been already described as the Core.

Furthermore, this gathering focus was not merely mirrored in the centre of the square, but, for the Norwegian architect, "the individual is at the centre," in a continual "tension between existential space and immediate egocentric space."[81] Hence, the centre was consequence of the humanisation process of the Heart described by Giedion, translated into a psychological process. The healthiness of the individual centre was dependent on the presence of a meaningful *milieu* where the individual can identify herself. Human life depends on this "system of meaningful places." The lack of both physical and symbolic *milieu* within the modern city was the main issue faced by the Heart idea, as described before. The heart, rather than the CBD centre, became the significant *milieu* which fully satisfies the need for identification of each individual psychological centre. This was conceived eternally valid, present, and even anticipator of later issues: "we understand thus, that the leaders of the modern movement already 20–30 years ago foresaw some of the most important problems we are facing now" – Norberg-Schulz concluded – "Those who got stuck with the early images of a green city and standardized form, were the epigones and vulgarizes of modern architecture."[82]

Hence, the Core and its humanising process were still an open necessity. The Core idea was not just related to a post-war rhetorical discourse, but it is an idea of the city which finds continuity and coherence through history. It is strongly linked to

Figure 3.13 Christian Norberg-Schulz, 1948–49.

Source: gta/ETH Zurich, Hans Hofmann Archive, Semester 1948/49 catalogue.

the symbolic territorial *genius loci*, but also to Geddes' human *locus genii*[83] and in a broader architectural debate as already proposed by Welter, remaining a valid and current idea.

Finally, the Heart, betrayed and criticised by some of the youngest members of CIAM and colleagues of Norberg-Schulz, still affirmed its weight and legitimacy thirty years later within the main theory in the entire life of the endorsed representative of the young architects at CIAM 8.

The CIAM Summer Schools

The CIAM Summer School in London, 1949

As far as the CIAM Summer Schools are concerned, the first edition was held in London, at the Architectural Association, from August 8 to September 3, 1949.[84] The decision to establish it was made before the CIAM 7 held in Bergamo, July 22–31, 1949. As stated in a letter written by CIAM members in Paris, in March 9, 1949, the first course was decided to be held in London,[85] with Maxwell Fry, member of the MARS Group, as the director and Jaqueline Tyrwhitt as assistant director.

Regarding the topic of the "frankly experimental"[86] summer school, the MARS Group itself, which later organised the congress in Hoddesdon as well, considered

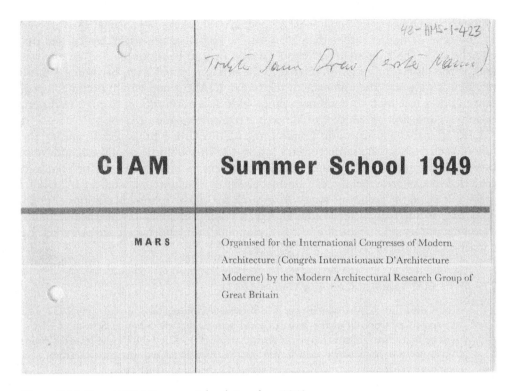

Figure 3.14 Flyer CIAM Summer School, London, 1949.

Source: gta/ETH 42-HMS-1–423.

four main subjects to propose to students: neighbourhood unit, office building, national theatre, city traffic problems. These were all related to actual sites in London which either had to face the reconstruction or had problems of unplanned growth, such as the "Elephant and Castle" area, considered by the MARS Group as an "Area of Extensive War Damage" in need of revitalisation.[87]

The participants were only post-graduates and they were "half drawn from the nominees of the various national groups of CIAM and half from residents in the British isles."[88] At the end of the summer school, sixteen schemes were finally prepared for the exhibition on September 1, where the projects were criticised by Professor C. van Eesteren from Amsterdam and Dr Ernesto Nathan Rogers from Milan, members of the Council of CIAM, by Maxwell Fry, the Director of the School, and by Robert Jordan, the Principal of Architectural Association.[89] Among the students who received a special merit,[90] there was also Oskar Hansen, who later participated to Team 10 and established his idea of "Open Form." This architectural-urban concept was presented at CIAM meeting in Otterlo in 1959, and it relied on principles of flexibility, indeterminateness and collective participation. Contrariwise, in London, the young Hansen designed blocks of flats for 3,000 people on Hampstead Ponds, whose section strongly reminded the closed and rational complexity of Le Corbusier's *Unité d'habitation* in Marseille, which was under construction at that time.

Finally, the CIAM Summer School in London, which became another "precursor"[91] of the Urban Design program at GSD according to Shoshkes, was primarily conceived as an organ of design rather than of research, "based upon researches carried out elsewhere."[92] The later summer schools would instead be more focused on analysis and on the discussion of issues related to the urban-regional level, becoming a more research laboratory. The influence of the Italian CIAM group would become important in order to enrich the summer school with discussions about history, tradition, continuity and context which would become relevant in later decades.

Last, after the first School in London, the MARS Group proposed organising the school each year, in the same country where CIAM would be organised, and "just before the Congress so that the work of members of the School can be seen and criticized by Congress members."[93] Instead, Venice, which never hosted a CIAM Congress, remained the recurrent focus of research for all the following editions. Apparently only in the lagoon the young architects could "obtain a better understanding of contemporary architectural and town planning problems which are presented by particular situation of Venice."[94]

The first CIAM Summer School in Venice, 1952

> The Council of CIAM which was held in Hoddesdon near London in July 1951, has accepted the proposal of the Italian CIAM groups that the Summer School of CIAM will be in Venice," affirmed a letter written in April 1952 by the CIAM Italian Group. "This town is particularly well set up for this type of school in its architectural and planning value and its ever increasing cultural expression which exist here.[95]

The appointed directors were Albini, Gardella, Rogers, Samonà, with Ms Trincanato as general secretary. Sixty-six participants attended the summer school (double than the number proposed by Albini at Hoddesdon) and twenty-three listeners, from fifteen different countries,[96] were present as well. Only ten of these students or young architects were Italian.[97]

Among the assistants there were Franco Berlanda, who was present at both the CIAM 7 Education Commission and at the CIAM Summer School in London, Gino Valle and Giancarlo De Carlo.[98]

Many architects and other key personalities were invited to lecture, such as Argan, Astengo, Piccinato, Holford, Bottoni, Ragghianti, Zevi, Bettini, Franco, Van der Broek, Satou and Lucio Costa, while the Honour committee even included Luigi Einaudi, President of the Italian Republic and Alcide De Gasperi, the President of the Council of Ministers and other senators, the mayor of Venice, ministers, and the Patriarch of Venice as well, highlighting the official character of the event.

Also, Giedion and Sert were listed on the Honour committee as members of CIAM. However, the main exponent of CIAM in Venice was Le Corbusier, who gave a lecture in "a classroom packed up to capacity."[99] The main topic of the lecture was Venice itself, as fundamental entity for further links with both his own theoretical and project works.[100] In particular, Le Corbusier emphasised the "humanity of Venice planning," as already deeply expressed in Hoddesdon. Piazzetta San Marco, its human scale and romantic-nostalgic essence was again stressed: "the pigeons mix with men, and the gondolas, like huge animals, swaying between the cross bars of their stables. Here, the human scale, lost in most modern cities, is preserved."[101]

Figure 3.15 Flyer CIAM Summer School, Venice, 1952.

Source: gta/ETH 42_AR_21_279.

As far as the students' work is concerned, the theme of the course regarded the attention on the link with the mainland. The assignment, proposed to the students through the "CIAM Grid," was described by the architect Gino Valle as concrete and potentially adequate topic in order to touch on the aspects concerning the whole Venice, in "its extemporaneous essence and in its present day life."[102] Indeed, the summer school tackled the issue of modern design in the historical city, as already introduced in Hoddesdon through the discussion on the reconstruction of historical centres. Venice had almost not been touched by the War. Nevertheless, it was a pivotal case study owing to its extremely weak equilibrium between modernisation and tradition, which is particularly evident in its point of contact and friction between the old historical structure and the new train and vehicle infrastructure.

Discussions were held among different groups of students, exhibiting different ideas and several project proposals. Among the young graduates and students, Vittorio Gregotti was also participating. He was the only Italian within an English group composed of Joseph Rykwert[103], Michael Burton, Patrick Crooke, William Ollis and John Turner. These latter individuals focused the attention on tourism, considered as a negative factor which destroys the social value of districts, parishes and autonomous communities. "If we do not insist anymore on the 'uniqueness' of Venice,"[104] then tourism could be limited to a certain quality, the group claimed.

This attempt to reconsider the historical structure of Venice as non-unique, normal, ordinary presence, was a striking proposal in relation to the potentialities of a new project within a pre-existing context.[105] Moreover, this accent on the ordinary of Venice seems to anticipate and to echo the later works of the young British architect John Turner, who later worked on the shanty towns and the squatter settlements of Peru, reconsidering the importance of the everyday life and self-building within a "Freedom to build."[106]

As far as the colleagues of Gregotti and Turner at CIAM Summer School are concerned, the (un)uniqueness of the city seemed to have been entirely forgotten by the group composed of Richard Fitzhardinge (UK), Gordon Hall (USA), Frank Meisler (UK), Michael Newberry (UK) and Ricardo Porro (Cuba) which proposed to "modernize" the Canal Grande, inserting modern buildings between the most important existing ones, "conserved thanks to their goodness,"[107] as Berlanda ironically observed: "they didn't deal with problems of a generic city, but of Venice, which is a sort of living, fragile miracle."[108]

Theoretically framed between the position of Gregotti's "loss of uniqueness" and Berlanda's "fragile miracle," other students tackled the urban issues of Venice with different solutions and attentions to the delicate context. Of particular interest was the proposal made by the group composed of Dutch, English and Swiss architects: Rita Ruprecht (CH), John Smith (UK), Jan Stockla (NL), Pieter Tauber (NL), Alan Wightman (UK). The young members used the CIAM Grid, which would be rejected by the students themselves in later editions, dividing Venice into four main scales (lagoon, Mestre-Venice, Venice and parish), which were then analysed through the main four functions of living, working, leisure and circulation. Remarkably, the parish was highlighted as a small and meaningful centrality in the city. On the one hand, it resonated with the Heart discourse; on the other, it grounded the functionalist, generic, aseptic grid of CIAM to the particular local social context of Venice. Finally, this rise of locality was mirrored

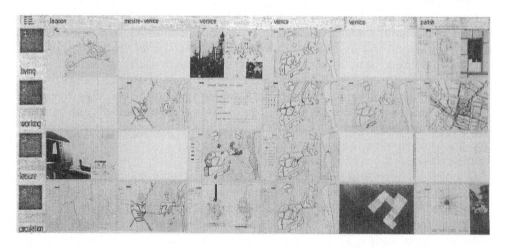

Figure 3.16 Ruprecht, Smith, Stockla, Tauber and Wightman. CIAM Summer School, 1952.

Source: Archivio Progetti IUAV, Venice, Trincanato 2, Attività Scientifica 2/011, 2/012, 2/013.

also in their proposal to redeem the autonomy of the island, and its cultural and social heritage, removing railways and the automotive connection from the city. Only a hidden underground metro, which interestingly foresaw later proposals,[109] would connect the mainland with Venice, passing through the lagoon, the Canal Grande to the Lido.

The second CIAM Summer School in Venice, 1953

In the second edition of the summer school in Venice, the theme was focused on the historical and tourist city, through the redesign of the Biennale Gardens. The Staff was composed of Albini, Gardella, Rogers, Samonà, Gentili Tedeschi, Myer, G. Valle, N. Valle, Cozzi and Venini. Conferences with Scarpa, Trincanato, Albini, Argan, Mercenaro, Belgiojoso were organised; Max Bill was also invited to be in the jury.

Ernesto Nathan Rogers presented the development of the second summer school in Venice, in the first issue of his *Casabella Continuità*. It is no coincidence that the article entitled "*Attualità di una scuola*"[110] ("Actuality of a School") written by Giancarlo Guarda, was presented in the same issue of the magazine with the well-known article "*Continuità*" written by Rogers himself, implicitly highlighting the link between the CIAM discourse started at Hoddesdon on the historical continuity of the Core and the Venice Summer School.

Nevertheless, during the Second CIAM Summer School, the projects were less influenced by the historical context, than in the other editions: the pavilions in the Biennale Gardens were mostly free buildings inside nature, in relationship only with the water of the canals and lagoon. However, in some of them, such as in Flavio Raboni's proposal, the description and reinterpretation of the Venetian structure was imbedded in the project, with many resonances for instance with the later project by Le Corbusier for the Hospital of Venice, in the early 1960s.

Lastly, in 1953, the local influence of the summer school of Venice, described by Guarda as different from any others since "there is an open waiver to any predetermined system,"[111] became more tangible. The Italian CIAM member, director of the University in Venice, Giuseppe Samonà praised the importance of the International course during his speech at the Opening of the Academic Year, since "it has let us know our technical and artistic activity making it enter into the concrete field of the city."[112] The work of the summer school therefore became the seed for a deeper, longer and more intensive work on the city, with the concrete aim of transforming and solving the problems of its planning. Samonà asserted:

> It is for this reason that the IUAV has decided to offer the city, the state, its work of collaboration; it decided to define an urban study of Venice, which might be useful as a concrete instrument in order to formulate the problems of the city . . . and offer it to the city.[113]

The third CIAM Summer School in Venice, 1954

The third edition took place from September 3 to October 3, 1954, at the University Institute of Architecture. The directors were again the CIAM members Albini, Gardella, Rogers and Samonà, while twenty-nine students or young architects from

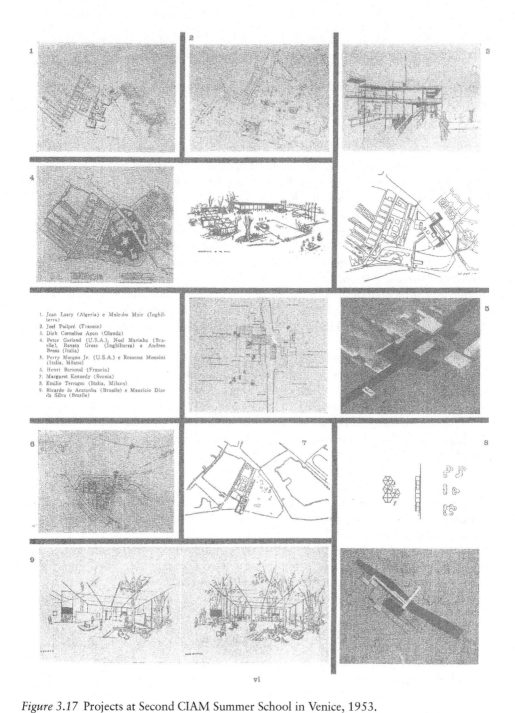

Figure 3.17 Projects at Second CIAM Summer School in Venice, 1953.

Source: Giancarlo Guarda, "Attualità di una scuola," *Casabella Continuità*, 199 (December 1953–January 1954): v.

ten different countries were attending the course. The other architects included the Italian CIAM members Bottoni and Pollini, while Alfred Roth was invited to judge the works. Finally, the architects Buzzi-Ceriani, Crooke, Kowalski and Gino Valle collaborated as assistants and Nani Valle as secretary.

During the first presentation the identity of the summer school was stressed yet again as not an academy "but a working congress attacking the most vital problems of our times."[114] The assignment was therefore centered on the main issue concerning the lagoon city in the 1950s and later: "the bridgehead[115] and its harmonious relation to the city."[116] This theme coherently followed, in a more specific frame, the research started with the first edition held a couple of years previously, on the relation between the mainland and the lagoon island.

The interest on the contrast revealed in the bridgehead "which is pivoted at the nervous centre between mechanization and man,"[117] echoed the rift between mechanisation and the human scale in the organic metaphor of the Heart as discussed at Hoddesdon and claimed by Giedion, for instance. The organic reference was explicit in some students' sketches where, for instance, Venice was symbolised as a heart, as the "responsible center of the lagoon" (Drews and Samper [Colombia], Letz [Austria], Liskamm and Spreiregen [USA]), or where the flux of persons from the mainland into the city was represented as an organism with arteries passing through the city's

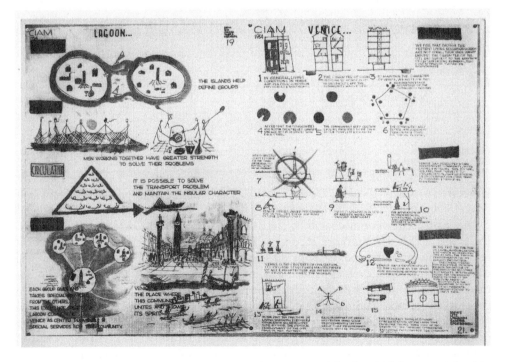

Figure 3.18 Drews, Letz, Liskamm, Samper and Spreiregen. Third CIAM Summer School in Venice, 1954.

Source: Università IUAV di Venezia Archivio Progetti, fondo Egle Renata Trincanato 2. Attività scientifica/2/011.

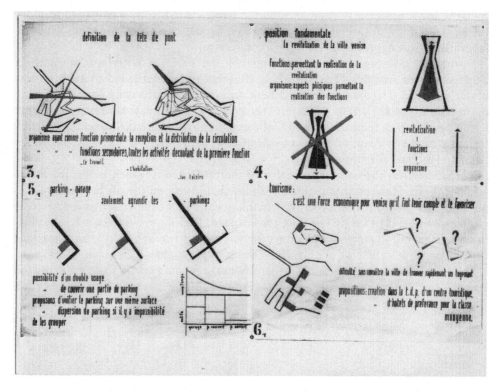

Figure 3.19 Aristegui, Cleves, Deplano, Francesco, Petre and Velasco. Third CIAM Summer
School in Venice, 1954.

Source: Università IUAV di Venezia Archivio Progetti, fondo Egle Renata Trincanato 2. Attività
scientifica/2/011.

structure (Aristegui [Spain], Cleves and Velasco [Colombia], Deplano [Italy], Francesco [Switzerland], Petre [Belgium]).

Other projects were discussed by the assistants Buzzi and Crook in *Casabella*, in
December 1954. The summer school, as the assistants affirmed, favoured common
research among participants from different backgrounds. This sharing of knowledge and experience even enhanced a common position of thought to arise among
the different young architects in different parts of the world, influencing an entire
generation. Hence, this legacy of the summer school mirrored the expectations
of the TEAM editors a few years before. Moreover, "today [the school] can be
defined more easily through the negation of some terms and in their critics"[118] rather
than in the affirmation of some radical objective universal beliefs, as Buzzi and
Crooke claimed. These criticisms, which were also evident during CIAM 9 held the
year before, were clear in Venice, for instance, in the work of the students Drews,
Letz, Liskamm, Samper and Spreiregen. These latter individuals, at the end of the
course, publicly rejected the functional hierarchy of the four functions because their

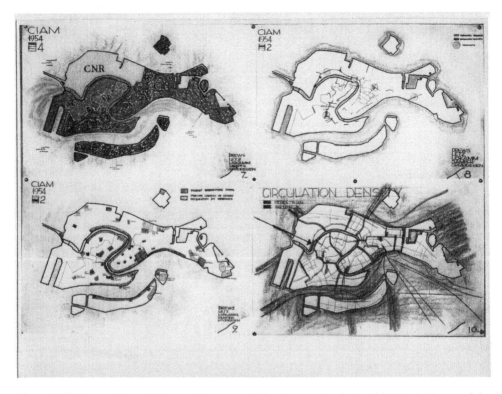

Figure 3.20 Drews, Letz, Liskamm, Samper and Spreiregen. Analysis of Venice in Terms of the
Four Functions of CIAM, CIAM Summer School, 1954.

Source: Università IUAV di Venezia Archivio Progetti, fondo Egle Renata Trincanato 2. Attività scientifica/
2/011.

inefficacy was evident when dealing with the complexity of urban relations, in particular, in Venice.

Other groups underlined different critical points of the contemporary urbanism. For instance, the group of the young Reima Pietilä[119] (Finland), together
with Jennewein and Swartz (USA), explored a preliminary study of land use and
zoning of Venice in-between the tourism from the sea and the commercial flow
from the mainland. Bovy (Belgium), Caramel, Mazzeri, Pastor, Venier (Italy)
and D'Amelio (USA) focused their attention on the necessity of reconsidering
the time of the project, affirming that "it is absurd to give an ideal form of a
hypothetical content": the final proposal was a dynamic *"organe planifiant
permanent"* (permanent planning organs) which changed according to the new
needs in different periods of time. The proposed method of planning, rather
than the project of a new street tangent to Venice, was the most relevant result
of the group. This was the demonstration, as Crooke and Buzzi highlighted,
that "the aim of the school is in particular to clarify some principles, and to
define through them the action of the architect,"[120] in direct coherence with the

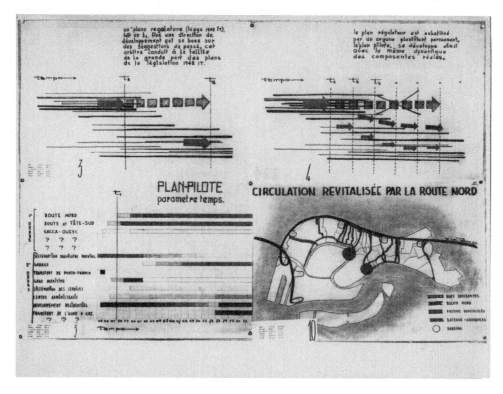

Figure 3.21 Bovy, Caramel, Mazzeri, Pastor, Venier and D'Amelio. "Plan Pilote," CIAM Summer School, 1954.

Source: Università IUAV di Venezia Archivio Progetti, fondo Egle Renata Trincanato 2. Attività scientifica/2/011.

didactic proposals within the ten points presented by Norberg-Schulz in Hoddesdon in 1951.

The issue of the time of the project was also considered by the team composed of Kondracki (USA), Kozlowski (France) and Lombaerts (Belgium), who investigated the consequences of the historical evolution of the city. Indeed, they compared the "synthesis of new relationships" with the "tissue of existing life," where the privileged areas, mostly concentrated along the Canal Grande, were defined "at the expense of the rest of the city." As proposal, the functions of the bridgehead were finally integrated with the rest of the city, connecting all the present-day unconsidered social parts of the urban tissue and transforming the entire Venice as a lagoon-centre.

Also, the group composed of Cohen (USA), Gunther (Peru) and Smith (USA), identified the social inequities, "the collapse of the communities" present in Venice, likewise the previous group, proposing new services where lacking. Interestingly, Venice was represented and identified through abstract schemes which interpreted the structure of the city only through social systems of relationships, equilibriums and polarities.

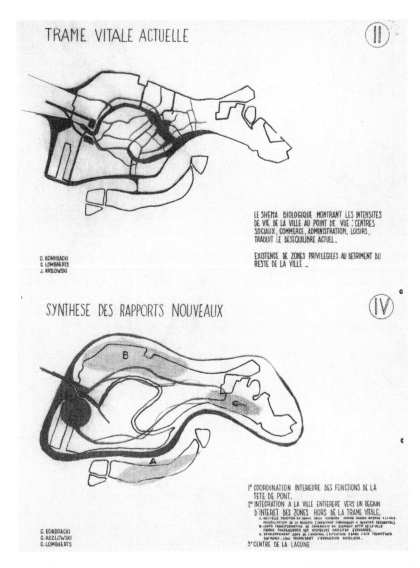

Figure 3.22 Kondracki, Kozlowski and Lombaerts. "Synthesis of New Relationships," CIAM Summer School, 1954.

Source: Università IUAV di Venezia Archivio Progetti, fondo Egle Renata Trincanato 2. Attività scientifica/2/011.

This social interest and abstract representation of the city echoed again theoretical nuances of the Heart of the City theme, as the first attempt to reject the rigidity of the four functions scheme with the introduction of a new interest on ordinariness, human scale and social values.

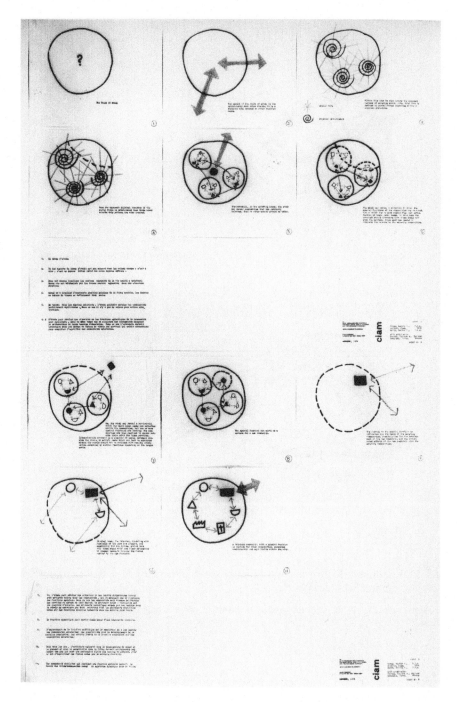

Figure 3.23 Cohen, Gunther and Smith. Schemes about Centres of Social Life, CIAM Summer School, 1954.

Source: Università IUAV di Venezia Archivio Progetti, fondo Egle Renata Trincanato 2. Attività scientifica/2/011.

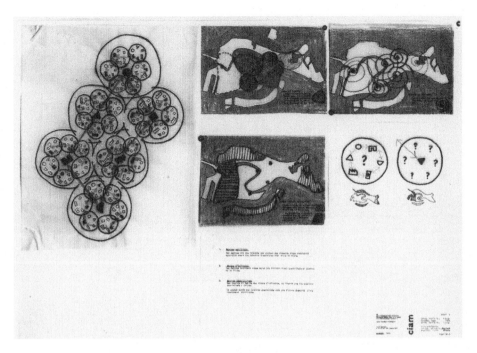

Figure 3.24 Cohen, Gunther and Smith. Centralities and Social Relationships, CIAM Summer School, 1954.

Source: Università IUAV di Venezia Archivio Progetti, fondo Egle Renata Trincanato 2. Attività scientifica/2/011.

The fourth CIAM Summer School in Venice, 1956

The edition of the summer school in 1955 was cancelled because of organisation reasons and overlapping meetings.[121] After this interruption, the fourth edition of the CIAM Summer School in Venice took place from September 6 to October 6, 1956. The directors were again Albini, Gardella, Rogers and Samonà but with the collaboration of Giancarlo De Carlo.[122] Bakema, Quaroni and Gino Valle attended as visiting critics. Conferences were held by De Logu, Deluigi, Melograni, Olivetti, Piccinato, Quaroni and Trincanato.

The year 1956 was the same year of the First Urban Design Conference organised at Harvard by Sert and of the initial dissolution of CIAM as well. The summer school took place exactly one month after CIAM 10 held in Dubrovnik (August 3–12, 1956). De Carlo and Bakema,[123] members of Team 10, were an imposing presence at the summer school, witnesses of a closed experience of CIAM. Not by coincidence, the 1956 summer school remained the last one which directly referred to CIAM.

In particular, in Venice, De Carlo's radical position of rift with the old CIAM's axioms raised up during the discussion on the role of the civic centre, which shared many resonances with the topic of CIAM 8 as well. On September 19–20, the Italian Team 10 member criticised the attempt to either restore symbols as Le Corbusier did for Chandigarh (presented at CIAM 8) or to re-create a medieval centre, being guilty of sentimentalism, as Sert for instance was coevally referring to. *Vis-à-vis* the plurality of contemporary life and "the confusion of the social situation, we reach the conclusion that only a plurality of centers can exist . . . The center can have just functional buildings, the rest is rhetoric," as De Carlo criticised, abhorring any

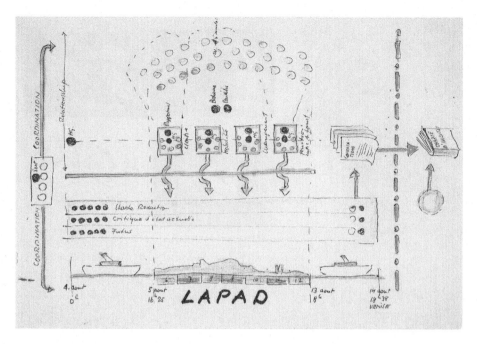

Figure 3.25 Sketch Showing the Program of CIAM 10 in August 1956.

From Padova to Lapad to Venice, where the Fourth Summer School is organised in September 1956. Bakema and Candilis are elected as exponents of the Young Groups.

Source: gta/ETH 42_SG_47_222.

symbolic and rhetoric attempts to redefine the Core-centre and to imitate forms of the past in favour, instead, of more complex socio-spatial centralities of plural character. But how to relate the plurality of centralities to the plurality of society? "We cannot consider the life of society as a whole. 'Communists' and 'Daughters of Mary' activities,"[124] De Carlo concluded. With this ironic answer, on the one hand, the Italian architect proposed to students a rupture with the absolutist attitude of the first CIAM to regulate the city as a whole, with zones and function distinctions; on the other, somehow he hinted at both the concrete limits and the impossible neutrality of the role of the architect facing the growing complexity of society.

Interestingly, at the Fourth Summer School, this interest on complex centralities raised in parallel with the necessity to consider Venice on its territorial scale, beyond the physical limits of the island.

In 1956, "The theme," the introductory text of the CIAM Summer School, proposed to focus on the future of Venice and its complexity, in particular, on the continual expansion of the Venice mainland, Mestre/Marghera,

> which is pushing for an indiscriminate building in a NO PLAN WORLD. Today, the problem has become urgent. We expect a doubling of the population in the next ten years, this is the moment when planning action becomes possible and necessary.[125]

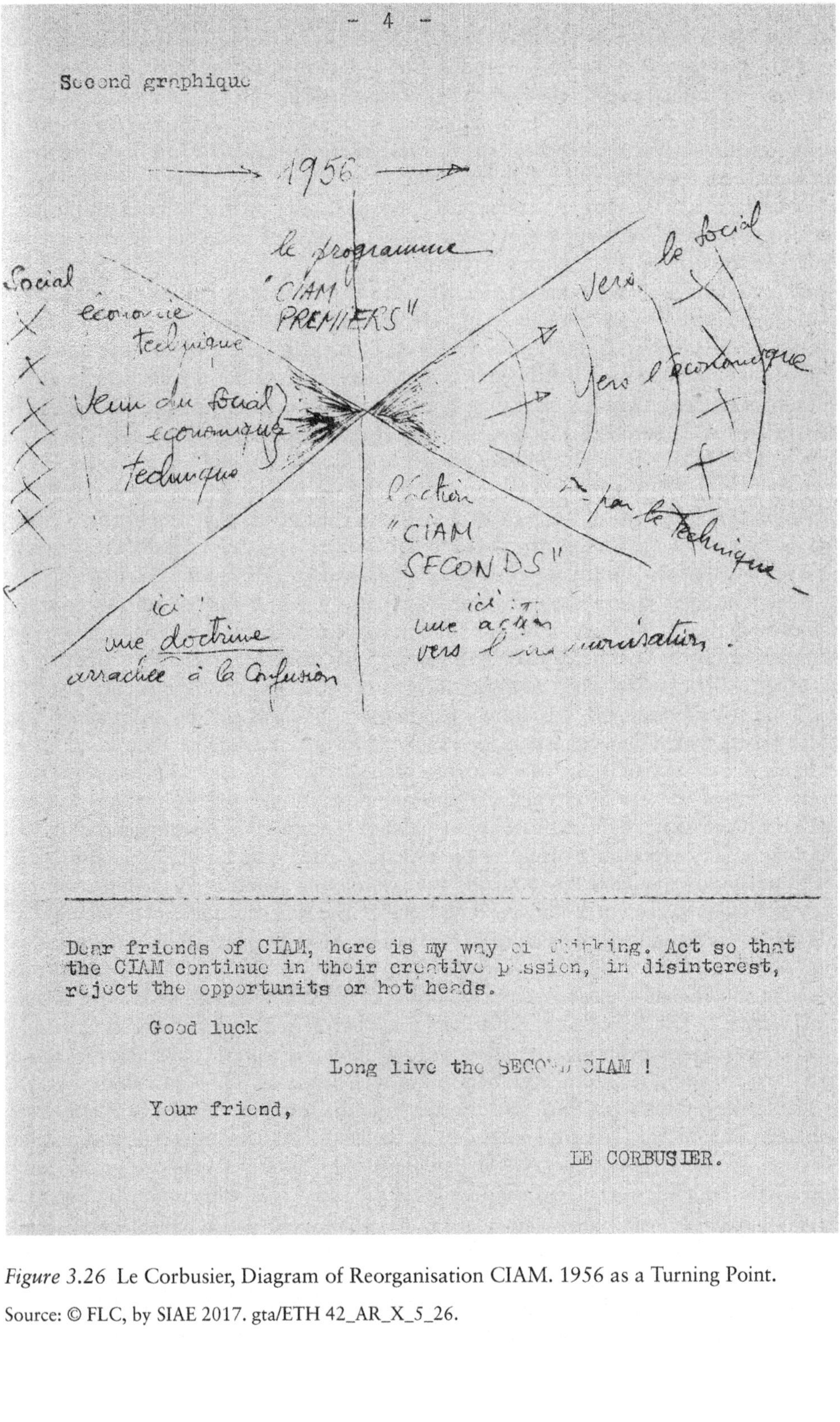

Second graphique

Dear friends of CIAM, here is my way of thinking. Act so that
the CIAM continue in their creative passion, in disinterest,
reject the opportunits or hot heads.

    Good luck

        Long live the SECOND CIAM !

    Your friend,

                LE CORBUSIER.

Figure 3.26 Le Corbusier, Diagram of Reorganisation CIAM. 1956 as a Turning Point.

Interestingly, the issue of "no plan world" shared similarities with the danger of the uncontrolled sprawl in the USA considered by Sert at First UD at Harvard. Moreover, whereas Sert in his speech relied on the younger generation for a solution, also in the summer school, the pivotal role of education and awareness of the responsibility of young architects were stressed for the future evolution of the city, on both the structural and conceptual levels.

Differently from the First UD at Harvard, in Venice, the lectures which tackled the main theme of the school exposed several nuances and perspectives related to the Venetian and Italian context: from the historical study of Venice (Trincanato's "The Election of the Doge"), to more general aspects on "Italian construction" (Melograni), to the necessity of planning (Gardella) to the compulsion of a cultural movement which could enhance a new social idea of Urbanism and of Venice itself, beyond the mere image of the "live museum" (Piccinato).[126] Among the CIAM members, Le Corbusier contributed a Conference at Ca' Giustinian on September 27, reiterating again the main topic of CIAM 8, the separation pedestrian and automobiles which particularly characterized the "miracle" of Venice: "il faut remettre la roue à sa place, il faut séparer le piéton de l'automobile et donner la primauté au piéton. Vous, gens de Venise, vous avec chez vous ce miracle."[127] Finally, Ludovico Quaroni strikingly revealed the need to consider the "territorial organism" of the City. In this vast organism, the Church, the political party office ("*sede del partito*"), the Chamber of Work and the social centres were considered significant urban elements, reinterpreting the discussion on social centralities and gathering points through the strong role of the political forces in the development of the city in Italy. Moreover, Quaroni underlined that town planning had to be considered closely connected with man's life, since the "space which man lives is an organism, where numberless forces are in action."[128] "Being concerned with the more general problems of territorial planning," which was also the main assignment of the Fourth CIAM Summer School, was the only way to enhance new humanistic values of in the role of Architecture, to allow architects to get more in contact with society and to regain unity of cultures overcoming the specialisations of the profession which occurred since the Renaissance. Only in this way the architect "succeeded in becoming again part of the cultural life, in operating again for the society, in gaining back the object of his activity,"[129] Quaroni expounded the social and cultural role and charge of the architect through the territorial investigation of the city, in his lecture "The Architect and Town Planning."

This new dimension of the territorial scale, of the later megastructure of the so-called *città-territorio*,[130] became later evident in Venice itself, in 1959, when Quaroni proposed in San Giuliano in Mestre, a new "urban heart which is alternative to the insular one [Venice],"[131] as described by Tafuri, dal Co. This unbuilt projects was composed by a cluster mega-semi-cylindrical buildings, with flexible structures which filter the lagoon and the mainland, the natural and the artificial, the historical and the modern.

The territorial scale presence and urgency was disclosed also in the projects of the students in 1956. The Group composed by Crumlish (USA), Dewhirst (UK), Gottwalles (France), Richards (UK), Sauer (USA), Saulnier (USA), Stuart (Australia), Virdis (Italy) and Virta (Finland) considered the family as the only significant unit which can be adopted, together with individuals, in order to define the structure of the society place by place and time by time, again with many resonances with the limited and incomplete private "*coeurs*," as discussed at CIAM 8.[132] The result, as Scimemi described it in *Casabella*, was a multiplicity of overlaying spheres of relations, each one with a certain centrality. These relations overcame the alleged symbolic value of the centre which, "if it is imposed, it reveals a fragile basis of preconceptions and prejudices."[133]

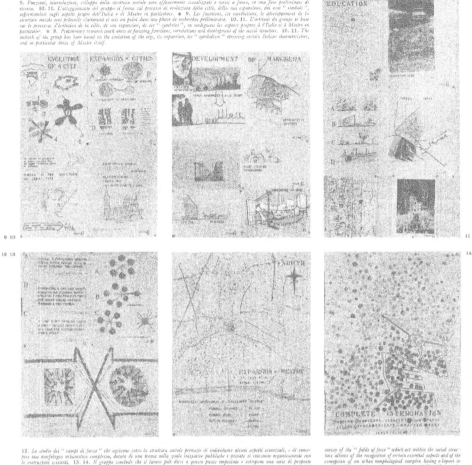

Figure 3.27 Crumlish, Dewhirst, Gottwalles, Richards, Sauer, Saulnier, Stuart, Virdis and Virta. CIAM Summer School, 1956.

Source: Gabriele Scimemi, "La quarta scuola estiva del CIAM a Venezia," *Casabella Continuità, n.213,* (1956): 73.

The group of Bindi, Garzena and Levi (Italy) and Rodriguez (Colombia) instead proposed an analysis of different phases of the extension of Mestre and Marghera which revealed "a spontaneous attempt of the community to settle around the 'core-street',"[134] in open contradiction with the Athens Charter. This core-street (sometimes called centre-street, or *rue-centre* in French or *strada-centro* in Italian) was explained as an attempt to propose traffic circulation – instead of residential entities – as the central concern for the

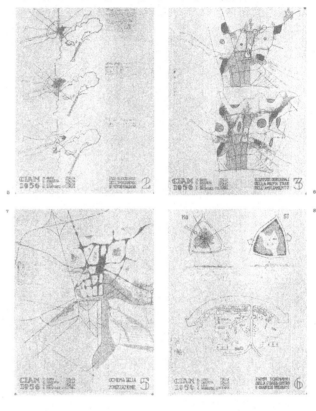

(continua da pag. 70)

timane), fece del suo meglio per governare la rotta, cercando di individuare le correnti ai lumi della propria bussola. E tuttavia non è stata una navigazione tranquilla. Il che non ci stupisce, anzi, (a parte ogni eccessivo ottimismo), ci soddisfa particolarmente. La vivacità degli atteggiamenti, la polemicità di molte posizioni ci sembrano chiaro indice di una acquisizione dei problemi quanto mai aderente alla realtà. Ed è anche una prova della validità degli interventi individuali. Veri e propri attacchi e contrattacchi hanno caratterizzato lo svolgersi del corso, investendo posizioni di principio, questioni di dettaglio, atteggiamenti metodologici, in un clima, come già si disse, di continua crisi. Se il CIAM stesso è in crisi (« crisis or evolution? » si domandavano preoccupati i più autorevoli membri del CIRPAC al recentissimo Congresso di Lapad), perchè non dovrebbe esserlo la Scuola del CIAM? La Scuola stessa esiste oggi più che come una emanazione del Congresso, come un utile, indispensabile incontro tra i giovani architetti di tutti i Paesi, nell'intento di affrontare i comuni problemi in uno spirito di democratica discussione. E la natura stessa di questi problemi non è tale da conciliare un atteggiamento di supina contemplazione. Il tema specifico degli insediamenti di Venezia in terraferma, e le soluzioni proposte in particolare dalla Scuola sono state deliberatamente trascurate in questa breve relazione. Se ne troverà qualche documentazione nelle illustrazioni e nelle didascalie che l'accompagnano. Ci è sembrato più significativo soffermarci su quelle posizioni, su quegli apporti che investono problemi di carattere universale, e che per la loro urgenza sono imprescindibili da ogni attività urbanistica contemporanea: dovunque localizzata, comunque condizionata, e da chiunque intrapresa. Quei problemi cioè che meglio degli altri possono e devono essere trattati su un piano di collaborazione internazionale. Se tale è e sarà il significato della Scuola del CIAM, ci auguriamo che questa esperienza possa ripetersi in avvenire con continuità e successo.

72   Gabriele Scimemi

Gruppo:
Biudi, Garzena, Levi, Rodriguez

Figure 3.28 Bindi, Garzena, Levi and Rodriguez. CIAM Summer School, 1956.

Source: Gabriele Scimemi, "La quarta scuola estiva del CIAM a Venezia," *Casabella Continuità*, n.213, (1956): 72.

planning of new and growing settlements. An "integrative tools of the technology in the society, as culture fact"[135] was privileged, rather than the pedestrian nature of the island of Venice itself or "*La royauté du piéton*" stressed at the Hoddesdon meeting in 1951 as well as at the CIAM Summer School in 1956 by the master Le Corbusier. The attention to modern technology and car traffic was optimistically considered as part of the contemporary structure of society, coherently with some later proposals of Team 10 and in particular of Bakema, who also reinterpreted the Core-street idea, as later exposed.

Among the other groups, Hoshour (USA) and Muzzillo (Italy) then highlighted the correspondence between "creation of new centers" as "the creation of new symbols."[136]

Five years after CIAM 8, the Core-centre as "the symbol of the city"[137] as praised by Sert, was mainly perceived as a pre-fixed entity inside the city. This was manifested in the opinion of students and critics as well, such as De Carlo who again highlighted the necessity to relate symbols, if their presence is really necessary, to the nearest texture of the city, to the concrete social aspirations, without being determined beforehand.

Finally, Denise Scott Brown was also present at the Fourth CIAM Summer School, in the same group with her first husband Robert Scott Brown (South Africa) and Campbell (North Ireland), Chipkin (South Africa), Heinemann (Germany), Hultberg (Scotland), Jackson and McKay (Australia), Paredes (Peru) and Townsend (Australia). Their research sought to ensure maximum opportunity of contacts among urban entities with either different or the same grades of connections: from individual house, to square, to neighbourhood, to town and between house and house, neighbourhood and neighbourhood, and so on.

The main aim was to elaborate and reveal the complexity of the city itself and to seek "efficient human relationships."[138] As Scimemi underlined, Venice represented a perfect case study where both associations could be investigated. Four scales are schematised in the first project panel, from the individual house (first scale) to the street and piazza (second scale) to the neighbourhood with a central space of connectivity (third scale). Finally, a vertical arrow on the left passes through all three different scales (individual, street, neighbourhood) indicating at the end the fourth scale, the Town, as the result of the addition, integration and intersection of the previous scales.

Under the "Town structure" schemes, the students then highlighted the complexity of Venice, which, in section, looks very different in contrast with new models of the city such as Howard's Garden City or Le Corbusier's Ville Radieuse. Comparison of these three sections, in the "Existing solutions" scheme, seems therefore to denounce the lack of complexity, of disjunction between social needs and physical structure which characterised Modern new city models. The complex three-dimensional stratified structure of Venice was instead progressively conceived as a better solution for integrating the urban scales as described previously. Historical Venice became suddenly more meaningful, fruitful, charged with a deeper significance than others, with a view to the future design of new and more adequate city models.

Furthermore, the students proposed a fast, suburban transport network as the backbone of the new plan for "Mestre-Venice-industry-new settlements." Denise and Robert Scott Brown had already planned a similar solution the previous year, as students in the AA's Tropical School, when they redesigned the city of Lima in Peru as a linear city which resonated with *Miljutin*'s projects and which was connected by a 300km/hour mass transport system.[139] From Lima to Venice, the attention of the transport infrastructure on the territorial scale was positively envisaged as a structural entity for the condensation and renovation of urban settlements, as shown in the third and fourth panels. Here, different solutions of relationships between living centres and the fast traffic arterial roads are studied. The multinational group considered either direct connections, secondary roads or parallel arteries connected to the residential strip through a mix of secondary arteries. In this last proposal, new settlements would even grow as encounters with new "bridge-heads" were generated by the fast highway. Therefore, in 1956 the mainland of Venice became the principal territory for the integration of technological mechanisation and social-urban gathering, in total contrast with the previous beliefs of CIAM 8, the programmatic and theoretical origin of the CIAM Summer School in Venice.[140]

Last, this territorial, socio-spatial focus on the highway and the interest in the symbolical, deep presence of historical Venice were destined to echo in further research and projects of paramount importance in the USA. From "Venice to Venice Beach"[141]

Tema: gli insediamenti di Venezia in terraferma

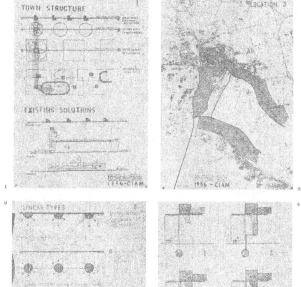

Gruppo: Campbell, Chipkin, Heinemann, Hultberg, Jackson, McKay, Paredes, D. e R. Scott-Brown, Townsend.   71

Figure 3.29 Denise Scott Brown, Robert Scott Brown and Campbell, Chipkin, Heinemann, Hultberg, Jackson, McKay, Paredes and Townsend. CIAM Summer School, 1956.

Source: Gabriele Scimemi, "La quarta scuola estiva del CIAM a Venezia," *Casabella Continuità*, n.213, (1956): 71.

and to Las Vegas, a transatlantic flow of influences, references and resonances engaged the activity of Denise Scott Brown, a young architect present at the Fourth edition of the CIAM Summer School.

Digression: Denise Scott Brown

Denise Scott Brown described the focus of the summer school in 1956 as the same concern discussed by Brutalists, but with "an Italian accent," with more emphasis on tradition and heritage, on "the pre-industrial and peasant societies rather than with an urban mass society."[142]

Interestingly, for her, Venice itself embodies "an extension of Brutalist thought"[143] in contrast with the Ville Radieuse, as already shown in the project panels. Venice's ability to adapt, its unpredictable future, its expression of time through "brick sizes and combination" which questions the fundamentals of orthodox Modernity, became formative for her architectural thinking.

"New Brutalism" derived from a transfusion and (mis)interpretation of the Swedish "new Humanism" into the young English architectural milieu at the beginning of the 1950s, as proposed by Banham.[144] It was another movement of thinking among the younger architects, in stark contrast with the old architectural establishment and yet uncomfortable and profuse architectural stream. It was a counterforce to the romanticism exhibited for instance at the "*frou-frou* of the Festival of Britain"[145] which was coeval to CIAM 8 in 1951, to the current doctrinaire urbanism and the conventional and conformist idea of beauty against which the Brutalists casted a more ethical truth, genuineness and directness as the real, deep concern. In short, "an ethic, not an aestetic," where beauty is derived from a second interior and deeper sight, from an honest though apparently agonising solution based on social realism.

Moreover, Brutalism was intrinsically connected with the rise of Team 10, thanks to the presence of the "Brutus"[146] Smithson, and the rift with the old CIAM which was mirrored at the 1956 edition of the CIAM Summer School in Venice as well. Here, the Brutalist plea for "fresh eyes and to stay out of aesthetic ruts"[147] was fully embraced by the young South African Architects in particular as a method of research, investigation and experience of life in the old lagoon through photography. Remarkably, in Venice, their awareness of photography as a critical tool became more clear: it was a fresh "Wayward Eye"[148] which enhanced the flow "from recording to analysing" and from composed architectural pictures to straight (without thinking, without filters) instinctive life snaps. "The reflected interplays between government, church, and people, is and ought to be, real and virtual,"[149] the complexity of timeless and immediate movements of the city, of urban and nature's superimpositions were explored with immediate shots of the city.

Finally, after the summer school, the South African couple had the opportunity to work in Giuseppe Vaccaro's office for six weeks on the project *INA-Casa* in the *Tiburtino* quarter in Rome. Ludovico Quaroni, who lectured at the CIAM Summer School in Venice, introduced them to the Roman architect. In Rome, through Vaccaro's design and the city itself, the young architects fermented their curiosity in the overlapping of structures, spaces, orders and "learning from Mannerism, in the collision of systems and in their folding and breaking to arrive at unique conditions."[150] Venice and Rome became important professional and life experiences for their whole future careers, "preparing us for urbanism in America,"[151] as Denise Scott Brown claimed.

Once adopted and transplanted in the American context, the nourishing of a new personal-architectural awareness of the photography tool as a "subdiscipline of architecture,"[152] the absorption of the Mannerist complexity and contradictions of the Italian urban structure in Rome[153] as well as in the Brutalist Venice, the juxtapositions of ambiguous and synchronic conditions, scales and uses, highly reverberated in later projects and well-known research.

From the CIAM Summer School in Venice to Rome, the Italian *milieu* resonated in Denise Scott Brown and Venturi's research on Architecture engaging symbolism, Brutalist-directness and Mannerist-ambiguities, influencing architectural thinking right up until today.

Figure 3.30 CIAM Summer School, 1956. Students and Tutors in Piazza San Marco, 1956.

Source: Collection Het Nieuwe Instituut, Rotterdam, BAKE.110300874, BAKE_f21–1.

The international summer seminar of architecture of Venice, 1957

The fifth and last edition was held from September 7 to 28, 1957 and it was called the "International Summer Seminar of Architecture" since it was no longer institutionally recognised by CIAM.

However, the focus on Venice and the directors – the CIAM members Albini, Gardella, Rogers and Samonà[154] – remained the same. Gillo Dorfles, Riccardo Morandi, Enzo Paci and Aral Korsmo expounded as external speakers while the internal ones were Scimemi, Piccinato and Trincanato.

As far as the reference to the Heart of the City is concerned, the most intriguing and outstanding lecture during the Summer Seminar was given by the Existentialist philosopher Paci. In his opinion, the foundations of Existentialism could be found in the relational theme, understood as a condition of existence of all the events that constitute the world, as a new concept which should be sought, cultivated and kept continuously authentic even though conflictual.[155] On September 16, 1957, Paci presented his lecture "Relationism and Architecture,"[156] where the philosopher underlined the meaning of Relationism "characterized by a desire to study the relations existing between the various aspects of reality and not the isolated realities – or substances." Only through forms, materials or proportions, can the architect discover that he is

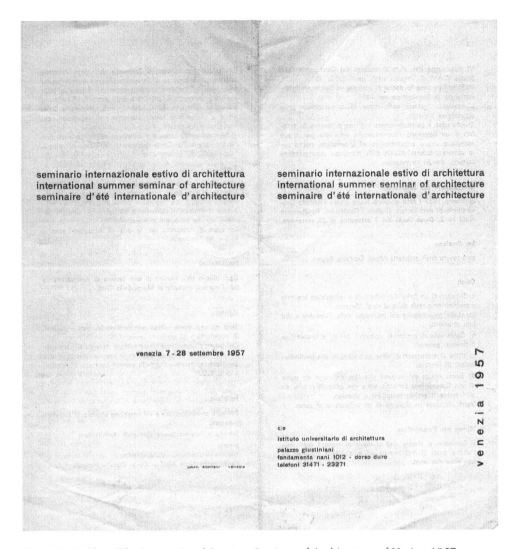

Figure 3.31 Flyer, The International Summer Seminar of Architecture of Venice, 1957.

Source: Università IUAV di Venezia Archivio Progetti, fondo Egle Renata Trincanato 2.Attività scientifica/2/014.

able to express all his faith in the relations he creates, his faith in a town as well as in the entire world yet to come, rather than in abstract functions. And whereas "to be 'organic' means to be poet . . . then the Organic Relationism is, at least in philosophy, a fecund synthesis of what architects call 'functionalism' and 'organicism'."[157] At the very finale of this pivotal international pedagogical experience of the Venice CIAM Summer School, the Italian philosopher praised the organic and relational process as a duty of the architect. In light of this responsibility and awareness, he indirectly reiterated also one of the most important interpretative arteries expressed at CIAM 8 in Hoddesdon by Bakema: the Heart of the City as relationship.

In conclusion, the CIAM Summer Schools underlined that the CIAM, rather being closed congress, was as much a fecund open cultural *milieu* in which new insights and perspectives were generated. The editions of summer schools added different issues and topics to the CIAM idiom and, above all, they grounded and confronted CIAM principles and knowledge to the real complexity and ambiguity of everyday life of a particular city as Venice, through the particular perspective of the young generation of architects. Thereby, they made the CIAM theories, methods and perspectives – in particular the Heart of the City as continuity – more resilient and its legacy more consistent also for our contemporary debate.

Notes

1 ("It is necessary to put the wheel in its place, we must separate the pedestrian from the automobile and give the primacy to the pedestrian. You, people of Venice, you with this miracle . . . Venice remains, in the midst of a modern order, a gift of God that is present and must not be touched, which must not be destroyed.") Le Corbusier is invited by the CIAM Summer School to attend a conference in Ca' Giustinian, on September 27, 1956. Le Corbusier, "Presentation in Venice," Trincanato 2. Attività scientifica/2/011, Archivio Progetti IUAV, Venice.

2 (Originally in Italian: "*peraltro, proprio al CIAM di Hoddesdon, anche attraverso il tema del 'Heart of the City', comincia a emergere la questione che si dimostrerà centrale per i quarant'anni successivi: il problema dell'ascolto del contesto, del progetto come dialogo con esso in quanto forma depositata della storia del luogo specifico. Si trattava, è vero, della formulazione della questione nei termini del continuismo rogersiano delle pre-esistenze ambientali o in quelli antropologici dei valori di permanenza di civiltà alternative, con una netta resistenza contro ogni richiamo agli stili storici, ma purtuttavia si era avviata la questione del valore e della difesa della città storica, della conservazione dei tessuti e non solo dei monumenti isolati, del tema della memoria e della tradizione come materiali importanti del progetto.*") Vittorio Gregotti, "Editoriale – Gli Ultimi CIAM," *Rassegna*, 52, no. 4 (1992): 4.

3 (Originally in Italian: "*la storia come terreno del progetto*") Vittorio Gregotti, *Il territorio dell'architettura* (Milano: Feltrinelli, 1966; third edition 2014), 1.

4 "In founding anti-history and presenting their work not so much as anti-historical, but rather as above the very concept of historicity, the avant-gardes perform the only legitimate act of the Time." Manfredo Tafuri, *Teorie e storia dell'architettura* (Bari: Laterza, 1968); quoted in Adrian Forty, *Words and Buildings: A Vocabulary of Modern Architecture* (London: Thames and Hudson, 2000), 198.

5 Forty, *Words and Buildings*, 198.

6 Alex Tzonis, Liane Lefaivre, "The Grid and the Pathway. An Introduction to the Work of Dimitris and Suzana Antonakakis," *Architecture in Greece*, 15 (1981). Kenneth Frampton, "Towards a Critical Regionalism: Six Points for an Architecture of Resistance," in *The Anti-Aesthetic: Essays on Postmodern Culture*, ed. Hal Foster (Seattle: Bay Press, 1983).

7 See Dirk van den Heuvel, "Another Sensibillity. The Discovery of Context," *Oase: tijdschrift voor architectuur*, 76 (2008): 21–46.

8 Rowe, Koetter, *Collage City*.

9 OMA, Rem Koolhaas, Bruce Mau, *S,M,L,XL* (New York: Monacelli Press, 1995), 640.

10 Forty, *Words and Buildings*, 132.

11 Ernesto Nathan Rogers, "Continuità," *Casabella Continuità*, 199 (December 1953/January 1954): 2.

12 For the difference between *contesto*-context-contextualism-*ambiente-preesistenze ambientali*, see Forty, *Words and Buildings*.

13 (Originally in Italian: "*cosiderare l'ambiente significa considerare la storia*") Ernesto Nathan Rogers, "Editoriale," *Casabella Continuità*, 204 (1955). Ernesto Nathan Rogers, "Preexisting Conditions and Issues of Contemporary Building Practice." In *Architecture Culture*, ed. Joan Ockman (New York: Rizzoli, 1993), 200–204.

14 Interestingly, according to Leo Spitzer, "*Ambiente*" is first found in Italian "*aria ambiente*" in 1656 with Galileo, one of the first proponents of a decentralised space in contrast with

dogmatic Man's universal barycentric position. It therefore becomes another important reference for the historical, social, cultural and physical relationships between the existent and the new project which are considered as the basic design materials. Moreover, "*Ambiente*" is one of the "indigenous terms" which resonate in imperfect synonyms of French *milieu*, German *Umwelt*, Spanish *medio*, English *Environment*: "the concept of an aggregate of influence or conditions which shape or determine the being, development, life, or behaviour of a person or a thing."

Leo Spitzer, "Milieu and Ambience: An Essay in Historical Semantics." *Philosophy and Phenomenological Research*, 3, no. 2 (December 1942): 205–206.

15 (Originally in Italian: "*omaggio a una Milano che la speculazione aveva praticamente distrutto*") Manfredo Tafuri, Francesco Dal Co, *Architettura Contemporanea* (Milano: Electa, 1976; XVI edition Electa, 2012), 339.

16 Rossi himself worked as collaborator of Rogers at *Casabella* since 1955. The importance of the ideas of Rogers on Rossi is mentioned also by Eric Mumford: "*well before Aldo Rossi, Rogers had introduced the concept of the 'preesistenze ambientali,' emphasizing how preexisting urban conditions continue to shape those of the present.*" Eric Mumford, *Defining Urban Design: CIAM Architects and the Formation of a Discipline, 1937–69* (New Haven and London: Yale University Press, 2009), 115.

17 (Originally in Italian: "*ma è la conoscenza del passato che costituisce il termine di confronto e la misura per l'avvenire.*") Rossi, *L'architettura della città* (Padova: Marsilio, 1966; Novara: Citta' Studi, 2006), 44.

18 Domhardt, Konstanze Sylva. "From the 'Functional City' to the 'Heart of the City.' Green Space and Public Space in the CIAM Debates of 1942-1952," in *Greening the City: Urban Landscapes in the Twentieth Century*, ed. Dorothee Brantz, Sonja Dümpelmann (Charlottesville: University of Virginia Press, 2011), 150.

19 "Every time you draw a line you should do it as if it is thought to stay forever." Ernesto Nathan Rogers, "Resume of Open Session, Wednesday July 11," in an unpublished CIAM 8 Session, CIAM JT-6-16-75. Quoted in Mumford, Eric. "The Emergence of Urban Design in the Breakup of CIAM," in *Urban Design*, eds. Alex Krieger, William S. Saunders (Minneapolis, London: University of Minnesota Press, 2009), 26.

20 "Far from becoming weaker, the sense of opposition existing between one generation and another will acquire a new importance if the younger ones, instead of opposing the work of their elders, will, in the full conscience of their own strength, fall into place, alongside, and travel the same road together." Ernesto Nathan Rogers, "Architectural Education, First Session, CIAM 8, 1951" 42-JT-7-473/475, gta/ETH.

21 Ernesto Nathan Rogers, "*Nous considérons aussi la question des jeunes sous le signe du groupe unique. Ils sont invitées a adhérer a notre groupe mais en gardant toute leur autonomie.*" CIAM, *Le Documents de Sigtuna*, 14.

22 CIAM, *Le Documents de Sigtuna*, 17.

23 Rogers, "Architectural Education, First Session, CIAM 8, 1951."

24 "1/ We must make a complete break with the name CIAM [. . . .] 2/ We now think that a 'New CIAM of 30' is quite wrong" Smithson Alison and Peter, The Future of CIAM, To Team 10 and old CIAM Council, December 9, 1956." Alison Smithson, *The Emergence of Team 10 Out of CIAM* (London: AAGS Theory and History Papers 1.82, Architectural Association, 1982), 75–76.

25 "The function of the Continuity Organization would be to further define the new methods of attack on the Problem of Habitat started by the TEAM 10 (Cluster, Growth and Change, Mobility), and ultimately to organise a Congress to carry on the work started at CIAM X" Alison and Peter Smithson, Letter August 23, 1957, TTEN0002, Team 10 Smithsons, folder 16, Het Nieuwe Instituut, Rotterdam. It was "an effort to meet demands of CIAM delegates." Smithson, *The Emergence of Team 10 Out of CIAM*, 81.

26 During the last CIAM (in 1959 in Otterlo), "where the Death of CIAM is formally announced" (Architectural Design, October 1959), the role of the debate between Rogers and the Smithsons on the Torre Velasca project "which some later historians have linked to the beginning of postmodern historicism in architecture" is important. Mumford, *The CIAM Discourse on Urbanism*, 261.

27 (Originally in Italian: *"noialtri abbiamo illustrato le nostre opera . . . [che] intendono tutte di superare lo schematismo astratto del linguaggio 'moderno' per conferire un nuovo grado di modernità all'architettura."*) Ernesto Nathan Rogers, "I CIAM al Museo," *Casabella Continuità*, 232 (1959): 2–3.

28 Rogers, "I CIAM al Museo."

29 (Originally in Italian: *"in questo senso io parlo di continuità. E vi sarà molto da accogliere e da trasformare attivamente negli anni che verranno perché nessun giovane potrà prescindere, nel suo operare, da questa fertile realtà che è costituita per tutti dall'esperienza dei CIAM."*) Ibid., 3.

30 CIAM 8, "Discussion on Italian Piazzas," in *The Heart of the City: Towards the Humanisation of Urban Life*, ed. Jaqueline Tyrwhitt, Josep Lluís Sert, Ernesto N. Rogers (London: L. Humphries, 1952), 74–80.

31 Rogers, "The Heart: Human Problem of Cities," in *The Heart of the City*, 73.

32 Rogers, "Discussion on Italian Piazzas," 74.

33 Sert, "Discussion on Italian Piazzas," 77–78.

34 Ibid., 76–78. Peressutti focused his attention instead on the Piazza San Pietro in Rome, as did Giedion, while Paulson also talked about Piazza della Signoria in Florence and Piazza Vittorio Emanuele.

35 Giedion, "Conversation at CIAM 8," 39.

36 Le Corbusier, "The Core as a Meeting Place of the Arts," in *The Heart of the City*, 46.

37 There was the idea to organise the summer school in Venice also in 1950 and 1951, but it faced economic difficulties. Ernesto Nathan Rogers, "Letter to Le Corbusier, June 13, 1950," D2-19-265-001, Le Corbusier Archive, Paris. AM1970-18-162, Forbat Archive, ArkDes Archive, Stockholm.

38 CIAM 8, "Report on Architectural Education," in *Report of Hoddesdon Conference*, 115.

39 This comment was suggested by Tom Avermaete.

40 "His project, which would have occupied a prominent location on the Grand Canal, provoked passionate argument inside Italy and abroad about the suitedness of modern architecture to historic sites, and about the degree to which Wright's design did or did not take sufficient account of its surrounding." Forty, *Words and Buildings*, 133.

41 CIAM, D2-19-274-002, Le Corbusier Archive, Paris.

42 (*"E' nostra opinione che i temi prodotti per il prossimo congresso sono caratteristici di quella situazione e sono ovviamente privi dell'influenza della generazione più giovane, che pure non ha assunto una posizione di responsabilità."*) Proposal made by Merkelbach as president of the "Architectenvereeniging de 8," April 8, 1947. Quoted in Bosman, "I CIAM del dopoguerra: un bilancio del Movimento Moderno," 10.

43 Sigfried Giedion, *A Decade of New Architecture* (Zurich: Girsberger, 1951), 1.

44 "No one can foretell how things will develop, but my observations of the generation now about twenty-five years of age leads me to believe that this trend exists today in all countries of the western civilization." Giedion, "Historical Background to the Core," in *The Heart of the City*, 17.

45 Nicholas Bullock highlights that it was the first congress attended by the Smithsons, the Howells and the Voelckers (even though their names are not listed in CIAM 8 documents) who met other young Dutch and French counterparts: if CIAM 9 had always been considered the starting point of a new generation in opposition to the founders of CIAM, "the issues that were to divide CIAM were already evident at the CIAM 8." Bullock, *Building the Post-War World, Modern Architecture and Reconstruction in Britain*, 137.

   Dirk van den Heuvel and Max Risselada also affirm that Alison and Peter Smithson attended the congress in Hoddesdon in 1951 to hear Le Corbusier speak. Risselada, van den Heuvel, *TEAM 10 1953–81: In Search of a Utopia of the Present*, 11.

46 "A decisive moment of change had been represented by the students' projects in Hoddesdon. These ones raised the questions of the project study inspired by CIAM . . . through the idea of 'center' these could be understood as a new and global coherent approach." (Originally in Italian: *"un momento decisivo di cambiamento fu rappresentato dai progetti studenteschi di Hoddesdon. Questi sollevarono la questione dello studio progettuale ispirato ai CIAM . . . ; attraverso l'idea di 'centro' questi potevano essere intesi come approccio coerente nuovo e globale."*) Bosman, "I CIAM del dopoguerra," 13.

47 Third Commission, CIAM 7. *Reforme de l'enseignement de l' architecture et de l'urbanisme.* President: Ernesto Rogers. Vice-president: Jane Drew. 42-x-116 a-b, gta/ETH. See Walter Gropius, "In Search of Better Architectural Education," in *A Decade of New Architecture,* 41–46.

48 Commission 3, Architectural Education (Gropius, Rogers, van Eesteren, Giedion, Chermeyeff, Tyrwhitt). CIAM 8, *Report of Hoddesdon Conference,* 112.

49 Norberg-Schulz, Commission 3A (Young Architects), Report on Architectural Education. CIAM 8, *Report of Hoddesdon Conference,* 113.

50 Ibid., 114.

51 Maddalena Scimemi, "Venezia internazionale. La CIAM Summer School 1952–1957," *IUAV Journal,* 83 (2010): 5. Accessed on April 28, 2017, www.iuav.it/Ateneo1/chi-siamo/pubblicazi1/Catalogo-G/index.htm#dieci

52 "Leaping from one subject to another, at Hoddesdon in 1951 a discussion was held on 'The Core of the City' and around this such a large quantity of inaccurate and worldly nonsense was collected which, on re-reading the Report today after a lapse of time, makes one wonder how it was possible for the many serious-minded persons who were present – some of whom had assisted in drawing up the Athens Charter – to agree with or even stand it." Giancarlo De Carlo, "Summary," *Architectural Design* (May 1960): 204–205, E-017, Smithson Collection, GSD/Harvard.

53 Giancarlo De Carlo, Letter to Peter Smithson about ILAUD, December 12, 1977. Biblioteca civica d'arte Luigi Poletti, Fondo ILAUD, NOTE GDC, 1997. Published in Giovanna Borasi, ed., *The Other Architect: Another Way of Building Architecture* (Montreal: Canadian Centre of Architecture, Spector Books, 2015), 24.

54 "For me, personally, Team 10 was followed by ILAUD. ILAUD was a completely different business, though when I founded it, I obviously carried over a lot of ideas from Team 10." Clelia Tuscano, "How Can You Do Without History? Interview With Giancarlo De Carlo. Milan, Via Pier Capponi 13, 23 May 1990, 20 February 1995, and 24 November 1999," in *Team 10 1953–81: In Search of a Utopia of the Present,* 343.

55 From several personal discussions in 2012, 2013 and 2016 and a conference held at IUAV on September 2, 2013 ("Il Cuore della Città – CIAM 8," participants: Gregotti, Rykwert, Secchi, Viganò, Avermaete, Zuccaro Marchi).

56 "We are concerned with the situation of the young trained architect, the practicing graduate, the architectural student to-day. Ours is the first generation following the pioneers, and we inherit an already far advanced and extensive, rich architectural vocabulary. The architecture of our time exists posed in all its essential problems, and their many individual solutions.

   Our situation now confronts us with a threefold task.

   Synthesis of medium, integration of methods, reorganization of architectural schooling." Christian Norberg-Schulz, "Eduard Neuenschwander, 'TEAM 1', May 1, 1951," 42-x-150, gta/ETH.

57 Christian Norberg-Schulz, "Eduard Neuenschwander, 'TEAM 2', February 1952," 42-SG-39-62, gta/ETH.

58 Ibid., 7–8.

59 Ibid., 4.

60 "A junior Group was formed in Oslo in autumn 1949 as a result of Dr. Giedion's direct appeal and inspiration . . . In autumn 1950 the group was admitted to the CIAM group in Oslo, which had been reformed after the war by architect Arne Korsmo, with Korsmo and Erik Rolfsen, the Town Planning Officer of Olso, as delegates." Norberg-Schulz, "Neuenschwander, 'TEAM 2'".

61 PAGON, "CIAM," BYGGEKUNST nr. 6/7 (1952): 93. 42-x-14, gta/ETH.

62 Other architects are listed only as collaborators: Rolfsen, Korsmo, Norseng, Corwin and Esdale. PAGON, "Tveten panel, 1951" NAMT.ako061, The National Museum of Art, Architecture and Design, Oslo.

63 The district core contains facilities for about 25,000 people, who live in nearby neighbourhoods, and hosts a tramway station, storage, car parks, shops, offices, restaurants, cinemas, a market square, community building, secondary school, gymnasium, health centre and car workshop.

64 Christian Norberg-Schulz, "Letter to Giedion, Oslo, February 5, 1951," 42-SG-X-133, gta/ETH.

65 CIAM, "Letter of Extraordinary Council Meeting, Paris, May 14, 1952," CIAM Collection C11, GSD/Harvard.

66 Ibid.

67 Christian Norberg-Schulz, "On the Creation of Junior Groups, Sigtunta June 26, 1952," 42-JT-10-70, gta/ETH. CIAM, *Le Documents de Sigtuna*.

68 "Il a lu la question posée par Norberg-Schulz, 'why do we join CIAM?' Il faut y répondre: une société doit avoir un symbole d'appel et d'unité: c'est pour nous le combat pour l'architecture modern. Notre but n'a pas change mais nos méthodes . . . Et c'est significatif pour CIAM de faire notre ouvre en respectant les différences dans nos vus et nos tempéraments. C'est en insistant sur ces différences individuelles et nationales que nous pouvons construire une société libre et démocratique." Ernesto Nathan Rogers, CIAM, *Le Documents de Sigtuna*, 18.

69 Christian Norberg-Schulz, "Eduard Neuenschwander, 'TEAM 3': CIAM Junior Groups – *Groupes des jeunes*, September 1952," 42-SG-37-73 and 42-WM-X-1, gta/ETH.

70 It seems that Giedion, who was in direct contact with Norberg-Schulz during his studies at ETH at the end of the 1940s and who inspired the formation of the PAGON group, proposed calling the young members preparing the CIAM X "for instance Team Ten." Sigfried Giedion, "Letter to C. van Eesteren, January 15, 1956," Giedion CIAM Archive, gta/ETH. In Jos Bosman, "Team 10 Out of CIAM," in *TEAM 10 1953–81: In Search of a Utopia of the Present*, 247. Furthermore, during CIAM 9 the editors of TEAM were among the candidates for the election of the young members of CIAM. Bakema and Wogenscky were instead elected, while Howell and Candilis remained on the Council. See Bosman, "Team 10 Out of CIAM," 247.

71 At the Lapad Congress, July 10 1956, Norberg-Schulz and the PAGON group were present, though not mentioned among the Team 10 members. Their discourse at CIAM X remained focused on the education issue: "it is also important that well prepared work will give an understanding of the methods and outlines of CIAM among architectural students. Such work is already established in several universities and has the advantage of economical possibilities for both study and research as well as publication . . . The aim should be to have a worldwide cooperation within the universities to get student work and research directed toward solutions for the habitat." PAGON Group, "Notes, Norway, Lapad Congress, July 10, 1956," 42-JT-15-339/340, gta/ETH.

72 "The ancient poets animated all sensible objects with Gods and Geniuses," wrote "William Blake in The Marriage of Heaven and Hell, and particularly they studied the genius of each city and country, placing it under its mental deity." Christopher Tunnard, *The City of Man, a New Approach to the Recovery of Beauty in American Cities* (New York: Charles Scribner's Sons, 1953), 29.

73 Christian Norberg-Schulz, *Genius Loci: Towards a Phenomenology of Architecture* (New York: Rizzoli, 1980), 195.

74 Rowe, Koetter, *Collage City*.

75 Norberg-Schulz, *Genius Loci*, 168.

76 For instance, the Greek *polis* is based on the symbolic movement of meaning of landscapes into buildings. "It is a grand conception, indeed, to visualize the qualities of a landscape by means of a man-made structure, and then to gather several landscapes symbolically in one place!" Norberg-Schulz, *Genius Loci*, 170.

77 Norberg-Schulz, *Genius Loci*, 195. The quote of Giedion is from Giedion, *Architecture You and Me*, 127.

78 "The new Regionalism has as its motivating force a respect for individuality and a desire to satisfy the emotional and material needs of each area," in *Architectural Record*, January 1954, "The State of Contemporary Architecture, the Regional Approach." Also in Giedion, *Architecture You and Me*, 138. Norberg-Schulz, *Genius Loci*, 195.

79 "to visualize the genius loci, and the task of the architect is to create meaningful places, whereby he helps man to dwell." Norberg-Schulz, *Genius Loci*, 5.

80 The idea of the "genius loci, the spirit of the place" Norberg-Schulz talks about in his book, finds its origins directly within the discourse of Heidegger. Indeed Norberg-Schulz

affirms that man "*is 'thing' among 'things'*." He talked about "*an Übereinstimmung, a correspondence, between his own psychic states and the 'forces' of nature,*" which become "*meaningful*" when man finds "*a personal 'friendship' with things.*" The "*thing*" is then another outstanding theme for the author of the *Genius Loci*. Its original meaning is again "*gathering,*" as the author affirms, referring to the work of the philosopher Heidegger, who writes "*The Thing*" in 1950. Norberg-Schulz, *Genius Loci*, 5, 195.

81 Christian Norberg-Schulz, *Architecture: Meaning and Place* (New York: Electa, Rizzoli, 1988), 30.

82 Norberg-Schulz, *Genius Loci: Towards a Phenomenology of Architecture*, 195.

83 Interestingly, the *genius loci* was already adopted by Geddes, whose theory deeply influenced the definition of CIAM 8 as already argued. Volker M. Welter highlighted that Geddes considered the discovery and the capture of the *genius loci* as a passive action, which requires almost nothing to do. "*Wait in reverence for the genius loci of the place to work its miracle in its own way*" Geddes affirmed. Geddes, *Cities in Evolution*, vii, vi quoted In Welter, "From Locus Genii to Heart of the City," 41.

84 Also in 1948, a CIAM Summer School was organised. "CIAM Summer School, London 1948. You may already have heard that the first CIAM Summer School will be held in London this year from 19th July to 6th September." MARS Group, "Letter to Giedion May 14, 1948," 42-SG-19-4, gta/ETH. On June 14: "the greatest difficulty at the moment appears to be in attracting students and we are making renewed efforts to this in England" Cocks, MARS, "Letter to Giedion, June 14, 1948." Also, Ellen Shoshkes mentioned the summer school in 1948. See Shoshkes, *Jaqueline Tyrwhitt: A Transnational Life, in Urban Planning and Design*. Chapter: "CIAM International Summer School" 112. However, the edition held in August 1949 was last described as the first one. "The first CIAM Summer School was held in London from August 8th to September 2nd, 1949." Fry, Maxwell, "Letter to CIAM, November 24, 1949," 42-JT-4-215, gta/ETH. "CIAM [. . .] is now established firmly enough to justify the opening of a series of International Post-graduate Summer Schools. The first of these, which is frankly experimental, will be held in London in August 1949." CIAM, "Flyer, CIAM Summer School 1949," 42-HMS-I-424, gta/ETH. See also CIAM Collection B5.

85 Giedion, Le Corbusier, "Syrkus, Paris, March 9, 1949," CIAM Collection B5, GSD/Harvard. In a letter of November 24, 1949, we read that "The First CIAM Summer School was held in London from August 8th to September 2nd, 1949," 42-JT-4-215, gta/ETH.

86 MARS Group, "CIAM Summer School, Information Sheet," 42-JT-3-219, gta/ETH.
    Tyrwhitt had already been involved in the organisation of the TPI (Town Planning Institute) Summer School in 1944. Geddes himself, Tyrwhitt's main reference and influence, also organised a series of international summer schools between 1887 and 1899, the Edinburgh summer meetings, with the same aim to implement the conventional education through a multidisciplinary, international experience: "Fifteen years passed. Geddes' influence had come to be recognized. He had personally initiated slum clearance schemes in darkest Edinburgh; . . . had started a famous series of Summer Schools . . . And this was almost if not entirely voluntary work." Jaqueline Tyrwhitt, "The Valley Section. Patrick Geddes' World Image," 62.

87 MARS Group, "CIAM Summer School 1949, Program for a New Elephant and Castle," 42-JT-3-203, gta/ETH. *The Elephant and Castle Area Is Related to the Traffic Issue.* Other Areas are the South side of Hapstead Health, near Parliament Hill (housing), a site between Knightsbridge and Hyde Park (office), South side of Regents Park (national theatre). MARS Group, "CIAM Summer School, Information Sheet." Moreover, each theme of study had its own Tutor: C. K. Capon (theatre), A. Korn (traffic junction), H. T. Cadbury (office block), Peter Shepheard (housing scheme).

88 MARS Group, "CIAM Summer School, Information Sheet."

89 MARS, "Letter, November 24, 1949," 42-JT-4-215, gta/ETH.

90 42/JT/4/215, gta/ETH.

91 "In focusing on 'architectural aspects of the central urban planning' this summer school [1948] served as precursor to the urban design program that Tyrwhitt assisted CIAM president Jose Luis Sert and Giedion to establish at Harvard a decade later." Shoshkes, *Jaqueline Tyrwhitt: A Transnational Life in Urban Planning and Design*, 112.

92 "It is not intended that the school should be primarily an organ of research, but rather of design, based upon researches carried out elsewhere. But we are aware of the importance in architecture today, of factory production solutions of building problems, and we hope that the subject matter will give opportunity for the development of this aspect of contemporary design along with others of more general hearing." MARS, "Draft, Letter to CIAM Groups, 'CIAM Summer School: London 1949'," SG-19-31b, gta/ETH.

93 Notes of a meeting of the members of this school held at the Architectural Association, 34, Bedford Square, London, W.C.1., on September 2, 1949, 42-JLS-11-147, gta/ETH.

94 In the flyer for the CIAM, "CIAM Summer School 1952," 42-JLS-27-91, gta/ETH.

95 CIAM Italian Group, "Letter April 1952, CIAM Summer School, Architectural School in Venice, Palazzo Grassi, Fondamenta Nani," 42-JLS-23-51, gta/ETH.

96 Franco Berlanda, "Considerazioni sulla scuola estiva C.I.A.M. A Venezia," *Prospettive*, 5 (1953). AP-Originali/TXT/015 Np=043094 x-0012/7 in Archivio progetti IUAV, Venice.

97 Franco Berlanda, "La Scuola del C.I.A.M. A Venezia," *Urbanistica*, 13 (1953): 83–86.

98 Other assistants include Vittorio Boracchia, Piero Bruscagnin, Thomas McNulty, Giorgia Scattolin, Andrea Vianello-Vos. "From one the Flyers of the CIAM Summer School 1952," 42-JLS-27-90, gta/ETH.

99 Berlanda, "Considerazioni sulla scuola estiva C.I.A.M. A Venezia," *Prospettive*.

100 "The subject of the conversation was Venice, but for Le Corbusier it was all about his work, his books, his prophecies, and the accomplishments he was doing in India." (Originally in Italian: *"l'argomento della conversazione fu Venezia, ma per le Corbusier si tratto' di legarla a tutta la sua opera, ai suoi libri, alle sue profezie, e alle realizzazioni che sta attuando in India."*) Ibid., the conference is published with the title *A propos de Venise* in Venezia-Architettura (1, 1953).

101 (Originally in Italian: *"ecco la piazzetta S.Marco: il limite e' l'orizzonte della laguna che si confonde con il cielo, la città si afferma con le due alte colonne che portano i simboli del drago e del leone e tutto diventa unita', 'le bestiaire fraternel', la famiglia, i cittadini, la città. I piccioni si mescolano agli uomini, e le gondole, come enormi animali, si dondolano tra i battifianchi delle loro stalle. La scala umana, persa nella maggior parte delle città moderne, qui è conservata."*) The quote is made by Berlanda talking about the discourse made by Le Corbusier. It is probably a summary or a paraphrase of the original speech. Ibid.

102 Gino Valle, "Il Collegamento Venezia-Terraferma, tema per il C.I.A.M.," Trincanato 2 Attivita' Scientifica 2/011, Archivio Progetti IUAV, Venice.

103 As admitted by Rykwert himself by personal email July 19, 2917.

104 Gregotti and others, "Trincanato 2. Attivita' Scientifica 2/011," Archivio Progetti IUAV, Venice.

105 Remarkably, forty years later, at the first edition of the CIAM Summer School in Venice, Gregotti himself proposed a new system of Maritime station, place of arrival and departure of all commercial tourist cruise liners. The aim was to design a "more public permeability" between city activities and the "touristic monoculture" defined by Gregotti as "a culture which is impossible to give up but which must be governed." Vittorio Gregotti, "La Stazione Marittima di Venezia," *Casabella*, 589 (1992): 40–41. Gregotti, *Venezia Citta' della Nuova Modernita'*, 29.

106 John Turner, *Freedom to Build: Dweller Control of the Housing Process* (New York: Macmillan, 1972). See Shane, *Urban Design Since 1945*, 256–259.

107 (In Italian: *"Avanza poi la proposta di 'modernizzare' il Canal Grande inserendo edifici moderni fra i palazzi più significativi, che ha la bontà di conservare."*) Franco Berlanda, Considerazioni sulla scuola estiva C.I.A.M. A Venezia, *Prospettive*, 5 (1953), in Archivio progetti IUAV, Venice, AP-Originali/TXT/015 Np=043094 x-0012/7.

108 Ibid.

109 For instance, a similar proposal was contained in the later project by Trincanato and Samonà, the *Novissime* of 1964, where the bridge is destroyed and substituted by a suspended monorail, while Piazzale Roma, where all the cars arrive, is flooded. This resonance is proof of the influence of some of the summer school ideas and project proposals on the later design of Venice itself.

110 Giancarlo Guarda, "Attualità di una scuola," *Casabella Continuità*, 199 (December 1953–January 1954): v–vi.

111 (In Italian: "*ciò che distingue il corso estivo CIAM da un normale corso di architettura è nell'aperta rinuncia a qualunque sistematica prestabilita.*") Guarda, "Attualità di una scuola," v–vi.

112 (In Italian: "*questo corso internazionale ha avuto grande importanza per noi, ha fatto conoscere ancor più la nostra attività tecnica e artistica facendola penetrare nel campo degli interessi concreti della città.*") Giuseppe Samonà, *Annuario a.a. 1952–53, 1953–54* quoted in Ernesto N. Rogers, *Architettura, misura e grandezza dell'uomo. Scritti 1930–1969*, ed. Serena Maffioletti (Padova: il Poligrafo, 2010), 474.

113 (In Italian: "*e' per questo che l'istituto di architettura ha deciso di offrire alla città, al paese, la sua opera di collaborazione, ha deciso di intraprendere e definire uno studio urbanistico di Venezia, che serva da concreto strumento per formulare in modo urbanistico i problemi della città . . . e offrirlo alla città.*" Giuseppe Samonà, "Necessita' di uno studio di Venezia per la Pianificazione Urbanistica delle sue esigenze moderne," Opening speech of the Academic Year 1953–54, IUAV, November 1953 in Giuseppe Samonà, *L'unita' Architettura-Urbanistica, Scritti e progetti: 1929–1973*, ed. Pasquale Lovero (Milano: Franco Angeli, 1975), 248.

114 CIAM Summer School, "The Theme, 1954," Trincanato 2. Attività scientifica/2/011, Archivio Progetti IUAV, Venice.

115 The first bridge linking Venice with the mainland was opened in 1846 for trains, and it was built by the Austrian Empire which dominated Northern Italy and Venice as well. The road-traffic bridge was added under Fascism in 1933.

116 CIAM Summer School, "The Theme."

117 Ibid.

118 (In Italian: "*essa oggi può essere definite più facilmente nella negazione di alcuni termini e nella loro critica.*") Franco Buzzi, Pat Crooke, "La terza scuola estiva dei CIAM a Venezia," *Casabella Continuità*, 203 (1954): 84.

119 Reima Pietilä (1923–1993) participated also to the CIAM 10 in Dubrovnik in 1956. See Mumford, *The CIAM Discourse on Urbanism*, 248–250.

120 (In Italian: "*la sua funzione è stata soprattutto quella di chiarire dei principi e di definire per mezzo di essi l'azione dell'architetto.*") Ibid., 85.

121 "This Year the Congress of CIAM takes place in Algiers during September and . . . we have decided that this year the Summer School will have to be held over." CIAM Italian Group, "Letter to CIAM members, Venice, May 1955," CIAM Collection C15, GSD/Harvard.

122 Assistants: Francesco Tentori, Piero Moroni, Edoardo Vittoria, Gabriele Scimemi. Secretary: Giorgia Scattolin, Nani Valle, Dolores Stringaro, Maria Teresa Muffato.

123 Bakema was already in the Veneto region, in Padova, on August 2–3, 1956, in order to attend a CIAM meeting at the Hotel Storione, with the aim of formulating a final program for CIAM 10. See Strauven, *Aldo van Eyck: The Shape of Relativity*, 265.

124 De Carlo, September 19–20, 1956, in CIAM Summer School, "General Recapitulation," Trincanato 2. Attività scientifica/2/011, Archivio Progetti IUAV, Venice.

125 CIAM Summer School, "The Theme, Venice, 1956," Bakema Archive, g51, Het Nieuwe Instituut, Rotterdam.

126 CIAM Summer School in Venice, "Trincanato 2. Attività scientifica/2/011," Archivio Progetti IUAV, Venice.

127 Translation at endnote 1, Conference at Ca' Giustinian, on September 27, 1956. Le Corbusier, Presentation in Venice, Trincanato 2. Attività scientifica/2/011, Archivio Progetti IUAV, Venice.

128 Archivio Progetti IUAV, Venice, "Trincanato 2. Attività scientifica/2/011 and Bakema Archive," g51, Het Nieuwe Instituut, Rotterdam.

129 Ibid.

130 See Banham, *Megastructure*, 64–67.

131 (In Italian: "*un cuore urbano alternativo a quello insulare*") Tafuri, Dal Co, *Architettura Contemporanea*, 352.

132 "*Cœur limité et incomplet.*" Ascoral, *Les "cœurs" en fonctions de l'importance du GROUPE SOCIAL* in Report of the Hoddesdon, 91.

133 (In Italian: "*il preteso valore simbolico del centro non può rappresentare identità della comunità' se non artificialmente; e non a caso quindi, qualora sia imposto, rivela una*

fragile base di preconcetti e di pregiudizi.") Gabriele Scimemi, "La quarta scuola estiva del CIAM a Venezia," *Casabella Continuità*, 213 (1956): 70.

134 Ibid., 72.

135 (In Italian: "*i moderni sistemi di comunicazione sono allo stesso tempo un efficacissimo mezzo di integrazione della tecnologia nella società, come fatto di culture.*") Ibid., 70.

136 CIAM Summer School, "Tuesday, September 27, 1956. Seminar: Exhibition of the Works of Each Team Debate on Them," Bakema Archive, g54, Het Nieuwe Instituut, Rotterdam.

137 "Sert: the Core is the symbol of the city. There are certain places which would no longer exist if the cores were removed, for example Paris; if certain spots were removed Paris would change." Sert, "The theme of the congress. Resume of the Open session of 8 July, Chairman J.L. Sert, in Conversation about the Core," in CIAM8, Report of Hoddesdon Conference.

138 Gabriele Scimemi, "La quarta scuola estiva del CIAM a Venezia," *Casabella Continuità* 213 (1956): 71.

139 Denise Scott Brown, "Urban Concepts. Denise Scott Brown," *Architectural Design Profile* 83 (1990): 9.

140 Scimemi, "La quarta scuola estiva del CIAM a Venezia," 69.

141 Denise Scott Brown, "From Venice to Venice Beach: Denise Scott Brown's 'Wayward' Eye," *Metropolis Magazine*, July 13, 2016. Accessed on July 28, 2016, www.metropolismag.com/July-August-2016/From-Venice-to-Venice-Beach-Denise-Scott-Browns-Wayward-Eye/

142 Robert Venturi, Denise Scott Brown, *Architecture as Signs and Systems: For a Mannerist Time* (Cambridge and London: Belknap Press of Harvard University Press, 2004), 111.

143 Scott Brown, "From Venice to Venice Beach: Denise Scott Brown's 'Wayward' Eye."

144 Reyner Banham, *The New Brutalism: Ethic or Aesthetic?* (Stuttgart: Karl Krämer Verlag, 1966), 10.

145 Venturi and Scott Brown, *Architecture as Signs and Systems*, 109.

146 "Peter Smithson was known to his friends during his student days as 'Brutus.'" Banham, *The New Brutalism*, 10.

147 Denise Scott Brown, "Team 10, Perspecta 10, and the Present State of the Architectural Theory," *Journal of the American Institute of Planners* 1 (1967): 44.

148 Scott Brown, "From Venice to Venice Beach: Denise Scott Brown's 'Wayward' Eye."

149 Denise Scott Brown, "Denise Scott Brown," in *Time Space Existence, Venice Biennale 2016, Palazzo Bembo*, ed. Global Art Affairs Foundation (Italy: Global Art Affairs Foundation, 2016), 252.

150 (Originally in Italian: "*i modelli di reti e forze che si sviluppano erano belli e perfino ispiranti, suggerivano nuovi modi di pensare il progetto urbano e l'architettura, ma per me, come per Vaccaro, il maggior interesse resta nel sovrapporsi di sistemi e nei nuovi ordini che questo sovrapporsi determina, negli spazi tra i sistemi e, imparando dal Manierismo, nella collisione di sistemi e nel loro piegarsi e rompersi per raggiungere condizioni uniche.*") Denise Scott Brown, "Imparare da Vaccaro," in *Giuseppe Vaccaro*, ed. M. Mulazzani (Milano: Mondadori Electa 2002), 72.

151 "I think we learned more from Vaccaro than we could have from other architects, whose more famous Tiburtino designs lacked this rationalist edge and seemed simply allusive to traditional societies. Working for Vaccaro helped prepare us for urbanism in America." Venturi and Scott Brown, *Architecture as Signs and Systems*, 112.

152 Scott Brown, "From Venice to Venice Beach: Denise Scott Brown's 'Wayward' Eye."

153 See Robert Venturi, Denise Scott Brown, Steven Izenour, "From Rome to Las Vegas," in Robert Venturi, Denise Scott Brown, Steven Izenour, *Learning From Las Vegas* (Cambridge, MA: MIT Press, 1972) 18.

154 Mentioned on *Gazzettino di Venezia*, and *Il Gazzettino* (September 4, 1957).

155 See Enzo Paci, *Tempo e relazione* (Torino: Taylor, 1954).

156 Enzo Paci, "Relationism and Architecture," Trincanato 2. Attività scientifica/2/014, IUAV University Archive, Venice.

157 Ibid.

4 Jaap Bakema

The Heart of the City as relationship

Henceforth space by itself, and time by itself, are doomed to fade away into mere shadows, and only a kind of union of the two will preserve an independent reality.[1]

Hermann Minkowski, 1908

Relationship

Jacob Berend (called Jaap) Bakema (1914–1981) was one of the young CIAM architects, attending his first meeting in Bridgewater in 1947. Bakema, who was the principal partner, with J.H. van den Broek (1898–1978), of one of the most famous and productive Dutch architectural firms after the war, took on a critical role within the CIAM organisation in the 1950. On the one hand, he was tasked by Le Corbusier and Giedion to continue the old CIAM tradition when its collapse was forewarned, and on the other, he was later so influential within the young group Team 10 that, in De Carlo's opinion, the cultural death of Team 10 coincided with the physical death of Bakema himself in 1981.[2]

As far as the complexity and productive vagueness of CIAM 8 is concerned, Bakema's crucial position as the generational and theoretical link between the old and new avant-gardes was already evident in Hoddesdon, and it was mirrored in his groundbreaking interpretation of the topic of the Heart. At CIAM 8, the 37-year-old Dutch architect presented a remarkable point of view about the Heart of the City which seemed different to, though not in contrast with, the other architects' statements:

> What I ask myself is, at what moment can we really speak of CORE – the Core that we can plan in architecture and in town planning.
>
> Perhaps we can answer this: There are moments in our life in which the isolation of man from things becomes destroyed: in that moment we discover the wonder of relationship between man and things.
>
> That is the moment of the CORE: the moment we become aware of the fullness of life by means of cooperative action.[3]

Interestingly, Bakema neither showed nor mentioned any public city centre projects as first examples. His ultimate expression of the "moment of the Core" was instead represented by a Cemetery. The Dutch architect recalled having visited Stockholm some months before the meeting in Hoddesdon where he was struck by the cemetery designed by Erik Gunnar Asplund and Sigurd Lewerentz:[4] "I think in this cemetery there is a core, though of a special kind. It is a place where the isolation of life from death has been altered into a wonderful relationship."[5]

Bakema shifted the significance of the Heart from a concentric, traditionalist organic metaphor to an open, social and abstract symbolic moment of a "relationship between man and things." He conceptually and provocatively transferred the Heart theme from a conception of civic life to the archetypical tension between life and death "subordinated to all-governing and connecting principles,"[6] from the inside to the outside, from the urban centre to landscape as a public space for a collective centrality.

Surprisingly, the fullness of life Bakema discovered in the Swedish Cemetery was also characteristic of a local sauna, his second example of Core: "I can assure you a Finnish steam-bath can be an element of a core."[7] From the Finnish Sauna to the Swedish Cemetery, the Relationship between and among things was the most important reality present in nature, independently of the dimension, scale or localisation of the Core. Contrary to the Capitalist fervour to increase possession of things, criticised by Bakema at CIAM 8, relations between things instead "turned out to be essential."[8] In this sense, the example of the cemetery richly and radically explored and visualised the main purpose of the Heart, namely to destroy isolation among people even when facing the silence of death and to fulfill the "goal of human life [which] is to become aware of the governing principles of a full life," expressed here in its extreme contact between life and death.

Furthermore, Bakema's belief about the Heart was fully imbued with resonances and references to all kinds of knowledge that theoretically and experimentally supported the Relationship as the only presence in nature. "The developments of science have made it clear that the things we see in nature and culture are not really there," Bakema continued at CIAM 8, "Every day we discover the only thing that exists is relationship."[9]

This interest and awareness was already recurrent within all sciences of nature, as coevally highlighted by the French philosopher Georges Canguilhem in the early 1950s. From Newton's fluid as the intermediary between two bodies, to Lamark's "influencing circumstances" and "adaptations," Compte's "total set of external circumstances necessary for the existence of every organism," Ritter's and Humboldt's "relations between historical man and the environment" and Weiss' "environment of behaviour," Canguilhem built a genealogy of the idea of milieu which resulted in a "pure system of relations"[10] at the centre of required contemporary research. Then, since the rise and spread of the theory of Relativity, the main paradigm and foundation of the major transformations of "twentieth-century culture,"[11] (Kuhn, 1962; Strauven, 1998), the analysis of Relationship has become the main topic of an interdisciplinary investigation in nature (Einstein, Heisenberg) as well as in art (Cézanne, Picasso, Mondrian), in geometry (Riemann), in philosophy (Bergson), in literature (Joyce), in music (Schönberg) and so on. As Aldo van Eyck stated, "Our unbounded gratitude is due to them: to Picasso, Klee, Mondrian, and Brancusi: to Joyce, Le Corbusier, Schoenberg, Bergson, and Einstein: to the wonderful gang."[12]

Similarly to his Dutch colleagues, Bakema was fascinated by this new worldwide vision of the world, and he sought a conversion of these theories in Architecture. The latter regards the formation of space, and hence it should help the human being "in finding a good understanding (relationship) of the infinite (total) space in which he lives," where life itself is "a flowing process,"[13] a dynamic, creative process in a continual evolution from one condition to another.

Inasmuch as the moment of the Core appears during the intimate "wonder of relationship between man and things," the broader practice of building space is charged with the inescapable duty to relieve "man in his search for a good relationship with the wonder of his existence."[14] Rather than merely "deforming people into housing types"[15] the architect needs to respond to the individual's right to give significance and his "own expression to his conception of life," raising relationship as the archetypical activator and catalyst for a better existence within a new type of "open society."[16]

Abstract idea

"We all have to meet in this process
at the station called 'Idea'"[17]

Jaap Bakema, 1981

This compelling social role of Architecture and spatial conception, where all human activities should be possible in a common, collective way, was experimented in the second project of Pendrecht,[18] a district in Rotterdam-south, which was presented in Hoddesdon by the Dutch Opbouw Group.

Echoing the elementarist geometries, the "plurality of forms, lines, colours, and empty spaces [which] creates relationships"[19] typical of the art works of the compatriot artist Piet Mondrian and *De Stijl*'s art movement, the project gravitated around a centrifugal public central square which "can be taken as the expression of the totality

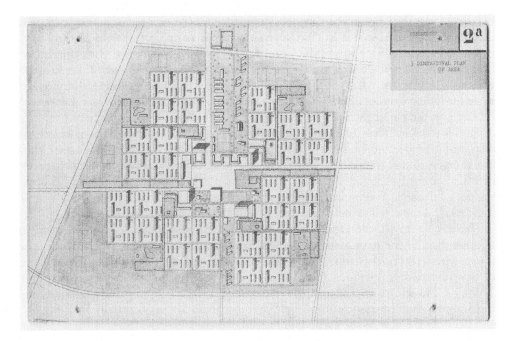

Figure 4.1 Opbouw, Plan of Pendrecht II, 1951.

Source: Collection Het Nieuwe Instituut, Rotterdam, BAKE t126.

of the core, as living heart of the locality."[20] The "locality," or "residential core," was mainly expressed by groups of five or six small multifunctional living units of 5–700 people, characterised by various building types with local activities. Whereas "community" embraced four localities and also contained light industry. The gradual three-dimensional relationship from living units, to locality, to community was aimed at a sense of continuity of space and balanced life at all the different scales without any danger of social segregation.

Interestingly, in the Pendrecht project, Bakema mostly used "Core" in order to describe both the physical public space and the theoretical idea of Heart. The Core was the central square and, in parallel, it somehow represented the symbol of the city's local identity. This double entity, the tangible and intangible essence of the Core-Heart was emphasised at the end of the report on Pendrecht II at CIAM 8, when Wissing summarised some very interesting theoretical conclusions evoked within the project which was missing in the published book of CIAM 8:

> 1e. the abstract core is not one point, or one space, or an expression of only one activity, but an idea, expressed now, by one, then by another activity, fluctuating from one place to another, reaching his extreme expression perhaps within a certain, but not distinctly bordered, region.[21]

The Heart as an idea, wandering from place to place until it condenses into a physical climax, definitely erased any contradictions between the functionalist metaphor and the abstract symbol of the heart.

The idea of the Heart and the Heart as idea were a counterforce to the functionalist, geometrical and financial centre of the Core CBD. Although the central square of Pendrecht was the Core of the City, its significance was recognised as a more complex theoretical issue and it was not possible to summarise its centrality in the city as a mere CBD. "The conception of the 'core' can no longer be identified with concentration of mass," Wissing and Hovens Greve stressed in their contribution "The Core or Physical Heart,"[22] at CIAM 8. The Pendrecht project had to be considered therefore as an intriguing overlap of both a concrete physical project and an abstract theoretical research on the Heart theme.

The Heart as an "idea" of Relationship both abstracted and visualised the most intense relationship among human beings, as already highlighted by Giedion, and between Man and things, or more transcendentally between "living-being-energy,"[23] "your being part of the total energy (space) system,"[24] as raised by Bakema. This relationship evolves within a "dynamic continuity" where each component and totality is physically and theoretically connected avoiding any functionalist, compartmentalised divisions.

Thereby, in 1951, the Heart as the idea of relationship heralded the "story of another idea,"[25] the main issue of the Dutch magazine *Forum*[26] in 1959, which was outspoken in its criticism of CIAM's analytical methods and instead favoured the rise of new approaches, methods and visions in architecture and urban planning within Team 10. The Heart as idea and as relationship therefore anticipated the later concepts about "human associations" proposed by Team 10, conceptually bridging the gap between the new avant-garde and the old.

Moreover, this definition of the Heart as idea seems coherent with the symbolical abstract emphasis given, for example, by Giedion to the Heart of the City and with its archetypical entity, with the "eternal present."[27] Van Eyck himself, in a reinterpretation of the Circles[28] presented in Otterlo in 1959, proposed the tradition of the spontaneous building of "the vernacular of the heart," where society is depicted between the "immutability and rest" of the Classical tradition and the "the change and movement"[29] of the Modern one. These forms of traditions have to be reconciled in a structural continuity with human society, represented by a group of embracing persons, enhancing the significant social role of architecture, which is eternally valid before the immutable identity of Humankind. This human continuous and constant human essence – "Man is always and everywhere essentially the same"[30] – whose balance should be always regained, was studied by the Dutch architect in archaic societies, such as the Dogon culture,[31] which is based on a sort of complex cosmology according to which everything in the world is immersed in analogous levels, connected like a chain, from the lowest scale level to the totality, the universe.

This proto-condition (proto-, gr. Πρωτο as "first, first element")[32] of the city and of the Heart, and its abstract essence, also resonated with "The idea of a town" by Joseph Rykwert, published in *Forum* in 1963. Rykwert was concerned with both an "Idea" of the City and with the worldwide recurrent foundation myth of ancient cities, based on the relationship between urban settlements and cosmos, in contrast with a contemporary functionally based urban design or with the abandonment of the urbanity by the architects.

As recalled also by Strauven,[33] Rykwert concluded his article highlighting that the failure of modern scientists to clearly depict the universe caused the impossibility to design our cities by relying on contemporary cosmology. Hence, rather than trusting uncertain cosmic landscapes, the solution should be revealed within: "We must

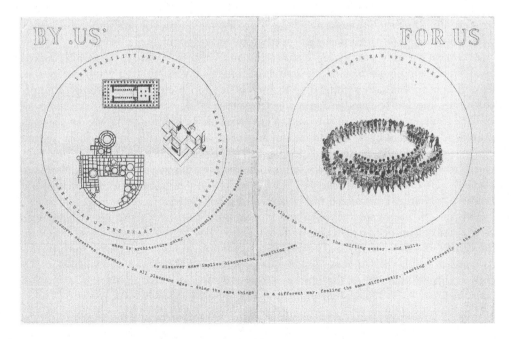

Figure 4.2 Aldo van Eyck, Slogan, Otterlo Circles.

Source: © Aldo van Eyck, from the Aldo van Eyck archive.

look for it inside ourselves: in the constitution and structure of the human person."[34] The opacity of human introspection should therefore be the main reference for the contemporary urban structure, rather than the perfect and immutable arrangements of the stars. This final hypothesis contrasted with any prefigured and fixed urban forms, as represented for instance by Ortega y Gasset's "canon" metaphor used by Sert. Rather than looking at the proportions and organic compactness of the Vitruvian human body, the city should echo human inwardness. In this sense, the Heart persisted as a still valid "abstract idea . . . fluctuating from one place to another"[35] as depicted at CIAM 8, resembling the psychological interior of the human being mirrored in the city "imperfectly controlled . . . , more like a dream than anything else."[36] It was then the profound duty of the architect to translate this un-framed Idea into a physical project, using architecture as "counter-form of the mind."[37]

In-between theory

> "*Qu'il nous est difficile*
> *De Trouver un abri*
> *Même dans notre cœur*
> *Toute la place est prose*
> *Et toute la chaleur*"[38]

Jules Supervielle, *Forum* (1959)

Both Bakema and van Eyck reiterated the importance of Relationship relying on examples of bilateral interactions, describing for instance Architecture and society exposed between "creation or routine, way of living or aesthetics, freedom or dictatorship, simultaneity of hierarchy, integration or chaos, town-planning or administration, structure or decoration, function of architecture or functionalism."[39]

According to Aldo van Eyck, Architecture and Urbanism were "inseparably linked as all basic twin phenomena: . . . part-whole, unity – diversity, large-small, many-few, as well as others equally significant – inside outside, open-closed, mass-space, change-constancy, motion-rest, individual-collective, etc. etc."[40]

The "twin phenomena" of the human existence of the human being was also shown graphically by van Eyck in 1965: people seated concentrically in a hollow gazing inwards towards the centre and people seated concentrically on a hill gazing outwards towards the horizon. "Two kinds of centrality, two ways of being together – or alone?" van Eyck asked himself – "The Man is both centre-bound and horizontal bound . . . Neither centralized nor decentralized but centred in every place."[41]

This insightful interpretation of the human condition had many resonances with the existentialism of Sartre, as quoted by Giedion at CIAM 8, which was focused on the centrality of the individual rather than on the universal supremacy and centrality of Man inside the Universe, as previously discussed. The "neither centralized nor decentralized" position of the Human being was echoing also the Italian *Relazionismo* of Enzo Paci. The Italian philosopher admired Bakema's position at CIAM 8, and he literally adopted his relational thought considering the Heart as Relationship between a compressed systolic and dilated diastolic moment, "as the focus moment of relations, . . . [as] a social problem which closely connects architectural design and urban planning."[42]

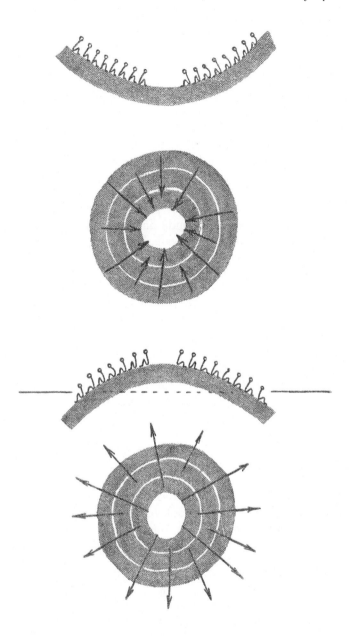

Figure 4.3 Aldo van Eyck, Diagram, Two Kinds of Centrality.

Source: © Aldo van Eyck, from the Aldo van Eyck archive. Original Pink.

All these positions clearly show the shift from an organic centred view of the world to a decentred conception of the Universe, where, as described by Canguilhem in the 1950s, "Man is no longer in the middle (*'au milieu'*), but he is a mid-point (*'un milieu'*) a mid-point between (*'milieu entre'*) two infinities, between nothing and everything, between two extremes."[43] This new awareness of the human condition as a "medium" between two extremes, rather than the barycentric – "the middle" – one, resonated as main concern also for Bakema, van Eyck and all Team 10. This consciousness manifested itself in a new interest in the ordinary everyday life, in a passage from a universalist order to the "ordinariness and banality"[44] and concrete reality of everyday spatial practices, from an analytical and compartmentalised functionalist study of human practices to a more anthropological praxeology of human habitat. This exploration of ordinariness, totally imbued with the influence of Lefebvre,[45] was mirrored in the research of the gradual relationship and threshold between humans and their surrounding context, in order to relieve them of "curbing polarities from which we are still suffering: -individual-collective; -physical-spiritual; -internal-external; -part-whole; -permanence-change."[46]

In Architecture, the overcoming of these polarities, which, in their new blurred relations, still afflict our contemporary condition, was symbolised by the simplest element of transition between public and private, from street to home: the doorstep. If the Heart was the elementarist symbol which should "spring directly to our senses,"[47] the doorstep was the simplest architectural element through which we corporeally experience the primary interaction between man and man, between man and things as abstractly symbolised by the Heart itself. This doorstep is the "place of a wonderful human gesture: conscious entry and departure"; it is the "place for an act that is repeated millions of times in a lifetime between the first entry and the last exit"[48] as revealed by van Eyck and embraced by the Smithsons in their notion of "hierarchy of human associations"[49] based on real entities of the city: house, street, district.

"From doorstep to city"[50] Bakema and van Eyck expressed their ideas about the archetypical conception of the threshold, as a "singular ethnological squint"[51] looking towards both sides like a double-faced Janus, when editors of the magazine *Forum* from 1959 to 1963. During these years, they presented and explored the topic of "the shape of the in-between" which was rooted in the idea of the Heart as relationship and was investigated by many young architects from all over Europe in the 1950s and 1960s.

The principal suggestion was the "in-between" theory of the Austrian Jewish philosopher Martin Buber who wrote the book *Ich und Du*[52]("I and Thou"), in 1923. Buber's theory was grounded on the relationship and dialogue as counterforce to isolation and monologue. It was a philosophy of faithful existentialism focused on the concrete encounter, on the interchange with a "Thou" in order to achieve the condition of fully human beings. "The fundamental condition of being is man with his fellow man," as Buber affirmed, naming this sphere as "the 'sphere of the in- between'. It is a primary category of human reality. It will be the starting point for the real third."[53] Unsurprisingly, the reference to the in-between theory of Buber was coherent with and reiterated the main aim "to reestablish an equipoise between the individual and the collective"[54] as highlighted by Giedion when he discussed the Heart of the City. Hence, it was no coincidence that the debate at CIAM 8 anticipated the Team 10 discourses on the "in-between" and that Giedion's book *Architecture You and Me*, where the historian stressed and restated the rise of the public "heart" as the basic condition for humanity itself, echoed the title of Buber's book.

As far as the influence of Buber's theory within CIAM is concerned, the young architects from Basel, Gutmann and Manz, who were also present at the Hoddesdon Congress, adopted and relied on Buber's theory for the first time at the CIAM preparatory meeting held in Sigtuna in 1952. Here, the Swiss Architects embraced the design of the in-between, called *"Zwischen"*[55] by the Austrian philosopher, for a concept of *habiter*-habitat as constituent and integrating element in the rest of the total human settlement. Gutmann and Manz, who "contributed though considerably to the formative discussion in CIAM"[56] according to van Eyck, were among the first, particularly through the theory of the in-between, to clearly criticise the role of the dwelling as an isolated function, of the compartmentalisation of the Functional City, depicted in CIAM in the 1930s.[57] According to them, the analysis of the Core at Hoddesdon finally demonstrated that it was implausible to conceive the Heart as a separate fifth function detached from its context. The quintessence of its complexity would have failed as in a similar later analysis of Habitat. Henceforth, the "analytical" methods of analysis and planning should have been replaced by a "synthetic" perspective which could approach the human settlement as "a whole, a living whole,"[58] reiterating Bakema's idea of heart as total relationship.

Symbolic and visual tools of relationship

Arch-o-Meter Man

The passage from the idea of the unadulterated Vitruvian Man as adopted by Sert to Bakema's "human-being-part-of-total-existence-called-energy"[59] was visualised and interpreted by the Dutch architect through diagrams which somehow functioned as symbolic tools for the reestablished relationship within the city.

For instance, Bakema's sketch the "Arch-o-Meter Man"[60] questions how "to discipline personal human emotions towards the approach of the total aspect of things."[61]

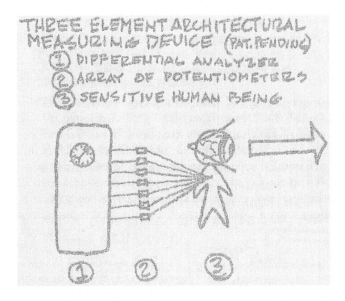

Figure 4.4 Bakema, Arch-o-Meter Man, Three Element Architectural Measuring Device, in "Notes about Theory," 1959–66.

Source: Collection Het Nieuwe Instituut, Rotterdam, BAKE_d264–4.

The head was drawn as a big, open eye looking towards an arrow indicating Bakema's writing about the importance of architectural history and examination of the buildings which have passed the test of time; from the chest – maybe from his heart – some lines come out, linking to a rectangle with a clock inside. The entire system was named by Bakema as the "handy Arch-o-Meter," or "a three-element architectural measuring device": man is the "sensitive human being," the lines with small boxes are the "array of potentiometers" while the clock in the rectangle is the "differential analyser."

The whole system seems to be a sort of playful experiment for the development of an analysis of the actual conditions and facts and decisions which caused the actual urban realm. It was also an important attempt to represent the relationship between the sense of human being and the physical aspects of the architecture and to encompass the differentiation between thinking and feeling as already stressed by Giedion. While Giedion himself referred to the existentialism-humanism of Sartre, under the sketch, Bakema copied some quotes from *The Architecture of Humanism*, written in 1914 by Geoffrey Scott, highlighting again the symbolic humanistic aspect of the Heart: "humanism is the effort of Men to think, to feel, to act for themselves and to abide by the logic of the results."[62]

As far as Scott's book is concerned, the subtitle reveals the character of the writing: "A Study in the History of Taste." As the author explained and Bakema rewrote in his notes, "We have few 'fully reasoned' theories." "If we desire clearness," Scott asserted, it is necessary to pass "from a priori aesthetics to a history of taste, and from the history of taste to *the history of ideas*"[63] (underlined twice in the notes). The Idea, such as the abstract Idea of the Heart as depicted by the Opbouw Group at CIAM 8, is therefore the final passage from Aesthetics to Taste and from Taste to Idea, for the definition of a proper sharp Theory,[64] which was the title of Bakema's notes and considered the only objective way to obtain "clearness" in design at any scale. From this point of view, a clear theoretical abstract discourse on the Heart might therefore be considered a unique opportunity for a later physical design of the city where the "cooperative action" symbolised by the Heart culminates in a vibrant, active social life.

Homo Ludens

The "sensitive human being" of the "handy Arch-o-Meter" somehow echoed the critical perspective of the "*Homo Ludens*"[65] ("man the player") described by the Dutch historian Johan Huizinga. The latter brought to the fore the social role of play, conceived as an archetypical cultural phenomenon which is older than culture itself: "Social life is endued with supra – biological forms, in the shape of play, which enhance its value. It is through this playing that society expresses its interpretation of life and the world."[66] Hence, play is crucial in society since it enhances the preservation of the modern human's individuality from mass culture or from the danger of lifeless and apathetic individuality, isolation as Huizinga already described in "Man and the Masses" (1918).[67] This reference to the social and cooperative role of play became a main reference for Bakema and van Eyck as well. "A Play with space"[68] was an expression used by Bakema, denoting the power of play to create spatial, emotional and cultural relationships inside the city, satisfying human need for variation and deep interaction.

Moreover, the definition of "play element" as a primary creative and cultural force was radically mirrored in van Eyck's famous design for children's playgrounds. The

Dutch architect designed more than 700 playgrounds between 1947 and 1978 in Amsterdam. This network polarised and embedded play as a public practice within the post-war urban structure. The youngest inhabitants, the city's children, also one of the main topics for the Swedish CIAM Group,[69] became an expression of a necessary diversity of social relationships, which was praised by Giedion at CIAM 8. It is no coincidence that the Swiss historian eulogised van Eyck's playgrounds at CIAM 8 in his discourse on the "Historical Background to the Core."

On the one hand, the simple elements designed by the Dutch architects were "grouped so subtly – with a background of the Stijl movement" that they inject "some kind of vitamin into the whole thing," helping the development of a child's imagination. On the other, playgrounds socially and physically fulfilled useless, wasted areas of the city which were revitalised into a new "active urban element. One need only provide the opportunity and we – the public, who are also maybe children of a kind – will know how to use it,"[70] Giedion concluded.

The friendship diagram

The most important image for the right relationship between different parts of the built environment through transitional elements was given by the image of the private family itself: from the hearth to the heart. Bakema drew the "Friendship Diagram," where a hierarchically disposed group of people simulates the proper arrangement and relationship of the buildings facing the street, from the external towers (the adults) towards the internal small buildings and canopies (the children) which are directly in contact with the human scale of the public space: "buildings could again make friends each other, the way it may happen to people through their children."[71] This sketch encapsulated the duty of Architecture to reconcile the right physical connection between the individual and her surrounding energy's forms.

Figure 4.5 Bakema, The Friendship Diagram.

Source: Collection Het Nieuwe Instituut, Rotterdam, BAKE_t42_1.

These different dimensional relationships, from the individual to the cosmos, were recurrent in Bakema's project sketches. In the master plan for Tel Aviv, in 1962, Bakema showed the gradual relationship between the different scale levels which make up the city, from interior furniture like the bed to the "Core-wall building"[72] or "backbone buildings" which served as a natural entrance for the national road to the city centre and embraced the old city square, the old Core.

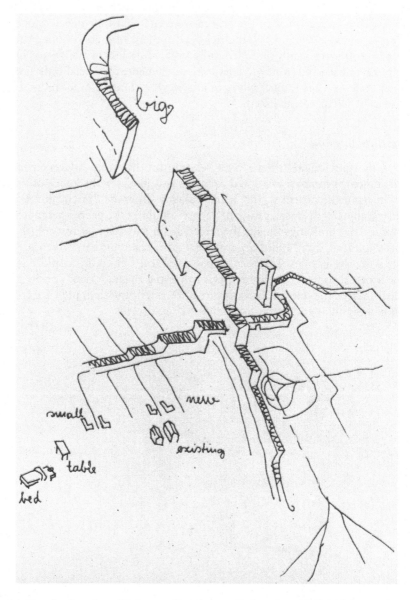

Figure 4.6 Van den Broek and Bakema, Sketch from Bed to Core Wall, Tel Aviv, 1962.

Source: Collection Het Nieuwe Instituut, Rotterdam, Archief d1315–1; BROX3092 (70–3092).

According to Bakema, the problem to solve was

> how to develop the heart of this township into real core . . . How to produce the visual reality called core, respecting both the permanent small scale of table and bed and desk and on the other hand the ever increasing scale of administration and traffic and (perhaps the most important thing to do) harmonizing the relationship between the two of them.[73]

Ten years after the CIAM 8, the Heart-Core as a relationship remained a permanent issue in order to tackle the right integration between private and public realms. While the "backbone building" and the other permanent "big scale elements shake hands with each other" like the taller adults in the diagram, the kids, the more temporary "small scale elements make the human mind possible to integrate itself step by step with the big scale elements and vice versa."[74]

Another intriguing project was the *"Lijnbaan"* Shopping Centre in Rotterdam (1951–53), considered one the first pedestrian urban shopping districts in the world. This was the first project which perfectly mirrored and embodied the idea of the "Friendship diagram" since it is characterised by canopies and by the floating volumes of the shops which serve as transition elements between the public spaces of the street and the high-rise slabs at the edges. "Europe's Fifth Avenue,"[75] born as reconstruction

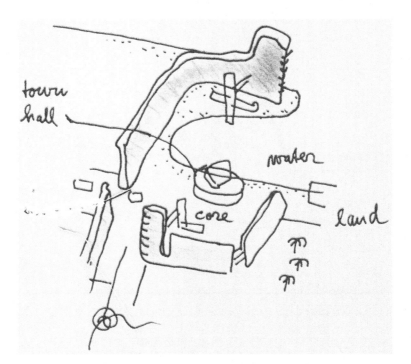

Figure 4.7 Van den Broek and Bakema, Sketch of the Core Wall Tel Aviv and Its Core.

Source: Collection Het Nieuwe Instituut, Rotterdam, Archief d1315–2; BROX3092 (70–3092).

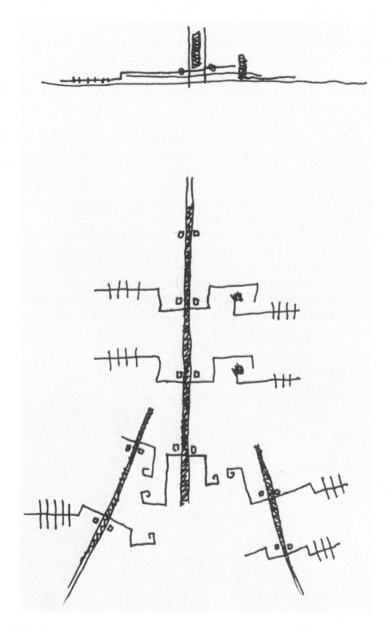

Figure 4.8 Van den Broek and Bakema, Sketch, Plan of the Core Wall Tel Aviv.

Source: Collection Het Nieuwe Instituut, Rotterdam, Archief d1315–3; BROX3092 (70–3092).

project inside bombed Rotterdam, combined the design of transitional elements with the emphasis on the free traffic street as highlighted by both CIAM 8 and Gruen, who lauded the project as "an outstanding pedestrian reserve"[76] and as a lesson for American downtown shopping centres.[77]

Figure 4.9 Van den Broek and Bakema, *Lijnbaan* Shopping Centre in Rotterdam, 1948–53.

Source: Collection Het Nieuwe Instituut, Rotterdam, BROX_907t55–1.

Visual groups

Within this theory of Relationship, Bakema then introduced the concept of "visual groups," which was first experimented in his firm and then proposed at CIAM. "The 'visual group' idea is purely based on relationships one can see,"[78] Bakema affirmed. It is interesting again to underline the use of the Idea as an abstract concept related to a tangible presence. In fact, the idea of the visual group regarded a physical "repeatable and variable cluster," whose design should follow the intermediate visual relationships and multiple social ways of living of "low, highrise and transitional types of housing: under, over and against the trees."[79] These three categories were therefore related to a vertical relationship with the height of a tree, instead of a horizontal walking distance between buildings. This vertical relationship was caused by the improved technology which has enabled Humankind to live, for the first time in history, above the trees "in contact with the horizon." In particular, Bakema considered the floors in sight of the treetops, from the first to the sixth, as in direct contact with the soil and with the other dwellings. Therefore, the different arrangements of dwellings should be regulated in order to consider the different possibilities of visual and physical relationships between them. Above the sixth floor, there is no more visual contact with the ground and the dwelling has to be conceived in relationship with the horizon.

This new dwelling's condition should also stimulate several housing solutions, using a more enlarged architectural vocabulary. In this way, every person should be able to

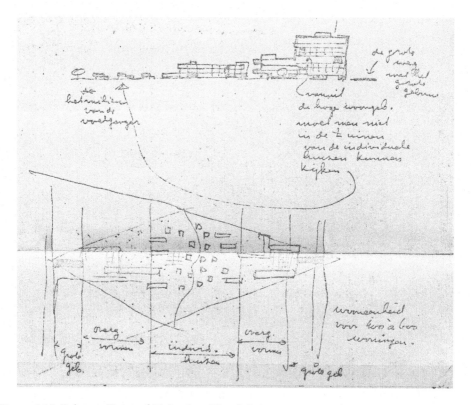

Figure 4.10 Bakema, Types of Living in a Visual Group.

Source: Collection Het Nieuwe Instituut, Rotterdam, TTEN_21–1 (detail) Team 10 Smithsons (761–0002).

dwell in a house "according to his [or her] character and capabilities," in a more democratic and personal relationship with the total space. The external open space should also be proportionally designed to the height and to the scale of the related building. These visual groups might even be used to make an urban master plan using the cluster as an urban transitional form between the house and the entire city. The extremes of this concept of changeable living scale was the "growing house" sketched by Bakema, Stokla and Kruyne first in 1959 for a new residential area in Eindhoven ("*'t Hool*"). The general aim was "to create a framework in which man will again be master of his own home, his own personal sphere, within the universe."[80]

Finally, in 1953, during the CIAM 9 Congress, the first made up widely by young participants, the "visual groups" became a linking Idea between the Heart of the City and Habitat for the Opbouw Group. Indeed, in the panel of the *Alexanderpolder* plan, the Dutch group reiterated the Heart of the City as both the "expression of interrelationship" of the Visual groups and "one of the indispensable conditions for 'habitat.'"[81] Therefore, the Heart of the City prepared the ground for a debate on the anthropological understanding of Habitat ensuring, as a theoretical in-between, a continuous line of inquiry, rather than an absolute rift, between CIAM and Team 10.

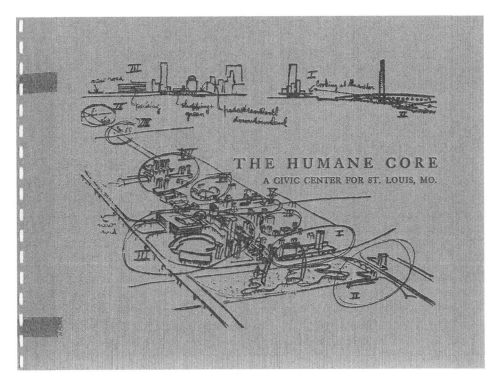

Figure 4.11 Bakema, Cover, "The Humane Core," 1959–60.

Source: Collection Het Nieuwe Instituut, Rotterdam, Bake d264.

From chair to city,[82] from the ground perspective of the child to the elevated view above the trees, from the critical cultural image of *Homo Ludens* to the gradual Family section and the humanist measuring Arch-o-Meter sensitive Man, the Heart of the City – as a moment of "cooperative action" and the Idea of total Relationship – became a terrific and prolific theoretical and urban design theme which influenced architectural debate in the 1950s and 1960s. And it has remained a fertile ground for further interpretations as well.[83] Last, Bakema emphasised a transatlantic continuity of the Heart theme and deepened his research on the Heart of the City as Relationship in the US, as shown in his St Louis project, which was proposed almost ten years after CIAM 8.

St Louis: the Humane Core

In 1959, Jaap Bakema was invited as Professor at the School of Architecture at Washington University, in the USA. The theme chosen for the urban design course was "The Humane Core – a New Civic Center for St Louis." As the Dutch professor explained, "Civic Center" includes the term "Civic," which is supposed to refer to Man as an integral member of society, and "Center," which loses any barycentric position in the city becoming the "central part of anything." Hence, the "Humane Core" or the Heart's concept was taught to students as the compression of the two terms in one concept, as the "heart in a settlement of a group of people being in enduring cooperation in order to maintain itself !!!"[84] Moreover, if we can consider "the architecture of the city as the structure of society," Bakema continued, "the core then indicates a place which is the heart of the matter."[85] Bakema's overlapping concept of the Humane Core reminds and anticipated Aldo Rossi's *Architettura della Città*, printed in 1966. Rossi underlined the need to reconduct Urban Science into the complex of the Human Sciences; moreover, the study of the city was an autonomous science only when it is considered as architecture, as a built existence within history.[86] The human condition of the city and its built essence, above other studies (sociological, political), were also stressed few years before by Bakema: the Dutch architect overlaid the structure of society (human value) with the structure of the city (its architecture, with its buildings, beams, pillars). The Core, as physical expression of the Idea of the Heart, existed where these two built entities, these two structures were melt into the ultimate intense interaction: "where the matter is." Bakema's interpretation of the Core-Heart was a progressive Idea towards a better future social condition. This perfect socio-spatial overlapping was as an ideal condition towards which the architect's project should tend, but which is doubtless not possible to obtain in a total realistic synergy.

As explained by Giedion at CIAM 8, querying a possible direct relationship between the social symbolical structure of the city and the physical structure of its Core,[87] this connection was not strictly proper: Newton already abolished this truth showing that the direct effect and cause couldn't exist any longer, and so also the tangible and intangible essence of the city.

Historical study of the heart

It's not by coincidence that in 1959, during his course about the Humane Core, Bakema attempted to trace the historical roots of the Heart like his Swiss CIAM colleague already did at Hoddesdon, in his lecture titled "Historical Background to the Core."

If in 1951 Giedion stressed the necessity of the historical revision of the heart because history "gnaws in the future" it serves "as a priceless container of human knowledge and experience,"[88] a few years later Professor Bakema praised the study of the Heart of the City in the past as a basic point in order to analyze the clearness of old urban structure in comparison with the chaotic modern one.

This analysis of the historical Heart seems coherent with the "Eternal Present" praised by Giedion and even more with the coeval interest of several members of Team 10 on the "perennial elements"[89] which persist in the city although serving different purposes, exigencies and functions. The Diocletian Palace in Split (fourth century AD), whose plan was sketched and archived together with Bakema's notes on St Louis, remained the most important example studied by the Dutch architect.[90] The castle-walls absorbed by the city and transformed in housing was a clear reference for his emphasis on the wall-like buildings and urban rooms, as shown in several projects, and on the necessity to structure long term traces as requested in St Louis.

Regarding the *aporia*[91] of the Heart of the City and of the origins of the "forces make a town,"[92] the Dutch architect drew insightful series of sketches representing the historical evolution of the Heart: from the crossing of traffic lines as expression of exchange, to military camps as answer to the necessary of protection from external enemies; from the castle as central point of political authority to the cathedral as a centre of religious transcendence; from the Industrial Revolution new urban grids

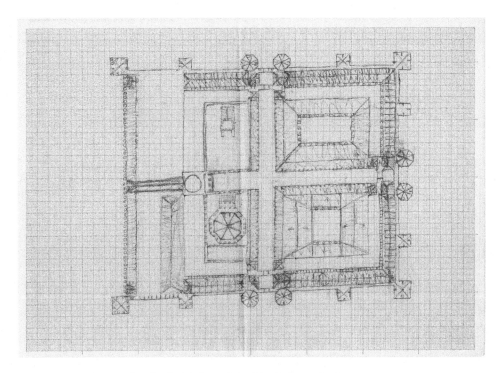

Figure 4.12 Bakema, Sketch of the Plan of the Diocletian Palace.

Source: Collection Het Nieuwe Instituut, Rotterdam, Bake d264.

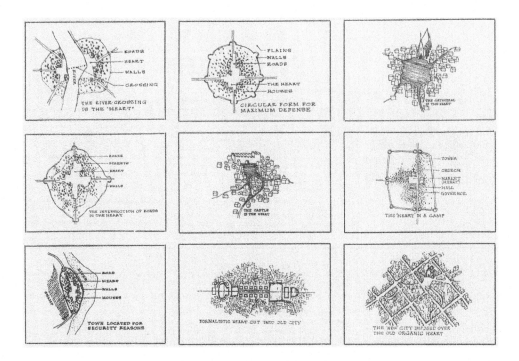

Figure 4.13 Bakema, "The Forces. A General History of Western City."

Source: Bakema, "The Humane Core," (1959–60) 2–3. Collection Het Nieuwe Instituut, Rotterdam, Bake d264.

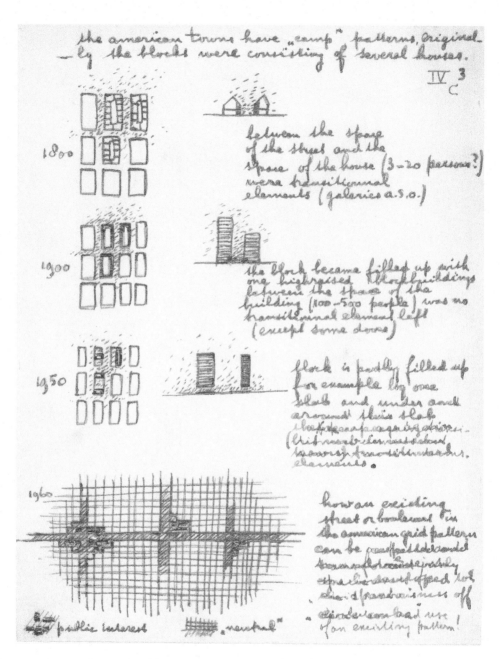

Figure 4.14 Bakema, Sketches about Space of the Street and the Disappearance of Transitional
    Elements.

Source: Collection Het Nieuwe Instituut, Rotterdam, Bake d264.

where "'Civic' became chaos" to the appearance of the first skyscrapers where the
transitional elements between the building and the street disappeared.

Interestingly enough, in this contemporary latter condition, the remaining relational element between the street pattern of the town and the huge new buildings is a

mere single door, with direct access to the street. The doorstep was thus transmuted from the symbol of a transitional positive element between interior and exterior, as expressed by Team 10, into a symbol of the lack of correlation between the new massive architecture and the social life, in Bakema's historical review. This issue was still present in 1960s, and its solution was one of the main challenges that his students should tackle for the redesign project of St Louis.

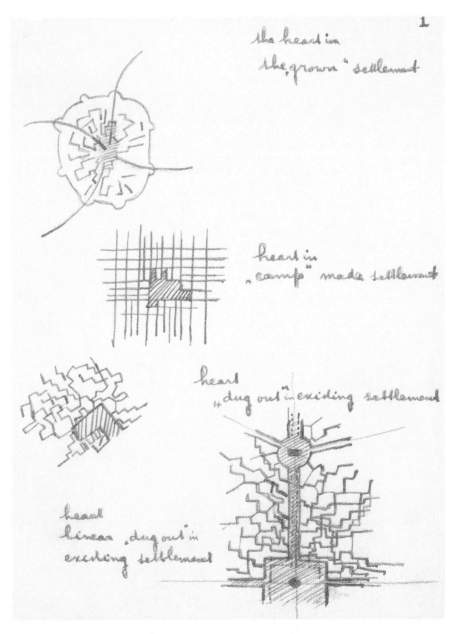

Figure 4.15 Bakema, Schemes, Historical Study about the Heart.

Source: Collection Het Nieuwe Instituut, Rotterdam, Bake d264.

Finally, among the sketches about the historical heart, Bakema introduced also the Heart of the City as expression of Power in "monumental formalistic solutions." It was the physical and symbolical part of the city which represents the non-discussable, even owner of God Power, Authority on the entire society, which still "speak to deep

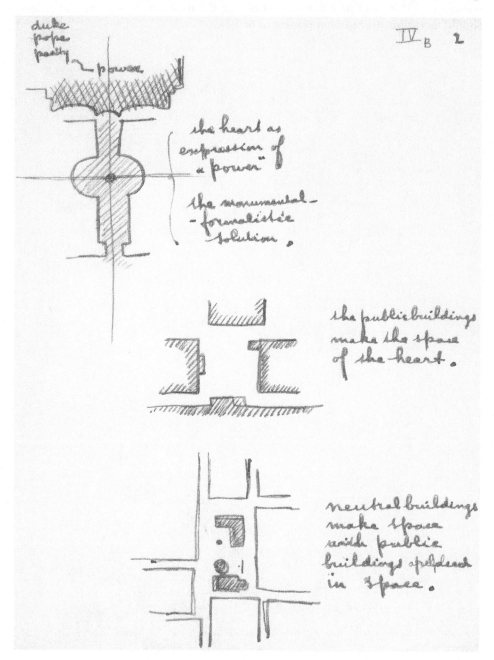

Figure 4.16 Bakema, Schemes, Historical Study and the Heart of Power.

Source: Collection Het Nieuwe Instituut, Rotterdam, Bake d264.

emotions of anxiety in people" and "yet we are still affected by those devices of rite and form,"[93] as Lynch later asserted. Remarkably, the Heart of Power inserted inside the existing pattern structure of the city, for instance in the Renaissance Formalism, was in contradiction with Giedion's idea of symbolic monumentality as ultimate crystallisation of community life. It mistrusted, queried and complexified that even too perfect, positive, naïve, hopeful conception of the Heart as "the centre where liberty consummates itself and explains itself"[94] – as it was embraced and acclaimed at CIAM 8.

Three-dimensional planning

The importance of the three-dimensional design was repeatedly stressed by the Dutch architect during the course lessons; its relevance for our daily life was even compared to that of "oxygen"[95] for our organisms. Similarly to Sert, Bakema considered the third-dimensional planning as a serious matter as far as the use and planning of the land was concerned. In particular, the post-war growth of population became a huge visible issue to tackle, especially where there was no available space for urban expansion, like in his home country, the Netherlands.

Bakema suggested that the typical Dutch concern about land use and the overwhelming necessity of coordination between planners and architect should be imported into the USA, where no physical limitations of the land instead favoured the explosion and the spread of cities over the country.

The result was an "enormous public space called USA," where single floor private expansions have contrary deprived the cities of any public identity, as already denounced by Sert at CIAM 8 as well as during the First Urban Design Conference. "City and nature are destroyed in the same instant," Bakema sustained. "There could be no harsher indictment."[96]

Second, the third-dimensional design had, in Bakema's mind, a humanistic value too. Only through the "3-dimensional language," Architecture, which has the "monopoly of Space,"[97] and Urbanism can indeed "explain to man what life is"[98] and "acknowledge every aspect of life: how to care about your body, the way you cook and eat, how you work, how you lie down and how you sit, how you walk and drive a car, how you feel the sun on your body."[99]

Facing these concerns, the three-dimensional structure in St Louis should be, first of all, the direct interpretation of the various aspects of its inhabitant's life. Indeed, this was supposed to be the basic step in order to transform the city into a "symbolic value, a monument which can be used by people and can use the people, stimulating peoples imagination about life,"[100] reverberating and repeating again CIAM 8's apprehensions and positions.

St Louis: Bakema's and students' project

As described by Dean Passenau during the meeting at GSD Harvard about the Human Scale[101] in April 1959, St Louis is characterised by two important formal elements: the river, which lacks of a relationship with the city, and the perpendicular axis of urban elements, connecting the river to the Washington University.

The general master plan proposed by Bakema followed and amplified these two main presences consisting of a "Spine Concept," a Linear Civic Center which developed from the eastern Missouri River where the City was born to the Forest Park on the West.

This linear spine included the main institutions, such as the Civil Courts Buildings, the Government buildings, the Union Station, the Mill creek, the St Louis University and the Cathedral, and it was thought to be further developed and expanded from East to West.

The spine idea was physically designed as an east-west double-deck road which penetrated towards the focus of the city near the bridge. "The visual expression can be stronger, as that of the river!"[102] – Bakema emphasised the strong linearity of and coherence between the natural and artificial infrastructures.

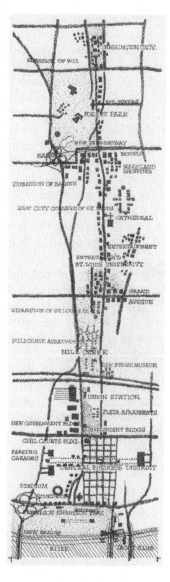

Figure 4.17 Bakema, A Linear Civic Center.

Source: Bakema, "The Humane Core," (1959–60) 11. Collection Het Nieuwe Instituut, Rotterdam, Bake d264.

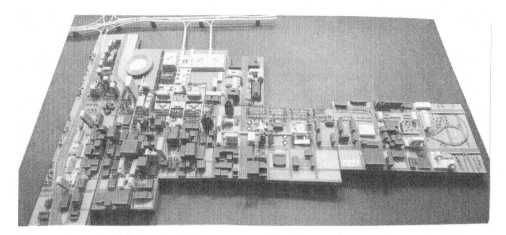

Figure 4.18 Bakema and Students, Model of the Spine Core.

Source: Collection Het Nieuwe Instituut, Rotterdam, BAKE_ph52–23.

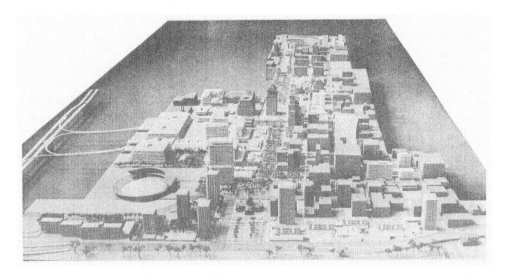

Figure 4.19 Bakema and Students, Model of the Spine Core.

Source: Bakema, "The Humane Core," 18. Collection Het Nieuwe Instituut, Rotterdam, Bake d264.

The choice to promote the passage of the main traffic line through the heart was supported by the conviction that the flow of the traffic is the basic element of the city which gives life to human settlements. The participants of the course believed that the "traffic lines can promote new structures in the heart,"[103] increasing the social relationships, rather than erasing them as conversely vehemently repeated at CIAM 8.

Indeed, the Spine Heart solution and these positive considerations about car mobility and traffic results were in total contradiction with the symbolic meaning given by

Giedion to the Heart as counterforce of the symbol of the "tyranny of mechanical tools"[104] and to the general acclaim at CIAM 8 for the right of the pedestrian, "*la royauté du piéton*" as it is celebrated by Le Corbusier, as one of the most outstanding traits of the Heart discourse.

Surprisingly, Bakema's linear spine concept in St Louis undressed the "humane core" of both its post-war humanist values in contrast with the machine and its organic metaphorical representations and resemblances.

Indeed, on the one hand the project emphasised the synergy and climax of the urban structure relying on technology and car mobility for the restoration humanity, social connections and urban life. On the other in the St Louis project the Heart surpassed its metaphorical interpretation, or literal interpretation, without using any anatomical analogies with the functional or dimensional characteristics of the human organ. The heart was mentioned in order to highlight the necessary overlap between the physical urban structure and the social one. But it was instead developed linearly, structured along the main traffic road, without any reference to organic form or structure.

The linear Heart was already mentioned at CIAM 8, by Wissing of the Dutch Opbouw Group, in parallel with the concentric Heart.[105] The different choice regarded more the dimension of the conglomeration and complexity of the activities and units to plan: the bigger and more complex they are, the easier and more appropriate it is to collect them in a linear form. However, this differentiation merely based on the dimension urban scale in St Louis was embedded also of symbolical meanings in tension between human scale and mechanical tools, artificial and natural dialogues between the linear presences.

Finally, the project for St Louis was published in "Team 10 primer," edited by Alison Smithson. As a footnote of the diagrams based on St Louis, Bakema wrote: "It is the architect who can demonstrate the special conditions that have to be recognized for the future development of the part."[106] The system of traffic and the central Spine seemed thus to be a right device for the architect for the design of a Civic Centre in evolution and in future expansion. Furthermore, the plan presented many similarities with Smithsons' traffic net for Berlin competition (1958),[107] which was published in "Team 10 primer" as well. Indeed, in both projects, the urban traffic infrastructure and the urban motorways defined the structure of the community. Moreover, the patterns of the streets appeared similar in their linear development and in their relationships with the River presences, the Missouri in St Louis and the Spree in Berlin. The "idea of mobility" as main characteristic of two plans was tangible and visible in both sketches. However, the St Louis project seemed to pay more attention on the pre-existing urban structure and therefore on the existing social connections which should be reactivated and enhanced; on the contrary, Smithsons overlaid a megastructure, "closely related but not touching . . . Superadjacencies"[108] as described by Venturi, in order to differentiate different layers of mobility, over the bombed city which nevertheless still revealed an existing texture, form, and urban structure.

Students' project

After a few reports of the urban analysis, on November 15, 1959, it was decided that students[109] would have to work on seven, later eleven, areas in which the city had been divided. Bakema remembered the participants to design the areas in coherence with the linear Spine concept, a sort of empty version of the later linear "Core Wall" of the

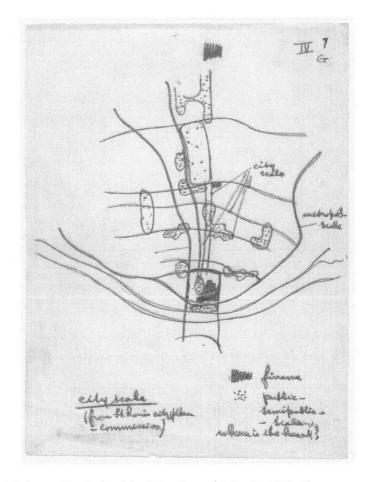

Figure 4.20 Bakema, City Scale of the Spine Core of St Louis, 1959–60.

Source: Collection Het Nieuwe Instituut, Rotterdam, BAKE_d264.

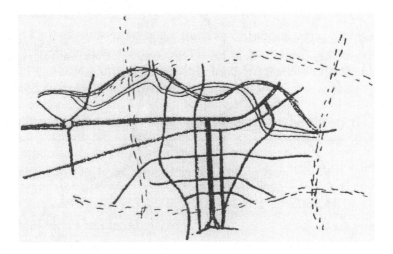

Figure 4.21 Smithsons, Traffic Net, Berlin Plan, 1958.

Source: Smithson, *Team 10 Primer*, Fig. 62, p. 58. Courtesy of Smithson Family Collection.

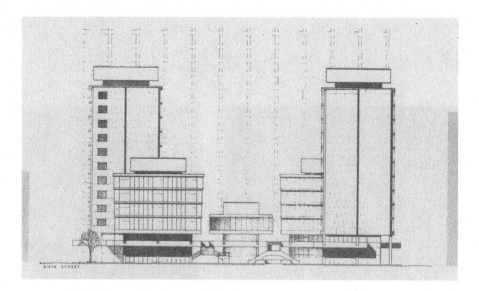

Figure 4.22 Bakema and Students, Team 4, Section of the Project in St Louis.

Source: Bakema, "The Humane Core," (1959–60) 19. Collection Het Nieuwe Instituut, Rotterdam, Bake d264.

already discussed Tel Aviv project, and he recommended to think about the need of the "3-dimensional expression."[110]

As shown in the sections of the projects, the presence of gradual and transitional elements was assured, with the main purpose to design a right overlapping between the social and physical structure of the city and to reconcile the right physical connection between the individual and his surrounding environment. Indeed, students' gradual hierarchical section perfectly mirrored Bakema's well-known "Friendship Diagram," paying attention to "the way in which high, low, big and small buildings are spatially related," with the ultimate social and humanist aim to "help man feel at home in total space,"[111] as Bakema taught.

Finally, the most astonishing project, among all students' projects, was certainly the proposal presented by Team 3 (Bonville, Ford, Johnson, Pruett, Smith), regarding the critical conjunction between the two linear urban elements, the urban spine and the river: it was a parking area in front of the River, saving part of the CBD for pedestrians.

The project was a romanticised version of medieval city walls; it consisted of two gigantic parking garages, hosting 9,000 cars, with a mound form like "literally hills defining car access to the city,"[112] whose shape followed the decrease of traffic flow in the upper floors. Finally, between the two mounds, which can be considered two Megastructures with their similar monumental character to the Philadelphia Garage project by Kahn, "a new dramatic entry for the CBD" was designed: "a large gasoline tank provides a modern focal point – the counterpoint of the medieval city's tower."[113]

As optimistic symbol of a modern mechanised present, in coherence for instance with Tange's interpretation of symbol, the project presented the humane core through the rise of traffic mobility, definitely emphasising the complexity and contradictions of the legacy of CIAM 8.

Figure 4.23 Students, Team 3, Model of the Parking Garage with Mound Form and Gasoline as Entrance to the City Center.

Source: Collection Het Nieuwe Instituut, Rotterdam, BAKE_ph52–12.

The parking garage from the crosswalk over Market-Locust Boulevard. The gasoline tanks serve as "entrance" markers to the downtown area.

Figure 4.24 Students, Team 3, View of the Parking Garage and Gasoline.

Source: Bakema, "The Humane Core," (1959–60). Collection Het Nieuwe Instituut, Rotterdam, Bake d264.

Figure 4.25 Students Discussing the Project, St Louis, 1959–60.

Source: Collection Het Nieuwe Instituut, Rotterdam, BAKE _ph47–3.

Figure 4.26 Bakema with the Plan of St Louis, 1959–60.

Source: Collection Het Nieuwe Instituut, Rotterdam, BAKE_ph47–10.

Figure 4.27 Bakema with Students, St Louis, 1959–60.

Source: Collection Het Nieuwe Instituut, Rotterdam, Bake_ph47–2

Notes

1 Hermann Minkowski, "Space and Time," in *The Principle of Relativity: A Collection of Original Memoirs on the Special and General Theory of Relativity*, ed. Hendrik A. Lorentz, Albert Einstein, Hermann Minkowski, and Hermann Weyl, (New York: Dover, 1923), 75.
2 "Team 10 ended because we stopped meeting; and this hapened when Bakema died and his post box was closed. We continued to see each other but there were no more meetings after Bakema died." Tuscano, "How Can You Do Without History? Interview with Giancarlo De Carlo," 343.
3 Bakema, "Relationship Between Men and Things," in *The Heart of the City*, 67.
4 "Some months ago I was walking in the cemetery of Asplund's crematorium in Stockholm – in this wonderful composition of trees, grass, halls, flowers, hills, rocks and living and dead people." Ibid.
5 Ibid.
6 Jaap Bakema, "Report on: Ethics and Aesthetics," Bakema Archive, g18, Het Nieuwe Instituut, Rotterdam.
7 Bakema, "Relationship Between Men and Things," 67.
8 Bakema, "Report On: Ethics and Aesthetics."
9 Bakema, "Relationship Between Men and Things," 67.
10 Georges Canguilhem, "The Living Being and Its Environment (milieu)," *Grey Room*, 3 (Spring 2001): 7–31. Originally in French: Georges Canguilhem, "Le vivant et son milieu," in *La connaissance de la vie* (Paris: Hachette, 1952).
11 Strauven, *Aldo van Eyck: The Shape of Relativity*. 423. Thomas Samuel Kuhn, *The Structure of Scientific Revolutions* (Chicago: University of Chicago Press, 1962).

12 van Eyck, Team 10, "The Role of the Architect in Community Building," 376.

13 Jaap Bakema, "New Architecture and Freedom," *Forum*, 2 (1948): 48–50. Francis Strauven, "Bakema," *Forum*, 34, no. 3 (1990): 24.

14 Jaap Bakema, *Van Stoel tot Stad, een verhaal over mensen en ruimte* (Antwerp: Uitgeversmaatschappij W. de Haan N.V., Zeist, N. V. Standaard Boekhandel, 1963); translated in English in Jaap Bakema, *From Doorstep to City: A Story about People and Space* (Urbana: University of Illinois, 711.4 B78vEw), 3.

15 "Now, we are doing no more (and not less) than deforming people into housing types." Bakema, *From Doorstep to City*, 15.

16 See Dirk van den Heuvel, "Towards an Open Society: The Unfinished Work of Jaap Bakema," 41 (2014): 3–3. Guus Beumer, Dirk van den Heuvel, "Open: A Bakema Celebration," *Dutch Pavilion, La Biennale di Venezia: Venice, Italy* (2014, June 7–2014, November 23).

17 "Of the basic question of human existence, What am I? Who am I? and Where am I?, the last one, to an architect, is the most important. Man functions in the total system. Built environment takes part in the process. We all have to meet in this process at the station called 'Idea.'" Jaap Bakema, *Thoughts about Architecture*, ed. Marianne Gray (London: Academy editions; New York: St. Martin's Press, 1981), 31.

18 The first proposal for Pendrecht, a district in Rotterdam-south, was submitted in 1949 at the CIAM meeting in Bergamo.

19 Piet Mondrian, *Plastic Art and Pure Plastic Art and Other Essays, 1941–1943* (New York: Wittenborn and Company, 1945), 44.
  For more in-depth analysis of Relationship and Relativity in different areas of knowledge, see Strauven, *Aldo van Eyck: The Shape of Relativity*.

20 Opbouw Group, "CIAM 8 Describing the Core of Pendrecht, Responsible Rapporteur: W. Wissing," Het Nieuwe Instituut, Rotterdam, Bakema Archive, g. 18.

21 "2e. there can be traced a certain scale of different importance as core-forming elements, that must be expressed by a different situation in relation to each of the various activities;
  3e. however this may not lead to a distinct separation between the primary and the secondary activities related to the core and between these and the residence;
  4e. on the contrary there must be a dynamic continuity of space, expressing the totality in every [one] of its components" Opbouw Group, 1951, g18, Het Nieuwe Instituut, Rotterdam.

22 Hans Hovens Greve, Wim Wissing, "Contribution to: The Core or Physical Heart. CIAM 8, July 1951," g18, Het Nieuwe Instituut, Rotterdam.

23 Bakema, "Report On: Ethics and Aesthetics."

24 Bakema, *Thoughts about Architecture*, 144.

25 Aldo van Eyck, "Het verhaal van een andere gedachte (The Story of Another Idea)," *Forum* 7 (1959). See Strauven, *Aldo van Eyck: The Shape of Relativity*, 339.

26 From 1959 to 1963, the *Forum* editorial board members were Bakema, van Eyck, Apon, Boon, Hertzberger, art pedagogue Hardy and graphic designer Schrofer.

27 See Strauven, *Aldo van Eyck: The Shape of Relativity*, 238. See also Sigfried Giedion, *The Eternal Present: I. The Beginnings of Art*, 1962; *The Beginnings of Architecture*, 1964. Giedion, "Historical Background to the Core," 17–25.

28 It consists again of two circles which represent the synergy between architecture on the left and human identity on the right.

29 For a detailed description see Strauven, *Aldo van Eyck: The Shape of Relativity*, 349–350.

30 van Eyck, quoted in Strauven, *Aldo van Eyck: The Shape of Relativity*, 349 and Oscar Newman, *CIAM '59 in Otterlo* (Stuttgart: Karl Krämer, 1961).

31 Dogon is in the South of former French Sudan.

32 *Oxford English Dictionary*.

33 Strauven, *Aldo van Eyck: The Shape of Relativity*, 390–391.

34 "We have lost all the beautiful certainty about the way the world works – we are not even sure if it is expanding or contracting, whether it was produced by a catastrophe or is continuously renewing itself. This does not absolve us from looking for some ground of certainty in our attempts to give form to human environment. It is no longer likely that we shall find this ground in the world which the cosmologists are continuously reshaping

round us and so we must look for it inside ourselves: in the constitution and structure of the human person." Joseph Rykwert, "The idea of a town," *Forum*, 3 (1963): 143.

35 Opbouw Group, "CIAM 8 Describing the Core of Pendrecht."

36 The town is "an artifact of a curious kind, compounded of willed and random elements, imperfectly controlled. If it is like any other piece of physiology at all, it is more like a dream than anything else" Rykwert, "The Idea of a Town," 100. See also in Strauven, *Aldo van Eyck: The Shape of Relativity*, 391.

37 van Eyck, quoted in Strauven, *Aldo van Eyck: The Shape of Relativity*, 391. Strauven affirms that van Eyck considered Rykwert's argument as an endorsement of the other idea, his view of architecture as the "counter-form of the mind." Ibid., 391.

38 "How difficult it is for us/To Find a Shelter/Even in our heart/The whole place is prose/And all the heat." Jules Supervielle, *Forum*, 7 (1959): 225.

39 Jaap Bakema, *Carré Bleu* (1961) in Smithson, *Team 10 Primer*, 30.

40 Aldo van Eyck, "Dutch Forum on Children's Home," in Smithson, *Team 10 Primer*, 100.

41 Aldo van Eyck, 1965, in Smithson, *Team 10 Primer*, 104.

42 In Italian: "*in quanto momento focale di relazione, il cuore della città è un problema sociale nel quale si congiungono strettamente il progetto architettonico e il piano urbanistico.*" Paci, "Il cuore della Città," vii.

43 Canguilhem, "The Living Being and Its Environment (milieu)": 25.

44 "Ordinariness and banality are the art source for new situation." Smithson Alison, Smithson Peter, typescript "The Ordinary and the Banal" preprinted in Claude Lichtenstein, Thomas Schregenberger, ed., *As Found: The Discovery of the Ordinary* (Baden, Switzerland: Lars Müller, 2001), 7. Avermaete, *Another Modern*, 95.

45 Eric Mumford mentioned in a hidden footnote that probably the invocation of the everyday life mentioned by CIAM members, in particular since the Sigtuna meeting 1952, could have been directly influenced by the ideas of Henri Lefebvre. Mumford, *The CIAM Discourse on Urbanism*, note 88, p. 329.

46 Bakema and Candilis, "The Great Reality of Doorstep," 1954 quoted in Avermaete, *Another Modern*, 86.

47 Sartre in Giedion, "Historical Background to the Core," 17.

48 Aldo van Eyck, 1965, in Smithson, *Team 10 Primer*, 96.

49 The "hierarchy of human associations" was based on four levels: house, street, district and city. The doorstep was first used at Aix-de-Provence in 1953, at CIAM 9.

50 Bakema, *From Doorstep to City: A Story about People and Space.*

51 The Threshold was an ancient figure, an archetype in the field of Architecture and Urbanism, from the rites of foundations to the myths of origin. Sergio Crotti explains that the threshold is an interval contested between two fronts, an ambiguous and inhabitable limited place, a context non-place, which is condemned to a "singular ethnological squint" looking towards both sides like a double-faced Janus. Sergio Crotti, *Figure architettoniche: soglia* [*Architectural Figures: The Threshold*] (Milan: Unicopli, 2000), 65–75.

52 See Martin Buber, *Ich und Du* (Leipzig: Insel-Verlag, 1923). Walter Kaufmann trans, *I and Thou a New Translation* (New York: Charles Scribner's Sons, 1970). Alexander Tzonis, Liane Lefauvre, *Aldo van Eyck, Humanist Rebel: Inbetweening in a Postwar World* (Rotterdam: 010 Publisher, 1999); Giuseppe Mantia, "Devices, lo spazio poroso figure e dispositivi," in *Comment Vivre Ensemble*, ed. Paola Viganò, Paola Pellegrini (Venezia: IUAV, Officina Edizioni, 2006), 194–196.

53 Buber, *Das problem des Menschen*. 1943. Joop Hardy, Herman Hertzberger, "Drempel en ontmoeting: de gestalte van het tussen," *Forum*, 8 (1959): 249.

54 Giedion, *Architecture You and Me*, 126.

55 Buber writes in his *Urdistanz und Beziehung*: "art is neither the impression of natural objectivity, nor the expression of soulful subjectivity; it is work and witness to the relation between the substantia humana and the substantia rerum, the in-between that has taken place." ("*Kunst ist weder Impression naturheiler Objektivität noch Expression seelenhaftor Subjektivität, sie ist Werk und Zeugnis der Bezichung zwischen der substantis humans und der substantis rerum, das gestaltgewordene Zwischen.*") in Rolf Gutmann, Theo Manz, "Ueberlegungen über das Wesen des Themas," in *Les Documents de Sigtuna*, 1952 and *Forum*, 7 (1959), 215.

56 Aldo van Eyck, "Ex Turico Aliquid Novum," *Archithese*, 5 (1981): 38 quoted in Pedret, *TEAM 10: An Archival History*, 86.

57 "The organic conception of habitat as 'totalities' challenged the analytical premise of the functional city that called for the separating of functions of living into autonomous sectors; the demand by habitat to respond to the specific conditions and greater differentiations between things challenged the universalizing premise the Athens Charter." Pedret, *TEAM 10: An Archival History*, 96.

58 "In this 'living' community there must be a relation between individuals and a relation between the individual and the whole." Report of the commission on the subject discussed during the Ninth Meeting of CIAM at Sigtuna – Sweden, *Forum*, 3 (1953), 42-WM-X-7, gta Archive, ETH Zurich.

59 Bakema, *Thoughts about Architecture*, 139.

60 Jaap Bakema, "Arch-o-Meter," d264, Bakema Archive, Het Nieuwe Instituut, Rotterdam.

61 Jaap Bakema, "Letter to Mr. Haskell," d264, Bakema Archive, Het Nieuwe Instituut, Rotterdam.

62 Geoffrey Scott, *The Architecture of Humanism: A Study in the History of Taste* (Boston and New York: Houghton Mifflin, 1914), 144. Quoted in Jaap Bakema, "Notes about Theory," d264, Bakema Archive, Het Nieuwe Instituut, Rotterdam.

63 Scott, *The Architecture of Humanism*, 7–8, in Bakema, "Notes about Theory."

64 These facts have to be explained by a Theory: "The first step in developing a Theory is to establish the facts to be explained . . . The handy arch-meter blue printed at the left would establish the facts with precision, but unfortunately it is still in a very crude stage of development." Bakema, "Notes about Theory."

65 Johan Huizinga, *Homo Ludens: A Study of the Play Element in Culture* (Boston: Beacon Paperback edition, 1955).

66 Ibid., 46.

67 See Cornelis Wagenaar, "Jaap Bakema and the Fight for Freedom," in *Anxious Modernism*, ed. Sarah Williams Goldhagen, Réjean Legault (Montreal: Centre Canadien d'Architecture; Cambridge, MA and London, UK: MIT Press, 2000), 268.

68 Strauven, *Aldo van Eyck: The Shape of Relativity*, 365.

69 During the congress in Hoddesdon, three subject proposals were mentioned for CIAM 9. Among the proposals, the second solution to organise the CIAM 9 in Stockholm, was proposed by the Swedish group, which was more interested in discussing the topic of "The child and the City." The discussion should have been focused on the consequences of changes in the family structure which have been analysed neither by architects, nor by sociologists or other experts.

70 Giedion, "Historical Background to the Core," 18.

71 Bakema, *From Doorstep to City*, 17.

72 The "Core-wall building" underlines the structure of a "linear Core" which will be later analysed in the St Louis case study.

73 "Architectenbureau Van den Broek en Bakema, Tel Aviv project, 1962, Archief d1315," BROX3092 (70–3092), Het Nieuwe Instituut, Rotterdam.

74 Ibid.

75 Robert Kiek, "Europe's Fifth Avenue," *Urban Land* 13 (October 1954): 6, quoted in Smiley, *Pedestrian Modern*, 235–236.

76 Gruen, *The Heart of Our Cities*, 241.

77 Smiley, *Pedestrian Modern*, 235.

78 "So the more the different human actions which have to be served by building-programs are expressed by specific elements (parts) in the built environment, the more the human quality to compare by seeing is stimulated and becomes vital." Bakema, *Thoughts about Architecture*, 139.

79 Ibid., 31.

80 Jaap Bakema, "The Growing Houses," in Bakema, *Thoughts about Architecture*, 131.

81 "The expression of the interrelationship (core) of the various dwelling types in repeatable units (visual groups) is one of the indispensable conditions for 'habitat'." See Bakema, *Van Stoel tot Stad*, 84; *Forum* 4 (1956): 105–106; Umberto Barbieri, ed., *Architectuur en Planning. Nederland 1940–1980* (Rotterdam: Uitgeverij 010, 1983), 57.

82 Bakema, *Van Stoel tot Stad*.

83 The Heart as relationship remains an open discourse for insightful interpretations of the public realm in our contemporary discussion. For instance, as far as the visual groups are concerned, the same idea of vertical relationship has been reinterpreted since the 1970s by Jan Gehl, though referring neither to Bakema nor to Team 10. The Danish architect analysed the same vertical relationships of the building, and he also considered the sixth floor as the "threshold" between the relationship with the ground and the relationship with the horizon. The main difference is that Gehl uses the same section as Bakema and Team 10, specifically in order to stress a physiological quality of the human scale in the public space instead of a democratic dwelling. See Jan Gehl, *Cities for People* (Washington, DC and London: Island Press, 2010), 41. Jan Gehl, *Life between Buildings: Using Public Space*, trans. Jo Koch (New York: Van Nostrand Reinhold, 1987), 98.

84 Jaap Bakema, "Problem: Civic Center for Metropolis St. Louis. Part IV," Bake d264, Bakema Archive, Het Nieuwe Instituut, Rotterdam.

85 Jaap Bakema, *The Humane Core: A Civic Center for St. Louis, MO* (Washington, DC: Washington University Press, 1960), 2.

86 Rossi, *L'architettura della città*, 12.

87 Giedion, "Historical Background to the Core," 25.

88 Giedion, "The Heart of the City: A Summing-Up," 162.

89 See Tom Avermaete, "Stem and Web: A Different Way of Analysing, Understanding and Conceiving the City in the Work of Candilis-Josic-Woods," 251–269. Accessed on June 9, 2017, www.team10online.org/

90 See Jacob Bakema, "An Emperor's House at Split Became a Town for 3000 People," *Forum*, 2 (1962): 45–78. Bakema, *Van Stoel tot Stad*, 95. Aldo Rossi in "*L'architettura della città*" (1966) studied the arenas in Nîmes and Arles as examples of persisting structures which overturned their original functions.

91 Aporia (Ancient Greek: ἀπορία: *impasse, lack of resources, puzzlement, doubt, confusion*), *Oxford English Dictionary*.

92 Bakema, "Problem: Civic Center for Metropolis St. Louis. Part II."

93 Lynch, *A Theory of Good City Form*, 79–81.

94 Rogers, "The Heart: Human Problem of Cities," 70.

95 Jaap Bakema, "Letter to Mr. Haskell, December 1959," Bake d264, Bakema Archive, Het Nieuwe Instituut, Rotterdam.

96 Jaap Bakema, "Enclosure A: The Modern Industrial City," Bake d264, Bakema Archive, Het Nieuwe Instituut, Rotterdam.

97 Scott, *The Architecture of Humanism*, quoted in Bakema, "Notes about Theory."

98 Bakema, "Problem: Civic Center for Metropolis St. Louis."

99 Bakema, Letter to Mr. Haskell.

100 Bakema, "Problem: Civic Center for Metropolis St. Louis. Part V."

101 The Human Scale Advanced Seminar for the Master's Class, conducted by Prof S. Giedion and Prof E. F. Sekler with the cooperation of Dean Jose Louis Sert, GSD Harvard University, Cambridge, Massachusetts, Spring Term 1959.

102 Bakema, "Problem: Civic Center for Metropolis St. Louis. Part IX."

103 Ibid.

104 Giedion, "Historical Background to the Core," 17.

105 "*L'idéal ci-devant peut est exprime en deux différents formes de Cœur:*

    a. *le cœur CONCENTRIQUE, où des activités est exprimé par la location de ces activités dans un certain nombre de cercles autour d'un noyau, qui est l'expression de l'activité la plus universelle du cœur.*

    b. *Le cœur EN LIGNE, où cet ordre est exprimé par la location d'eux d'un à-côté de l'autre selon un ligne quelconque qui est l'expression de l'activité universelle du cœur.*"

"Written comments on the Core from members of commission 1. W. Wissing, Holland, 'OPBOUW' CIAM 8, 1951, *Report of Hoddesdon Conference*.

106 Bakema, "Image 39. Diagram based on St. Louis," in Smithson, *Team 10 Primer*, 44.

107 This analogy was already highlighted in Eric Mumford, ed., *Modern Archietcture in St. Louis: Washington University and Postwar American Architecture, 1948–1973* (Washington: Washington University in Saint Louis, 2004), 58.

108 Robert Venturi, *Complexity and Contradiction in Architecture* (New York: The Museum of Modern Art, 1966), 64.

109 Sixth year design class project; October 1, 1959, to February 1, 1960. The class: Brewer, Bonville, Bortnick, Cannon, Day, Ford, Gilmore, Hanser, Heneghan, Henriken, Hosier, Johnson, Martin, Pruett, Richardson, Sarnoff, Skubiz, Smith, Torno, Vickery.

110 "It is not unreasonable that we should be able to communicate about life in our days in a way by 3-dimensional expression." Bakema, *The Humane Core: A Civic Center for St. Louis, MO*, 5.

Team 1 (Brewer, Henrekin, Vickery) redesigns the area adjacent and north to the Jefferson Memorial Park where a new workmen' s housing complex will be built. Team 2 (Gilmore, Sarnoff, Skubitz) has to rethink and area adjacent to and west of the Jefferson Memorial Park, to be developed as luxury and upper-middle class apartments. Team 3 (Bonville, Ford, Johnson, Pruett, Smith) designs the main parking area and the Lower Market, with the pedestrian entry into the CBD. Team 4 (Cannon, Torno, Veron) task is to revitalize the CBD area by a system of pedestrian walkways and brand new transitional spaces. Team 5 (Bortnick, Hanser, Heneghan, Richardson) redesigns the 12th Street Complex, a cultural government center bordering the Civil Courts Building, the City Hall and Kiel Auditorium. Team 6 (Day, Hosier, Martin) has the task to develop the area facing the Union Station, which should be considered as a new subcenter. Finally the other developments will involve the Mill Creek (Area VII), the Grand Avenue (Area VIII), the Cathedral Subcenter (Area IX), the Kingshinhway and Forest Park (Area X) and the Forest Park apartments (Area XI).

111 Jaap Bakema, "Architecture as an Instrument of Man's Self Realisation," *Forum*, 2 (1961): 56.

112 Bakema, *The Humane Core: A Civic Center for St. Louis, MO*, 29.

113 Ibid., 18.

Part III
Conclusions

Part II

Conclusions

5 Arteries of productive ambiguities and simultaneities

The heart, even in the age of its transplantability, is still viewed as the central organ of internalized humanity in the dominant language games of our civilization.[1]

Peter Sloterdijk, *Bubbles, Spheres Volume I*, 1998

The three actors – First UD and Gruen, CIAM Summer School and Bakema – enhanced the blossoming of the simplicity, Elementarism[2] – sometimes even trivialisation – of the Heart of the City into pivotal, complex and intricate layers of significance and interpretation. Within the reference of the branches of the phylogeny tree as presented within the introduction, the three actors revealed the productive ambiguity and the "imponderable nature"[3] of the Heart of the City, which is the main concern of this book.

The synchronic presence which is enshrined in the heart as both metaphor and symbol, mechanistic and vitalistic, reverberates in the juxtaposition and tension between cultural image, urban structure and social presence and between figures, concepts and projects.[4] In this perspective, the Heart of the City was, and remains, an important first attempt to simultaneously consider and tend towards the utmost synergy between the social and spatial categories and elements of the built environment. This synergy is ambiguous and unstable, difficult or impossible to express and frame into universalising and normative rules. *Vis-à-vis* this uncontrollability, the artifice or deviation of the metaphor/symbol is adopted, similarly to what happens in other disciplines, even scientific ones.[5] In fact, the inaccurate metaphor appears as the ultimate, necessary and inescapable expression for the definition of complexity and ambiguity of our built environment.

As far as the three actors are concerned, this overlapping social-spatial purpose of the Heart is particularly clear in Bakema's interest in transitional relationships, as exposed for instance in his "friendship diagram" and later tested in the "humane core" of St Louis. Not by coincidence, this synergy of the Heart anticipated later important demands for and research into the ordinariness of urban life, of the "social plastic"[6] design of everyday life which were manifested intensely in later debates on "Habitat for the greatest number"[7] within CIAM, Team 10 and still nowadays within the UN.

Furthermore, this social effect of the metaphor of the heart surprisingly also resonated within diverse disciplines and later fields of research which are not directly connected with the CIAM discourse,[8] somehow transforming the heart of the city into a broader paradigm of the social-spatial urban life.

However, these vectors of continuity are visible if the heart is not considered merely as an issue of urban reconstruction after the war, as generally thought. Instead, its humanist purpose has been imbedded in the renewal of "the human being as such – the bare naked man"[9] and his extensions in the city with regard to the "human crisis,"[10] in the dramatic words of Albert Camus, which occurred during the Second World War and somehow still persists. Architecturally speaking, this humanist claim also represented the crisis of the Modern Movement and the rise of other clouds of architectural thought, through which we are still hazily fumbling.

Giedion certainly had a pivotal role in framing the most important humanist expressions and interpretations of the Heart, chronologically and theoretically disclosing the research of the Heart between his critique of killing mechanisation and the search for the eternal principle of architecture, which are both imbedded in the topic of the CIAM 8.

As far as the killing mechanisation is concerned, both the symbolical and functional split between human beings and machines, for the preservation of both the right of the pedestrian and the human scale, as vehemently claimed during CIAM 8 by Giedion and other CIAM members, found divergent solutions, overlaps, contradictions and critiques within the three actors. Generally speaking, we can conclude that the more a three-dimensional design attitude was considered, the less the split between pedestrian and vehicle flows was simplistic and merely functionalist; all of this thanks to the efforts to merge urban structure with ever changeable and complex social exigencies. The new discipline of Urban Design raised and relied on this three-dimensional approach, which was imbedded in the topic of CIAM 8. In particular, the Urban Design experiments of Gruen's shopping centre tremendously and stably influenced the design and essence of public space until nowadays, thanks to its commercial strategies, arrangements and its elaborated proposals of differentiation of flows. Remarkably, the encounters between the avant-garde of CIAM and the mass consumption of Gruen's theories and projects resulted into ecological urban planning proposals which are worthwhile to rediscover and reexamine also within our urban condition.

Regarding the eternal principle, in the case studies analysed and in particular in the Italian continuity and in Bakema's relationship, the Heart becomes both an archetypical "proto-Idea" (proto- , *gr. Πρωτο* as "*first, first element*") and a progressive "pro-Idea" (pro -, *gr. Προ-* as "*in front of, before*") of the City.

On the one hand, it concerns the structure of perennial, archetypical, existential identity of a place, and the continuous transformation of social alienation into a gathering *focus* or *foci*. Somehow it resonates with Norberg-Schulz's "*genius loci*," with the "eternal present" by Giedion, as already described, with the purpose to enhance and "to maintain the perennity of culture, the immortality of the social soul."[11]

On the other, the Heart is a progressive idea of a better future social condition or physical space, translated into a real present urban form. The most exhaustive example was again Giedion's description of Michelangelo's Capitol, whose spatial composition was ahead of its time, symbolising democracy in Rome even though the city was still oppressed and latent under the despotism of the Pope.[12]

In this perspective, the Swiss historian depicted the humanism of the Core as the answer to the need for the human being of signs and symbols which are bare of any mediations, any filters, any preconceptions, any Maya's veil.[13] This unembellished, somehow "brutalist" figure of the Heart probably found its best expression in the "child and the city," in the playgrounds of van Eyck, in the act of playing as a brakeless cultural revelation as considered by Bakema.

Bakema himself and the Dutch group are merited with explicitly bringing to the fore the abstract entity of the Heart of the City as an Idea. Its abstraction reveals a deep and archetypical presence inside the existence of the city and of public space itself. Especially when the Symbol kills the Metaphor, when the abstract organic value prevails over the organic form, it solves in part that "great confusion" about the organic elements as expressed by Gropius in December 1949. The heart of the city shifts from a metaphorical-physical analogy, which is ambiguous with the "ingenuous functionalism,"[14] to an abstract theme, whose translation into a physical form is delegated to the ability of the architect, of the "great artist."[15]

Structures and relationships

As far as the structure of the city is concerned, the heart of the city was interpreted through a great variety of structures, forms and materiality. From Sert's adoption of Ortega y Gasset's conservative metaphor of the city as the hole of a cannon to Gruen's new archetypes of shopping centres as urban crystallisation points and cellular metropolis, from the Italian piazzas as both nostalgic and progressive social spaces to the bridgehead of Venice as the nervous centre between mechanisation and human being, from Bakema's linear spine Core, to Tyrwhitt's urban constellations with empty hearts, Opbouw's fluctuating and variable cores, and Bakema's heart as total Relationship, the heart of the city has assumed different and contradictory forms. Surprisingly and conflictingly, the heart, with its multiple infills, did not present a unique corporeal, organic structure, but rather multiple variations, alternatives and interpretations which were framed and balanced between totally hierarchical structures and more open compositions. This variety consequently mirrored also different grades of power-control and democracy.

However, all these translations of the heart had the common aim and hope, namely to propose a new image of the city, to restructure the city through centres of social life and to deal with brand new urban social-spatial fragmentation, illegibility and fear of uncontrollable expansion. In particular, despite all these different configurations, the authors stressed the common need of social condensation and multiple levels and forms of centralities. In the most interesting solutions and proposals, the latter do not necessarily overlap with the urban CBD or with the historical barycentre of the city, with "the captivity of center."[16] For instance, the Asplund Cemetery praised by Bakema as his first example of Heart of the City remains the most provocative and significant example of this shift presented here.

Moreover, adopting as reference Kepes' "The New Landscape" in 1951, which deeply influenced the theories of Jaqueline Tyrwhitt and other CIAM members, in the three actors the notion of centrality shifted from the radiocentricity of the Lichtenberg figure, where branching electric discharges stem from a well-defined circle-centre, towards the heterogenic cells of the transverse section of the wood where, adopting Lefebvre's thought, the "centrality now aspires to be total."[17] Differently from the hierarchical cell's structure considered for instance by Gruen, the wood cell has neither a nucleus nor cytoplasm and its position and form do not follow any hierarchy. It is instead a "positive space"[18] resulting from a complex equilibrium between internal and external pressures, between a proper centrality and that of the other adjacent

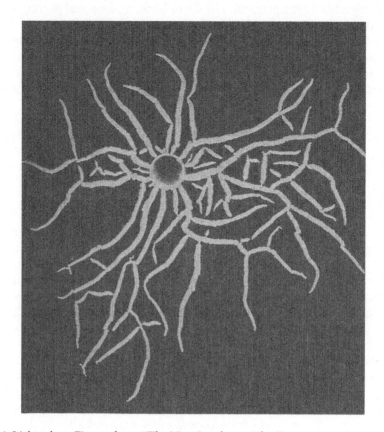

Figure 5.1 Lichtenberg Figure, from "The New Landscape" by Kepes.

Source: Courtesy of Julie Kepes Stone, published in *The Heart of the City: Towards the Humanisation of Urban Life*, ed. Jaqueline Tyrwhitt, Josep Lluís Sert, Ernesto N. Rogers (London: Lund Humphries, 1952), 84.

bubbles, as described by Christopher Alexander in his discourse about the "Heart of the City"[19] as a necessary binding force.

This balance between the interior and the exterior pressures, which also precipitates into a social idea of commons and in the presence of commonality within the "ambiguous and unstable . . . everyday urban spaces,"[20] shares similarities with the movement and fleeting balance, exposed by the Italian philosopher Enzo Paci, between the systolic condensation and the diastolic aperture of the Heart of the City. The latter is another example of synchronicity of the symbolical-anatomical movements of the heart, which are manifested in either more static or open forms and relationships.

Between the "cannon"[21] of Ortega y Gasset, the city structured on the Vitruvian Man as described by Sert, where the civic space has to be separated from the landscape, and the harmonious and total relationship of the "human-being-part-of-total-existence-called-energy"[22] presented by Bakema, the three actors present different "rate[s] of growth"[23] of the complexity of relationships.

According to the first actor, the relationship is univalent since it is focused only on a single entity. It concerns the "urban re-centralization,"[24] as praised by Sert and

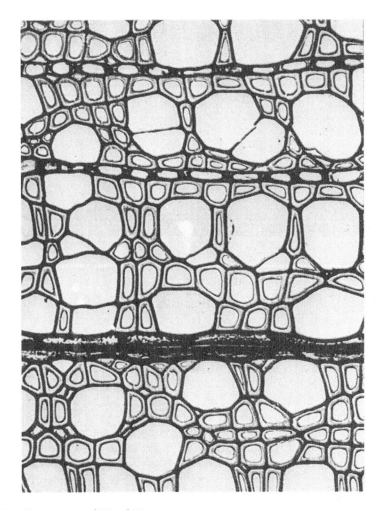

Figure 5.2 Cell Structure of Wood Tissue.

Source: Courtesy of Maggie Alexander, Center for Environmental Structure. Published in Alexander, *The Heart of the City*, 33.

Gruen, of the urban structure for high density centres in contrast with the urban sprawl which is considered responsible for both the loss of civic values and the death of environmental qualities.

In the CIAM Summer School in Venice, the second actor, there are two or multiple grades of relationships since attention is focused on the link between the new project inside a pre-existing historical surrounding, such as Venice, which becomes the starting point of a fundamental urban reflection and dialogue on the contemporary project with both the physical and historical context.

Finally, the third scheme considers the Heart of the City as fully represented by the Relationship concept itself. According to this last actor, the Relationship, together with three-dimensional design, results as one of the most important topics raised

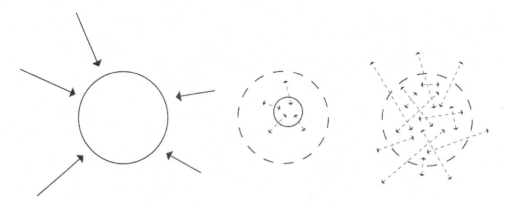

Figure 5.3 Rates of Relationships. First, Second and Third Actor.

Source: Author.

within the Heart of the City, for both a correct synergy between social and spatial levels of the city and for advantageous cooperation between different professional practices. This was later reiterated in *Architecture You and Me*[25] by Giedion and in the philosophy of dialogue in Buber's in-between theory of *Ich und Du*[26] which was adopted by the younger generation of architects, who rose up from CIAM 8 and the CIAM Summer School in Venice, as an alternative to CIAM's pre-war mono-functional analytical approach.

Finally, the Heart of the City can be interpreted, in its most intriguing layer of significance, as a complex interaction of both dynamic and submerged conditions. The Heart of the City is neither conservative, nor traditionalist, nor totally functionalist; it expresses eternal values and at the same time can become a progressive, active and anticipator element for the evolution of society in the built environment, in new forms of urbanity, through the design of a new socio-spatial idea of the public realm which remains a contemporary interest and necessity. It's an abstract idea which needs to be profoundly translated and tested by the architect.

Facing our age of rapid, uncontrolled, violent urbanisation, in front of the "failure of urban planning and the construction sector,"[27] of the lack of "a significant invention of new structure in the realm of urban space,"[28] the Heart remains an urgent urban element with the aim to reposition the social realm and the centralities of social life as originators of the design process of the city.

"The last word cannot be anything but the project itself."[29]

Notes

1 Peter Sloterdijk, *Bubbles: Spheres Volume I: Microspherology*, trans. Wieland Hoban (Los Angeles: Semiotext(e), 2011), 101. Originally published as Peter Sloterdijk, *Sphären I – Blasen*, Mikrosphärologie (Frankfurt: Suhrkamp, 1998).
2 See Paola Viganò, "Elementarismo Urbano, Materiali urbani e struttura della città," in *La città elementare*, 87. See also Theo van Doesburg, "Painting and Sculpture: Elementarism, (1927)," in *De Stijl*, trans., Hans L.C. Jaffé (New York: H. N. Abrams, 1971).
3 CIAM, "A Short Outline of the Core," 165.
4 See Secchi, Giulia Fini, *Il futuro si costruisce giorno per giorno*, 128.

5 The German physicist Werner Heisenberg used metaphors to describe the immateriality of the World, within the new quantum mechanics. See Jérôme Ferrari, *Le principe* (Kindle edition).
6 See Venturi and Scott Brown, *Architecture as Signs and Systems: For a Mannerist Time*, 109.
7 Michel Ecochard, "Habitation pour le plus grand nombre. Position du problème par rapport a l'habitat normal," Report United Nations, Conseil Economique et Social, Commission Economique pour l'Europe, Sous-comité de l'Habitat, 2, Bake0153, g19, Bakema Archive, Het Nieuwe Instituut, Rotterdam. See also Tom Avermaete, "From Knoxville to Bidonville: ABTAT and the Architecture of the French Welfare State," in *Architecture and the Welfare State*, ed. Mark Swenarton, Tom Avermaete, Dirk Van den Heuvel (New York: Routledge, 2015), 219–236.
8 For instance: "The description of the core (CIAM 8) resembles the definitions of the public sphere by Hannah Arendt, Jürgen Habermas and Richard Sennett," respectively, in 1958 (Arendt, *The Human Condition*), in 1964 (Habermas, *The Structural Transformation of the Public Sphere*) and in 1977 (Sennett, *The Fall of Public Man*). Tom Avermaete, Klaske Havik, Hans Teerds, ed., *Architectural Positions: Architecture, Modernity and the Public Sphere* (Amsterdam: SUN Publisher, 2009), 38.
9 Giedion, "Historical Background to the Core," 17.
10 Albert Camus, *La Crise de l'Homme*, Lecture at Columbia's McMillin Academic Theatre, March 28, 1946.
11 Geddes, *Cities in Evolution*, 143.
12 Giedion, "Historical Background to the Core," 25.
13 See Arthur Schopenhauer, *The World as Will and Idea*, 3 vols., trans. R.B. Haldane and J. Kemp (London: Routledge & Kegan Paul, 1883–1886; first edition 1818).
14 In Italian: "*critica al funzionalismo ingenuo.*" Rossi, *L'architettura della città*, 35.
15 Giedion, "Historical Background to the Core," 25.
16 "Generic City" (1995), OMA, Rem Koolhaas, Bruce Mau, *S,M,L,XL*, 1249.
17 Lefebvre, *The Production of Space*, 332.
18 Alexander, *The Heart of the City: The Necessary Binding Force that Creates the Core of Every City*.
19 Interestingly, Christopher Alexander recently embraced this organic wood cell image in his discourse about the Heart of the City as a possible image of the city and process for the production "of an endless system of positive space at many scales."
    "Look at the packing of kernels in a bit of wood tissue. While the tissue is growing, the wood cells press against one another, deforming their shapes, much as bubbles in a mass of bubbles keep their coherence under their own internal pressure, balanced against the pressure of nearby bubbles. Just so with the cells in the wood tissue, until each bit of space is made positive." Alexander, *The Heart of the City: The Necessary Binding Force that Creates the Core of Every City*, 33.
20 Margaret Crawford, "Blurring the Boundaries: Public Space and Private Life," in *Everyday Urbanism*, ed. John Leighton Chase, Margaret Crawford, John Kaliski (New York: The Monicelli Press, 1999), 22–35. See Henri Lefebvre, *Critique of Everyday Life* (London: Verso, 1991).
21 Ortega y Gasset, *The Revolt of Masses*, quoted in Sert, "Centres on Community Life," 3.
22 Bakema, *Thoughts about Architecture*, 139.
23 Similarly to Lynch, who criticises the organic metaphor preferring a "rate of growth" of the city rather than the "elusive concept" of a presumed optimum size of the city, we can consider this scheme as a "rate of growth" of the complexity of the relationships concerning the Heart of the City. Lynch, *A Theory of Good City Form*, 281.
24 Sert, "Opening Remarks to the Urban Design Conference," April 9, 1956.
25 Giedion, *Architecture You and Me*.
26 Buber, *Ich und Du*, 1923.
27 "So far, the failure of urban planning and the construction sector in matching demand for homes has resulted in a huge housing backlog that has led to the development of slums in a variety of contexts globally." UN-Habitat. Accessed on August 22, 2016, http://unhabitat.org/urban-themes/housing-slum-upgrading/
28 Alexander, *The Heart of the City*, 4.
29 (Original in Italian: "*l'ultima parola non può essere altro che il progetto stesso.*") Giorgio Grassi, "Premessa," in Carlos Martí Arís, *Le variazioni dell'identità*, 8.

Afterword

This book by Leonardo Zuccaro Marchi carefully reconstructs the issues under debate both before and during the CIAM held in Hoddesdon in 1951, significantly entitled "The Heart of the City," the critical comparison with the Modern Movement of those years (including the reference to the contemporary and often under-estimated conference in Darmstadt). If I could add something to this important work, this something would be represented so much more acutely by what happens today – with the difficult comparison between the professionalised methodologies of the Modern Movement and the formalism of disjunction driven by the post-war reconstruction policy – and by the issues of relations with the history of cities and fragments of urban contexts that constituted an essential part of that "heart of the city," especially the European one, but also in colonial north Africa, with all its consequences on the central theme of recapturing the urban personality for its own population.

But beyond the impact of this debate on my generation, divided not only between those who sought to develop a new heart of the future city using technologies and the different interpretations and reasons of urban and regional history as proposals for a new interpretation of the Modern Movement, there is also the progressive influence of US culture and the political pressures of the proletarian demands, that lasted until the early 1980s.

In 1992, I directed a special issue on this topic, and I thank Zuccaro Marchi for having cited it in his book.

Then the eclipse of industrial culture was gradually replaced by financial capitalism and the culture of new communication tools as essential elements also for the architecture of the cities, dealing with what, in one of my books of about ten years ago, I defined as the new and highly complicated "post-metropolis."

The first chapter of that book began by quoting a text by Jean-Luc Nancy entitled "The Distant City" (in his case, Los Angeles) where, in 1999, he described the features very effectively, obviously trying to read the contradictions and certainly not the perspectives which are the project's job, with the disintegration and homogenous and indifferent extension in which the supercity "has drowned all civil features of the historical city." As far as Nancy is concerned, the city of today (but also probably that of tomorrow) is generally "a scattered whole which is no longer supported by any sovereign firmness but just by glittering opulence." It is still a place where the unique something happens. This "something" is not "the civil but rather the restless heart, growth, and the assault on the civil."

I cited this text because the assault on urban concentration exists (even with the consequences of its sudden specialised emptying), especially in the areas of cities of rapidly developing countries and with an increase in density, that fuel their mercantile visibility and together with the idea of their progressive transitoriness, that also seems to want to pursue a "colossal created by building ever higher" ("*il colossale del sempre più alto*"). It also appears as an element demonstrating the power and independence from any context, often using an independent coating that seems to produce the luxury and superfluousness of its surface as temporary responses founded on the chaos against any definite rule, which in turn is considered an illusory symbol of an unlimited personal freedom while its connection with the powers is very solid.

All this not only is developed in the large concentrations of new towns but it becomes a rather sad and definitively destructive model of every "heart of the city," even in its provincial imitations of cities that have often been established for centuries but which deceptively believe that they have found symbolic evidence of their desire for development and modernity.

To all this we should add the loss of any sense of belonging, fostered by the extraordinary and indomitable development of intangible communications, by the arduous search for new production places equipped with better economic and bureaucratic conditions. All this occurs despite this transfer often also meaning the loss of the best tangible cultures, with an ease of transport that also offers alternative opportunities; all things that transform from tools into essential conditions and even the contents of life.

The production of architecture and urban design seems to be subjected to similar conditions. Today, increasingly, the project is produced by large construction firms, planning regulations and their related, though no less important, variants, marketing experts, engineering and system proposals and market economics. Instead of designer, the architect becomes the illustrator of all this, with images whose aim is primarily that of the product's mercantile visibility and its possible variations of use.

Architectural design, urban planning and the construction of objects have also lost the methodological unity proposed by the Modern Movement, and each part, with the incessant formalistic change without a critical eye on the contradictions of the reality and without any intention of proposing a fragment of truth that is possible and necessary for the present, has definitively also renounced any future reasons for establishing themselves in the specific area of their own history.

Besides the periods of decadence studied by history, our years seem to be characterised by a strong contradictory mix of technological progress and negative social consequences.

It seems less and less clear that the passage of time can be conceived according to a *telos*, a linear change as a progress to which all the processes of the history of the disciplines refer; at least all those conceived by Western civilisation, as it is presented.

The dire state of the relations between things "not as a distant future, but what is imminent, or already present," writes Franco Rella, "today seems without any visible redemption."

Where is the feeling of belonging to a place and the relationship with the heart of the city positioned among these conditions? Or perhaps has the city definitively lost its

Figure A.1 Conference "*CIAM 8. Il Cuore della Città,*" IUAV University, Room Tafuri, September 2, 2013, Venice. From left: Leonardo Zuccaro Marchi, Vittorio Gregotti, Joseph Rykwert, Bernardo Secchi. Tom Avermaete and Paola Viganò participated also.

Source: Photo by author.

ancient identity in the image and daily reality of its citizens, limiting itself to the needs of the working and living environment?

These ever-wider possibilities of the means, rather than positively comparing the valuable differences between cultures, seem to want to unify desires, goals and even hopes that sometimes focus on considering the means offered by the technological process as the reasons for the ends, namely as the heart not only of their city but of their striving for each value of the human collective.

Vittorio Gregotti,
Gregotti Associati International.

Bibliography

Published sources

Alexander, Christopher. "A City Is Not a Tree," *Architectural Forum*, 122, no. 1 (April 1965): 58–62.

Alexander, Christopher. "The Heart of the City. The Necessary Binding Force that Creates the Core of Every City," in *Center for Environmental Structure*, ed. Maggie Moore Alexander (2006), 5. Accessed on July 8, 2016, www.livingneighborhoods.org/library/the-heart-of-the-city-v18.pdf

Alexander, Christopher, Sara Ishikawa, Murray Silverstein. *A Pattern Language* (New York: Oxford University Press, Center for Environmental Structure, 1977).

Arendt, Hannah. *The Human Condition* (Chicago: University of Chicago Press, 1958).

Augè, Marc. *Non-Lieux, Introduction a une anthroplogie de la supermodernitè* (Paris: Le Seuil, 1992); John Howe trans., *Non-Places: Introduction to an Anthropology of Supermodernity* (London and New York: Verso, 1995).

Avermaete, Tom. "Stem and Web: A Different Way of Analysing, Understanding and Conceiving the City in the Work of Candilis-Josic-Woods," 251–269 (2003). Accessed on June 9, 2017, www.team10online.org/.

Avermaete, Tom. *Another Modern, the Post-War Architecture and Urbanism of Candilis: Josic-Woods* (Rotterdam: NAI Publishers, 2005).

Avermaete, Tom. "From Knoxville to Bidonville: ABTAT and the Architecture of the French Welfare State," in *Architecture and the Welfare State*, ed. Mark Swenarton, Tom Avermaete, Dirk Van den Heuvel (New York: Routledge, 2015), 219–236.

Avermaete, Tom, Maristella Casciato, *Casablanca Chandigarh: A Report on Modernization* (Montreal: Canadian Center for Architecture; Zürich: Park Books, 2014).

Avermaete, Tom, Klaske Havik, Hans Teerds, ed., *Architectural Positions: Architecture, Modernity and the Public Sphere* (Amsterdam: SUN Publisher, 2009).

Bacon, Mardges. "Josep Lluís Sert's Evolving Concept of the Urban Core," in *Josep Lluís Sert: The Architect of Urban Design, 1953–1969*, ed. Eric Mumford, Hashim Sarkis (New Haven and London: Yale University Press, 2008), 76–115.

Bakema, Jaap. "Relationship Between Men and Things," in *The Heart of the City: Towards the Humanisation of Urban Life*, ed. Jaqueline Tyrwhitt, Josep Lluís Sert, Ernesto N. Rogers (London: L. Humphries, 1952), 67–69.

Bakema, Jaap. *The Humane Core: A Civic Center for St. Louis, MO* (Washington, DC: Washington University Press, 1960).

Bakema, Jaap. "An Emperor's House at Split Became a Town for 3000 People," *Forum*, 2 (1962): 45–78.

Bakema, Jaap. *Van Stoel tot Stad, een verhaal over mensen en ruimte* (Antwerp: Uitgeversmaatschappij W. de Haan N.V., Zeist/N. V. Standaard Boekhandel, 1963). Translated in English as Bakema, *From Doorstep to City: A Story about People and Space* (Urbana: University of Illinois, 711.4 B78vEw).

Bakema, Jaap. *Thoughts about Architecture*, ed. Marianne Gray (London: Academy Editions; New York: St. Martin's Press, 1981).

Banham, Reyner. *The New Brutalism: Ethic or Aesthetic?* (Stuttgart: Karl Krämer Verlag, 1966).

Banham, Reyner. *The Architecture of the Well-Tempered Environment* (Chicago: University of Chicago Press, 1969).

Banham, Reyner. *Megastructure: Urban Futures of the Recent Past* (London: Thames and Hudson, 1976).

Barbieri, Umberto, ed. *Architectuur en Planning. Nederland 1940–1980* (Rotterdam: Uitgeverij 010, 1983).

Bardet, Gaston. *Le Nouvel urbanisme* (Paris: Editions Vincent. Freal et Cie 1948).

Barthes, Roland. "Semiology and the Urban (1967)", in *Rethinking Architecture: A Reader in Cultural Theory*, ed. Neil Leach (London and New York: Routledge, 1997), 166–171.

Bellamy, Edward. *Looking Backward 2000–1887* (Houghton: Mifflin Publication, 1888).

Berlanda, Franco. "Considerazioni sulla scuola estiva C.I.A.M. A Venezia," *Prospettive*, 5 (1953): 83–86.

Berlanda, Franco. "La Scuola del C.I.A.M. A Venezia," *Urbanistica*, 13 (1953): 83–86.

Borasi, Giovanna, ed. *The Other Architect: Another Way of Building Architecture* (Montreal: Canadian Centre of Architecture, Spector Books, 2015). Bosman, Jos. "My Association with CIAM Gave Me New Perspective," *Ekistics*, 52, no. 314/315 (September–December 1985): 478–486.

Bosman, Jos. "I CIAM del dopoguerra: un bilancio del Movimento Moderno," *Rassegna*, 52 (1992): 6–21.

Bosman, Jos. "Team 10 Out of CIAM," in *TEAM 10 1953–81: In Search of a Utopia of the Present*, ed. Max Risselada, Dirk van den Heuvel (Rotterdam: Nai Publishers, 2006), 246–251.

Buber, Martin. *Ich un Du* (Leipzig: Insel-Verlag. 1923); Walter Kaufmann, trans. *I and Thou a New Translation* (New York: Charles Scribner's Sons, 1970).

Bullock, Nicholas. *Building the Post-War World, Modern Architecture and Reconstruction in Britain* (London: Routledge, 2002).

Buzzi, Franco, Pat Crooke. "La terza scuola estiva dei CIAM a Venezia," *Casabella-Continuita*, 203 (1954): 83–85.

Canguilhem, Georges. "The Living Being and Its Environment (milieu)," *Grey Room*, 3 (Spring 2001): 7–31. Originally in French: Georges Canguilhem, "Le vivant et son milieu," in *La connaissance de la vie* (Paris: Hachette, 1952).

CIAM 8. "Conversation at CIAM 8," in *The Heart of the City: Towards the Humanisation of Urban Life*, ed. Jaqueline Tyrwhitt, Josep Lluís Sert, Ernesto N. Rogers (London: L. Humphries, 1952), 36–40.

CIAM 8. "Discussion on Italian Piazzas," in *The Heart of the City: Towards the Humanisation of Urban Life*, ed. Jaqueline Tyrwhitt, Josep Lluís Sert, Ernesto N. Rogers (London: L. Humphries, 1952), 74–80.

CIAM 8. "A Short Outline of the Core," in *The Heart of the City: Towards the Humanisation of Urban Life*, ed. Jaqueline Tyrwhitt, Josep Lluís Sert, Ernesto N. Rogers (London: L. Humphries, 1952), 164–167.

Ciucci, Giorgio. "The Invention of the Modern Movement," *Oppositions*, 24 (1981): 68–69.

Collins, Christiane C., George R. Collins. "Monumentality. A Critical Matter in Modern Architecture," *Harvard Architectural Review*, 4 (Spring 1984): 14–35.

Coppola D'Anna Pignatelli, Paola. "Cuore della città," in *Dizionario enciclopedico di Architettura e Urbanistica*, ed. Paolo Portoghesi (Roma: Gangemi, I edition 1968, II edition 2006), 120.

Crawford, Margaret. "The World in a Shopping Mall," in *Variations on a Theme Park: The American City and the End of the Public Space*, ed. Michael Sorkin (New York: Hill and Wang, 1992), 3–30.

Crawford, Margaret. "Blurring the Boundaries: Public Space and Private Life," in *Everyday Urbanism*, ed. John Leighton Chase, Margaret Crawford, John Kaliski (New York: The Monicelli Press, 1999), 22–35.

Crotti, Sergio. *Figure architettoniche: soglia [Architectural Figures: The Threshold]* (Milan: Unicopli, 2000).

Curtis, Barry. "The Heart of the City," in *Non-Plan: Essays on Freedom, Participation and Change in Modern Architecture and Urbanism*, ed. Jonathan Hughes, Simon Sadler (London and New York: Architectural Press, Routledge, 2000), 52–65.

Curtis, William J. *Le Corbusier: Ideas and Forms* (New York: Rizzoli, 1986).

Darling, Elizabeth. *Re-forming Britain, Narratives of Modernity Before Reconstruction* (London and New York: Routledge, 2006).

Das Darmstädter Gespräch, 1951. *Mensch und Raum* (Braunschweig: Vieweg, 1991).

de Bruyn, Gerd. *Fisch und Frosch oder die Selbstkritik der Moderne* (Basel: Birkhäuser, 2001).

De Carlo, Giancarlo. "Summary," *Architectural Design* (May 1960): 204–205.

de Grazia, Victoria. *Irresistible Empire: America's Advance Through Twentieth-Century Europe* (Cambridge: Harvard University Press, 2005).

de Solà-Morales, Ignasi. "Architecture and Existentialism," in *Differences: Topographies of Contemporary Architecture* (Cambridge: MIT Press, 1997), 41–56.

Deyong, Sarah. "An Architectural Theory of Relations: Sigfried Giedion and Team X," *JSAH*, 73, no. 2 (June 2014): 226–247.Domhardt, Konstanze Sylva. "From the 'Functional City' to the 'Heart of the City.' Green Space and Public Space in the CIAM Debates of 1942–1952," in *Greening the City: Urban Landscapes in the Twentieth Century*, ed. Dorothee Brantz, Sonja Dümpelmann (Charlottesville: University of Virginia Press, 2011), 133–156.

Domhardt, Konstanze Sylva. *The Heart of the City: Die Stadt in den transatlantischen Debatten der CIAM 1933–1951* (Zürich: Gta Verlag, 2012).

Filippuzzi, Fabio, Luca Taddio ed., *Costruire, Abitare, Pensare* (Milan and Udine: Mimesis/ Estetica e Architettura, 2010).

Fishman, Robert. *Bourgeois Utopias: The Rise and Fall of Suburbia* (New York: Basic Books, 1987).

Foucault, Michel. "Of Other Spaces, Heterotopias," *Architecture, Mouvement, Continuité*, 5 (1984): 46–49. Original Publication: Conférence au Cercle d'études architecturales, 14 mars 1967.

Foucault, Michel. "Security, Territory and Population, Lecture One 11 January 1978," in *Security, Territory and Population, Lectures at the College de France 1977–78*, ed. Michel Senellart et al., trans. Graham Burchell (New York: Palgrave Macmillan, 2009).

Forty, Adrian. *Words and Buildings: A Vocabulary of Modern Architecture* (London: Thames and Hudson, 2000).

Frampton, Kenneth. "Foreword," in Eric Mumford, *The CIAM Discourse on Urbanism, 1928–1960* (Cambridge: MIT Press, 2000), xi–xv.

Frampton, Kenneth. *Labour, Work and Architecture: Collected Essays on Architecture and Design* (London: Phaidon Press, 2002).

Fuchs, Thomas. *The Mechanization of the Heart: Harvey and Descartes*, trans. Marjorie Grene (Rochester, NY: The University of Rochester Press, 2001).

Patrick Geddes, *Cities in Evolution: An Introduction to the Town Planning Movement and to the Study of Cities* (London: Williams and Norgate, 1915).

Giedion, Sigfried. "Introduction," in *Can Our City Survive? An ABC of Urban Problems, Their Analysis, Their Solutions*, ed. Josep Lluís Sert (Cambridge: The Harvard University Press, Cambridge, 1944).

Giedion, Sigfried. "The Need for a New Monumentality," in *New Architecture and City Planning*, ed. Paul Zucker (New York: Philosophical Library, 1944), 549–568.

Giedion, Sigfried. *A Decade of New Architecture* (Zurich: Girsberger, 1951).

Giedion, Sigfried. "The Heart of the City: A Summing-Up," in *The Heart of the City: Towards the Humanisation of Urban Life*, ed. Jaqueline Tyrwhitt, Josep Lluís Sert, Ernesto N. Rogers (London: L. Humphries, 1952), 159–162.

Giedion, Sigfried. "Historical Background to the Core," in *The Heart of the City: Towards the Humanisation of Urban Life*, ed. Jaqueline Tyrwhitt, Josep Lluís Sert, Ernesto N. Rogers (London: L. Humphries, 1952), 17–25.

Giedion, Sigfried. *Architecture You and Me* (Cambridge: Harvard University Press, 1958).

Giedion, Sigfried. *Breviario di Architettura* (Milano: first ed. Garzanti, 1961; Torino: Bollati Boringhieri, 2008), 68. Originally published as *Architektur und Gemeinschaft* (Reinbek: Rowohlt, 1956).

Giedion, Sigfried. *The Eternal Present: 1. The Beginnings of Art* (New York: Bollingen Foundation, Pantheon Books, 1962).

Giedion, Sigfried. *The Eternal Present: 2. The Beginnings of Architecture* (New York: Bollingen Foundation, Pantheon Books, 1964).

Giedion, Sigfried. *Architecture and the Phenomena of Transition, the Three Space Conceptions in Architecture* (Cambridge, MA: Harvard University Press, 1971).

Giedion, Sigfried. "Man in Equipoise," in *Human Identity in the Urban Environment*, ed. Jaqueline Tyrwhitt, Gwen Bell (London: Penguin Books, 1972), 224–226.

Gladwell, Malcolm. "The Terrazzo Jungle," *The New Yorker* (March 15, 2004). Accessed on February 3, 2015, www.newyorker.com/magazine/2004/03/15/the-terrazzo-jungle.

Gregotti, Vittorio. *Il territorio dell'architettura* (Milano: Feltrinelli, 1966; third edition 2014).

Gregotti, Vittorio. "Editoriale – Gli Ultimi CIAM," *Rassegna*, 52, no. 4 (1992): 4.

Gregotti, Vittorio. *Venezia Città della Nuova Modernità* (Venezia: Consorzio Venezia Nuova, 1999).

Gruen, Victor. "Dynamic Planning for Retail Areas," *Harvard Business Review*, 32, no. 6 (November–December 1954): 53–62.

Gruen, Victor. "Cityscape and Landscape," *Experts From a Speech Recently Given at the International Conference of Design in Aspen, Colorado* (1955).

Gruen, Victor. *The Heart of Our Cities: The Urban Crisis Diagnosis and Cure* (New York: Simon and Schuster, 1964).

Gruen, Victor. *Centers for the Urban Environment: Survival of the Cities* (New York: Van Nostrand Reinhold Company, 1973).

Gruen Associates. *A Greater Fort Worth Tomorrow* (Los Angeles: Victor Gruen Associates, 1956), Fort Worth Public Library, LH 976.45315 G.

Gruen, Victor, Larry Smith. *Shopping Town USA: The Planning of Shopping Centers* (New York: Reinhold Publishing Corporation, 1960).

Guarda, Giancarlo. "Attualità di una scuola," *Casabella Continuità*, no. 199 (December 1953–January 1954): v–vi.

Hardwick, M. Jeffrey. *Mall Maker: Victor Gruen, Architect of an American Dream* (Philadelphia: University of Pennsylvania Press, 2004).

Hardy, Joop, Herman Hertzberger, "Drempel en ontmoeting: de gestalte van het tussen," *Forum*, 8 (1959): 249–278.

Harvey, David. *The Condition of Postmodernity: An Enquiry into the Origins of Cultural Change* (Malden: Blackwell Publisher, 1989).

Heidegger, Martin. "Bauen, Wohnen, Danken," in *Vorträge und Aufsätze* (Pfullingen: Günther Neske Verlag, 1954), 145–162. In English "Building, Dwelling, Thinking," in *Poetry, Language, Thought*, trans. Albert Hofstadter (New York: Harper Colophon Books, 1971), 145–161.

Hight, Christopher. *Architectural Principles in the Age of Cybernetics* (New York and London: Routledge, 2007), 131.

Hillier, Bevis, Mary Banham, ed. *Tonic to the Nation: Festival of Britain, 1951* (London: Thames & Hudson Ltd, 1976).

Holford, William. "The Commercial Core of London," in *The Heart of the City: Towards the Humanisation of Urban Life*, ed. Jaqueline Tyrwhitt, Josep Lluís Sert, Ernesto N. Rogers (London: L. Humphries, 1952), 97–102.

Howard, Ebenezer. *Garden Cities of To-Morrow* (London: Swan Sonnenschein & Co, 1902).

Hudnut, Joseph F. "Foreword," in *Can Our City Survive? An ABC of Urban Problems, Their Analysis, Their Solutions*, ed. Josep Lluís Sert (Cambridge: The Harvard University Press, Cambridge, 1944).

Hyde, Timothy. "Planos, Planes y Planificación. Josep Lluís Sert and the Idea of Planning," in *Josep Lluis Sert: The Architect of Urban Design, 1953–1969*, ed. Eric Mumford, Hashim Sarkis (New Haven and London: Yale University Press, 2008), 54–75.

Ibelings, Hans. *Supermodernism* (Rotterdam: Nai Uitgevers Pub, 1998).

Jacobs, Jane. *The Death and Life of Great American Cities* (New York: Random House, 1961).

Jacobs, Jane. "Do Not Segregate Pedestrians and Automobiles," in *The Pedestrian in the City*, ed. David Lewis (Princeton, NJ: Van Nostrand Company, Inc., 1966), 109–110.

Koolhaas, Rem, Chuihua Judy Chung, Jeffrey Inaba, Sze Tsung Leong. *Harvard Design School: Guide to Shopping* (Los Angeles: Taschen, 2001).

Krauss, Rosalind E. *The Originality of the Avant-Garde and Other Modernist Myths* (Cambridge: MIT Press, 1986).

Kroeber, Alfred Louis. *Anthropology: Race, Language, Culture, Psychology, Prehistory* (New York: Hacourt Brace Jovanovich, 1948).

Ketchum, Morris. *Shops and Stores* (New York: Progressive Architecture Library, Reinhold Publishing Corporation, Knickerbocker Printing Corp., 1948).

Kuhn, Thomas Samuel. *The Structure of Scientific Revolutions* (Chicago: University of Chicago Press, 1962).

Lathouri, Marina. "CIAM Meetings 1947–59 and The 'Core' of the City: Transformations of an Idea," in *La Città Nouva: The New City*, ed. Katrina Deines, Kay Bea Jones (Washington: ACSA International Conference Press, 2000), 403–407.

Le Corbusier. *Aircraft* (London: The Studio, 1935; New York: The Studio Publications (collection The New Vision), 1935).

Le Corbusier. *La Charte d'Athènes* (Paris: Plon, 1943). Translated by Anthony Eardley, *The Athens Charter* (New York: Grossman, 1973).

Le Corbusier. *When the Cathedrals Were White: A Journey to the Country of Timid People* (New York: Reynal and Hitchcock, 1947). Originally published as *Quand les cathedrals etaient blanches* (Paris: Plon, 1937).

Le Corbusier. "The Core as a Meeting Place of the Arts," in *The Heart of the City: Towards the Humanisation of Urban Life*, ed. Jaqueline Tyrwhitt, Josep Lluís Sert, Ernesto N. Rogers (London: L. Humphries, 1952), 41–52.

Le Corbusier, Presentation in Venice, Trincanato 2. Attività scientifica/2/011 (Venice: Archivio Progetti IUAV, 1956).

Le Corbusier, Pierre Jeanneret, Jane B. Drew, E. Maxwell Fry, "Chandigarh," in *The Heart of the City: Towards the Humanisation of Urban Life*, ed. Jaqueline Tyrwhitt, Josep Lluís Sert, Ernesto N. Rogers (London: L. Humphries, 1952), 153–155.

Lefebvre, Henri. *Critique of Everyday Life* (London: Verso, 1991).

Lefebvre, Henri. "Preface to the Study of the Habitat of the *Pavillon*," in *Henri Lefebvre: Key Writings*, ed. Stuart Elden, Elizabeth Lebas, Elenore Kofman (New York: Continuum, 2003), 121–135. Originally published in French as Henri Lefebvre, "Preface," in *L'Habitat pavillonnaire*, ed. Henri Raymond et al. (Paris: CRU, 1966), 3–23.

Lefebvre, Henri. *The Production of Space*, trans. Donald Nicholson-Smith (Malden, MA: Blackwell Publishing, 2010). Originally published in French as Henri Lefebvre, *La production de l'espace* (Paris: Anthropos, 1974).

Lefebvre, Virginie. *Paris-Ville Moderne. Maine Montparnasse et la Défense, 1950–1970* (Paris: ed. Norma, 2003).

Lichtenstein, Claude, Thomas Schregenberger ed., *As Found: The Discovery of the Ordinary* (Baden, Switzerland: Lars Müller, 2001).

Lin, Zhongjie. *Kenzo Tange and the Metabolist Movement: Urban Utopias of Modern Japan* (London and New York: Routledge, 2010).

Lotringer, Sylvère ed., *Foucault Live: Collected Interviews, 1961–1984* (New York: Semiotext(e), 1996).

Lynch, Kevin. *The Image of the City* (Cambridge, MA: MIT Press, 1959).

Lynch, Kevin. *A Theory of Good City Form* (Cambridge, MA: MIT Press, 1981).

Marshall, Richard. "The Elusiveness of Urban Design: The Perpetual Problem of Definition and Role," in *Urban Design*, ed. Alex Krieger, William S. Saunders (Minneapolis and London: University of Minnesota Press, 2009), 38–60.

Martí Arís, Carlos. *Le variazioni dell'identità. Il tipo in Architettura* (Torino: Clup, 1990).

Maki, Fumihiko. *Nurturing Dreams: Collected Essays on Architecture and the City*, ed. Mark Mulligan (Cambridge, MA: MIT Press, 2008).

Maki, Fumihiko. "Fragmentation and Friction as Urban Threats: The Post-1956 City," in *Urban Design*, ed. Alex Krieger, William S. Saunders (Minneapolis and London: University of Minnesota Press, 2009), 88–100.

Mattsson, Helena. "Designing the Reasonable Consumer," in *Swedish Modernism: Architecture, Consumption and the Welfare State*, ed. Helena Mattsson, Sven Olov Wallenstein (London: Black Dog Publishing, 2010).

Mennel, Timothy. "Victor Gruen and the Construction of Cold War Utopias," *Journal of Planning History*, 3 (2004): 116–150. Accessed on June 4, 2014, doi:10.1177/1538513204264755

Mondrian, Piet. *Plastic Art and Pure Plastic Art and Other Essays, 1941–1943* (New York: Wittenborn and Company, 1945).

Moholy-Nagy, Sibyl. "The Diaspora," *Journal of the Society of Architectural Historians*, 24 (March 1965): 24–26.

Mumford, Eric. "CIAM Urbanism After the Athens Charter," *Planning Perspectives*, 7 (1992): 391–417.

Mumford, Eric. *The CIAM Discourse on Urbanism, 1928–1960* (Cambridge, MA: MIT Press, 2000).

Mumford, Eric, ed. *Modern Architcture in St. Louis. Washington University and Postwar American Architecture. 1948–1973* (Washington: Washington University in Saint Louis, 2004).

Mumford, Eric. "The Emergence of Urban Design in the Breakup of CIAM," *Harvard Design Magazine* (2006): 10–20.

Mumford, Eric. *Defining Urban Design: CIAM Architects and the Formation of a Discipline, 1937–69* (New Haven and London: Yale University Press, 2009).

Mumford, Eric. "The Emergence of Urban Design in the Breakup of CIAM," in *Urban Design*, ed. Alex Krieger, William S. Saunders (Minneapolis and London: University of Minnesota Press, 2009), 15–37.

Mumford, Eric, ed. *The Writings of Josep Lluís Sert* (New Haven and London: Yale University Press. Cambridge: Harvard GSD, 2015).

Mumford, Lewis. "The Death of the Monument," in *Circle; An International Survey of Constructive Art*, ed. James L. Martin, Ben Nicholson and N. Gabo (London: Faber and Faber, London, 1937).

Newman, Oscar. *CIAM '59 in Otterlo* (Stuttgart: Karl Krämer, 1961).

Norberg-Schulz, Christian. *Genius Loci: Towards a Phenomenology of Architecture* (New York: Rizzoli, 1980).

Norberg-Schulz, Christian. *Architecture: Meaning and Place* (New York: Electa, Rizzoli, 1988).

Oechslin, Werner. "I Darmstädter Gespräche," *Rassegna*, 52, no. 4 (1992): 76–81.

OMA, Rem Koolhaas, Bruce Mau. *S,M,L,XL* (New York: Monacelli Press, 1995).

Ortega y Gasset, José. *The Revolt of Masses* (New York: W.W. Norton and Company Inc., 1932).

Ortega y Gasset, José. *Meditación de la técnica* (Madrid: Alianza Editoriale, 2002).Paci, Enzo. "Il cuore della città," *Casabella Continuità*, 202 (1954): VII–X.

Paci, Enzo. *Tempo e relazione* (Torino: Taylor, 1954).

Paulsson, Gregor. "The Past and the Present," in *The Heart of the City: Towards the Humanisation of Urban Life*, ed. Jaqueline Tyrwhitt, Josep Lluís Sert, Ernesto N. Rogers (London: L. Humphries, 1952), 26–29.

Peck, Bradford. *The World a Department Store: A Twentieth Century Utopia* (Lewiston: B. Peck, 1900).

Pedret, Annie. "Representing History or Describing Historical Reality?: The Universal and the Individual in the 1950s," in *Universal Versus Individual: The Architecture of the 1960s* (Finland: Alvar Aalto Academy; Alvar Aalto Museum: Helsinky; University of Art and Design: Jyväskylä, 2002), 82–85, Accessed on February 25, 2017, www.alvaraalto.fi/conferences/universal/finalpapers/annie.pedret.rtf

Pedret, Annie. *TEAM 10: An Archival History* (London and New York: Routledge, 2013).

Rannells, John. *The Core of the City: A Pilot Study of Changing Land Uses in Central Business Districts* (New York: Columbia University Press, 1956).

Riani, Paolo. *Kenzo Tange (20th Century Masters)* (New York: Hamlyn, 1971).

Richards, James M. "The Idea Behind the Idea," *Architectural Review*, 77 (1935): 203–216.

Ricoeur, Paul. *The Rule of Metaphor: The Creation of Meaning in Language*, trans. Robert Czerny with Kathleen McLaughlin, John Costello, SJ (London and New York: Routledge, 2010). Originally published in French as Paul Ricoeur, *La métaphore vive* (Paris: Editions du Seuil, 1975).

Rogers, Ernesto Nathan. "The Heart: Human Problem of Cities," in *The Heart of the City: Towards the Humanisation of Urban Life*, ed. Jaqueline Tyrwhitt, Josep Lluís Sert, Ernesto N. Rogers (London: L. Humphries, 1952), 69–73.

Rogers, Ernesto Nathan. "Continuità," *Casabella Continuità*, 199 (December 1953/January 1954): 2–3.

Rogers, Ernesto Nathan. "I CIAM al Museo," *Casabella-Continuità*, 232 (October 1959): 2–3.

Rogers, Ernesto Nathan. "Preexisting Conditions and Issues of Contemporary Building Practice." In *Architecture Culture*, ed. Joan Ockman (New York: Rizzoli, 1993), 200–204.

Rogers, Ernesto Nathan. *Architettura, misura e grandezza dell'uomo. Scritti 1930–1969*, ed. Serena Maffioletti (Padova: il Poligrafo, 2010).

Rossi, Aldo. *L'architettura della città* (Padova: Marsilio, 1966; Novara: Citta' Studi, 2006).

Rowe, Colin, Fred Koetter, *Collage City* (Cambridge, MA and London, UK: MIT Press, 1983).

Rykwert, Joseph. "The Idea of a Town," *Forum*, 3 (1963): 99–148.

Sadler, Simon. *The Situationist City* (Cambridge, MA: MIT Press, 1998).

Samonà, Giuseppe. *L'unita' Architettura-Urbanistica, Scritti e progetti: 1929–1973*, ed. Pasquale Lovero (Milano: Franco Angeli, 1975).

Sartre, Jean-Paul. *L' existentialisme est un humanisme* (Paris: Les Editions Nagel, 1946).

Scimemi, Gabriele. "La quarta scuola estiva del CIAM a Venezia," *Casabella-Continuità*, 213 (1956): 69–73

Scimemi, Maddalena. "Venezia internazionale. La CIAM Summer School 1952–1957," *IUAV Journal*, 83 (2010): 5. Accessed on April 28, 2017, www.iuav.it/Ateneo1/chi-siamo/pubblicazi1/Catalogo-G/index.htm#dieci

Scott, Geoffrey. *Architecture of Humanism: A Study in the History of Taste* (Boston and New York: Houghton Mifflin, 1914).

Scott Brown, Denise. "Team 10, Perspecta 10, and the Present State of the Architectural Theory," *Journal of the American Institute of Planners*, 1 (1967): 42–49.

Scott Brown, Denise. "Urban Concepts," *Architectural Design Profile*, 90 (1990): 1–2.

Scott Brown, Denise. "Urban Concepts. Denise Scott Brown," *Architectural Design Profile*, 83 (1990): 1–96.

Scott Brown, Denise. "Imparare da Vaccaro," in *Giuseppe Vaccaro*, ed. M. Mulazzani (Milano: Mondadori Electa 2002), 65–75.

Scott Brown, Denise. "Denise Scott Brown," in *Time Space Existence, Venice Biennale 2016, Palazzo Bembo*, ed. Global Art Affairs Foundation (Italy: Global Art Affairs Foundation, 2016), 252.

Scott Brown, Denise. "From Venice to Venice Beach: Denise Scott Brown's 'Wayward' Eye," *Metropolis Magazine* (July 13, 2016). Accessed on July 28, 2016, www.metropolismag.com/July-August-2016/From-Venice-to-Venice-Beach-Denise-Scott-Browns-Wayward-Eye/Secchi, Bernardo. *Il Racconto Urbanistico. La politica della casa e del territorio in Italia* (Torino: Einaudi, 1984).

Secchi, Bernardo. *La città del ventesimo secolo* (Bari: Laterza, 2005).

Secchi, Bernardo. "A New Urban Question 3: When, Why and How Some Fundamental Metaphors Were Used." in *Metaphors in Architecture and Urbanism: An Introduction*, ed. Andri Gerber, Brent Patterson (Bielefeld: Transcript Verlag, 2013), 123–129.

Sert, Josep Lluís. *Can Our Cities Survive? An ABC of Urban Problems, their Analysis, their Solutions* (Cambridge: The Harvard University Press; London: Humphrey Milford Oxford University Press, 1944).

Sert, Josep Lluís. "The Human Scale in City Planning," in *New Architecture and City Planning*, ed. Paul Zucker (New York: Philosophical Library, 1944), 392–412.

Sert, Josep Lluís. "Centres on Community Life," in *The Heart of the City: Towards the Humanisation of Urban Life*, ed. Jaqueline Tyrwhitt, Josep Lluís Sert, Ernesto N. Rogers (London: L. Humphries, 1952), 3–16.

Sert, Josep Lluís, Paul Lester Wiener, "Chimbote," in *The Heart of the City: Towards the Humanisation of Urban Life*, ed. Jaqueline Tyrwhitt, Josep Lluís Sert, Ernesto N. Rogers (London: L. Humphries, 1952), 128–130.

Sert, Josep Lluís, GSD, "Urban Design. Condensed Report of an Invitation Conference Sponsored by Faculty and Alumni Association of Graduate School of Design, Harvard University, April 9–10 1956," *Progressive Architecture* 37 (August 1956): 97–112.

Shane, David Grahame. "The Street in the Twentieth Century. Three Conferences: London (1910), Athens (1933), Hoddesdon (1951)," *The Cornell Journal of Architecture*, 2 (1983): 20–41.

Shane, David Grahame. *Urban Design Since 1945: A Global Perspective* (New York: John Wiley & Sons Inc, 2011).

Sharr, Adam. *Heidegger for Architects* (London and New York: Routledge, 2007).

Shoshkes, Ellen. "Jaqueline Tyrwhitt and Transnational Discourse on Modern Planning and Design, 1941–1951," *Urban History*, 36, no. 2 (2009): 263–283.

Shoshkes, Ellen. *Jaqueline Tyrwhitt: A Transnational Life in Urban Planning and Design* (New York: Routledge, 2013).

Sloterdijk, Peter. *Bubbles: Spheres Volume I: Microspherology*, trans. Wieland Hoban (Los Angeles: Semiotext(e), 2011). Originally published as Peter Sloterdijk, *Sphären I: Blasen, Mikrosphärologie* (Frankfurt: Suhrkamp, 1998).

Smiley, David. *Pedestrian Modern: Shopping and American Architecture, 1925–1956* (Minneapolis: University of Minnesota Press, 2013).

Smithson, Alison, ed. "Team 10 Primer 1953–1962," *Architectural Design*, 12 (December, 1962): 559–600.

Smithson, Alison, ed. *Team 10 Primer* (London: Great Britain by Studio Vista Limited, 1965).

Smithson, Alison. *The Emergence of Team 10 Out of CIAM* (London: AAGS Theory and History Papers 1.82, Architectural Association, 1982).

Smithson, Alison, Peter Smithson. "Cluster City," *The Architectural Review*, 422, no. 730 (November 1957): 333–336.

Soja, Edward W. *Thirdspace* (Malden, MA: Blackwell, 1996).

Spitzer, Leo. "Milieu and Ambience: An Essay in Historical Semantics," *Philosophy and Phenomenological Research*, 3, no. 2 (December 1942): 169–218.

Stanek, Łukasz. *Henri Lefebvre on Space: Architecture, Urban Research, and the Production of Theory* (Minneapolis: University of Minnesota Press, 2011).

Steadman, Philip. *The Evolution of Design* (Cambridge: University Press, 1979).

Strauven, Francis. "Bakema," *Forum*, 34, no. 3 (1990): 19–30.

Strauven, Francis. *Aldo van Eyck: The Shape of Relativity* (Amsterdam: Architectura & Natura, 1998).

Tafuri, Manfredo. *Teorie e storia dell'architettura* (Bari: Laterza, 1968).

Tafuri, Manfredo. *Architecture and Utopia*, trans. Barbara Luigia La Penta (Cambridge, MA: MIT Press, 1976). Originally published in Italian as *Progetto e Utopia* (Bari: Laterza, 1973).

Tafuri, Manfredo. *Venice and the Renaissance* (Cambridge, MA: MIT Press, 1995), X. Originally published in Italian as *Venezia e il Rinascimento* (Torino: Einaudi, 1985).

Tafuri, Manfredo, Francesco Dal Co. *Architettura Contemporanea* (Milano: Electa, 1976; XVI edition Electa, 2012).

Tange, Kenzo. "Hiroshima," in *The Heart of the City: Towards the Humanisation of Urban Life*, ed. Jaqueline Tyrwhitt, Josep Lluís Sert, Ernesto N. Rogers (London: L. Humphries, 1952), 136–138.

Tange, Kenzo. "Technology and Humanity," *Japan Architect* (October 1960): 11–12.

Tange, Kenzo. "Function, Structure, Symbol (1966)," in *Kenzo Tange 1946–1969*, ed. Udo Kultermann (Zürich: Verlag für Architecktur Artemis Zürich, 1970), 240–245.

Team 10, "The Role of the Architect in Community Building," in *Human Identity in the Urban Environment*, ed. Jaqueline Tyrwhitt, Gwen Bell (London: Penguin Books, 1972), 376–393.

Topalov, Christian, Laurent Coudroy De Lille, Jean-Charles Depaule, Brigitte Marin, *L'aventure des mots de la ville à travers le temps, les langues, les sociétés* (Paris: Robert Laffont, 2010).

Tunnard, Christopher. *The City of Man, a New Approach to the Recovery of Beauty in American Cities* (New York: Charles Scribner's Sons, 1953).

Tuscano, Clelia. "How Can You Do Without History? Interview with Giancarlo De Carlo. Milan, Via Pier Capponi 13, 23 May 1990, 20 February 1995, and 24 November 1999," in *TEAM 10 1953–81: In Search of a Utopia of the Present*, ed. Max Risselada, Dirk van den Heuvel (Rotterdam: Nai Publishers, 2006), 340–344.

Tyrwhitt, Jaqueline. "The Valley Section. Patrick Geddes' World Image," *Journal of the Town Planning Institute*, 37 (1951): 61–66.

Tyrwhitt, Jaqueline, ed., "Definitions of Urban Design," *Synthesis – GSD Harvard*, 1 (April 1957): 27–31.

Tyrwhitt, Jaqueline. "CIAM and Delos," *Ekistics*, 52, no. 314/315 (November/December 1985): 470–472.

Tyrwhitt, Jaqueline. "History of the CIAM Movement. An Unfulfilled Project," *Ekistics*, 52, no. 314/315 (1985): 486–487.

Tyrwhitt, Jaqueline, Gwen Bell, ed. *Human Identity in the Urban Environment* (London: Penguin Books, 1972).

Tyrwhitt, Jaqueline, Josep Lluís Sert, Ernesto N. Rogers, ed. *The Heart of the City: Towards the Humanisation of Urban Life* (London: Lund Humphries Ltd, 1952; New York: Pellegrini and Cudahy, 1952).

Tyrwhitt, Jaqueline, Josep Lluís Sert, Ernesto N. Rogers, ed. *Il Cuore della Città: per una vita più umana delle comunità*, transl. Julia Banfi Bertolotti (Milano: Hoepli editore, 1954).

van den Heuvel, Dirk. "Towards an Open Society: The Unfinished Work of Jaap Bakema," 41 (2014): 3–3.

van Eyck, Aldo. "Het verhaal van een andere gedachte (The Story of Another Idea)," *Forum*, 7 (1959): 198–239.

van Eyck, Aldo. "The Role of the Architect in Community Building, Team 10," in *Human Identity in the Urban Environment*, ed. Jaqueline Tyrwhitt, Gwen Bell (London: Penguin Books, 1972).

Venturi, Robert. *Complexity and Contradiction in Architecture* (New York: The Museum of Modern Art, 1966).

Venturi, Robert, Denise Scott-Brown, *Architecture as Signs and Systems: For a Mannerist Time* (Cambridge and London: Belknap Press of Harvard University Press, 2004).

Venturi, Robert, Denise Scott Brown, Steven Izenour, "From Rome to Las Vegas," in *Learning From Las Vegas* (Cambridge, MA: MIT Press, 1972).

Victor Gruen Foundation for Environmental Planning. "Die Charta von Wien," in *Das Über-leben der Städte: Wege aus der Umweltkrise: Zentren als urbane Brennpunkte*, ed. Victor Gruen (Wien: Molden, 1973).

Viganò, Paola. *La città elementare* (Milano: Skira, 1999).

Wagenaar, Cornelis. "Jaap Bakema and the Fight for Freedom," in *Anxious Modernism*, ed. Sarah Williams Goldhagen, Réjean Legault (Montreal: Centre Canadien d'Architecture; Cambridge, MA and London: MIT Press, 2000), 261–278.

Wall, Alex. *Victor Gruen: From Urban Shop to New City* (Barcelona: Actar, 2005).

Welter, Volker M. "From Locus Genii to Heart of the City: Embracing the Spirit of the City," in *Modernism and the Spirit of the City*, ed. Iain Boyd Whyte (London and New York: Routledge, 2003), 35–56.

Welter, Volker M. "In-between Space and Society. On Some British Roots of Team 10's Urban Thought in the 1950's," in *TEAM 10 1953–81: In Search of a Utopia of the Present*, ed. Max Risselada, Dirk van den Heuvel (Rotterdam: Nai Publishers, 2006), 258–263.

Williamson, dr. George Scott. "The Individual and the Community," in *The Heart of the City: Towards the Humanisation of Urban Life*, ed. Jaqueline Tyrwhitt, Josep Lluís Sert, Ernesto N. Rogers (London: L. Humphries, 1952), 30–35.

Zevi, Bruno. "Downtown come San Marco, una nuova Philosophy urbanistica nell'economia Americana." *Urbanistica*, 20 (1956): 116–117.

Zuccaro Marchi, Leonardo. "Cuore della Città e Urban Design: contraddizioni e ibridazioni nel Dopoguerra," *Territorio*, 72 (2015): 131–141.

Zuccaro Marchi, Leonardo. "Victor Gruen: the environmental Heart." *The Journal of Public Space*, Vol 2, No 2 (2017): 75–84. DOI: https://doi.org/10.5204/jps.v2i2.94 https://www.journalpublicspace.org/article/view/94/61

Relevant archive documents

"Architectenbureau Van den Broek en Bakema, Tel Aviv Project, 1962," Archief d1315, BROX3092 (70–3092), Het Nieuwe Instituut, Rotterdam.

Bakema, Jaap. "Letter to Mr. Haskell, December 1959," Bake d264, Bakema Archive, Het Nieuwe Instituut, Rotterdam.

Bakema, Jaap. "Letter to Mr. Haskell," d264, Bakema Archive, Het Nieuwe Instituut, Rotterdam.

Bakema, Jaap. "Notes about Theory," d264, Bakema Archive, Het Nieuwe Instituut, Rotterdam.

Bakema, Jaap. "Problem: Civic Centre for Metropolis St. Louis. Part IV," Bake d264, Bakema Archive, Het Nieuwe Instituut, Rotterdam.

Bakema, Jaap. "Report On: Ethics and Aesthetics," g18, Bakema Archive, Het Nieuwe Instituut, Rotterdam.

CIAM 8. "Report of Hoddesdon Conference," 1951, BIB 200583, CCA Library, Montreal.

CIAM. "CIAM Summer School 1952," 42-JLS-27-91, gta/ETH.

CIAM. "CIAM Summer School in London-1949," 42-JT-3-203, gta/ETH.

CIAM. "Document, D2-19-274-002," Le Corbusier Archive, Paris.

CIAM. "Flyer, CIAM Summer School 1949," 42-HMS-I-424, gta/ETH.

CIAM. "Le Documents de Sigtuna, June 1952, A0612," Forbat Archive Am 1970–18, Arkdes Stockholm.

CIAM. "Letter of Extraordinary Council Meeting, Paris, May 14, 1952," CIAM Collection C11, Frances Loeb Library, GSD Harvard, Cambridge.

CIAM. "Notes on CIAM Meeting Held on June 5, 1950 at 9 East 59th St. New York. Present: S. Giedion, L. Holm, A. Iriarte, J.L. Sert, J. Tyrwhitt, P.L. Wiener," 42 JLS-25-1, gta/ETH.

CIAM Italian Group. "Letter April 1952, CIAM Summer School, Architectural School in Venice, Palazzo Grassi, Fondamenta Nani," 42-JLS-23-51, gta/ETH.

CIAM Summer School. "The Theme, 1954," Trincanato 2. Attività scientifica/2/011, in Archivio Progetti IUAV, Venice.

CIAM Summer School. "The Theme, Venice, 1956," g51, Bakema Archive, Het Nieuwe Instituut, Rotterdam.

CIAM Summer School. "Tuesday, September 27, 1956. Seminar: Exhibition of the Works of Each Team Debate on Them," g54, Bakema Archive, Het Nieuwe Instituut, Rotterdam.

Fry, Maxwell. "Letter to CIAM, November 24, 1949," 42-JT-4-215, gta/ETH.

Giedion, Sigfried, Le Corbusier. "Syrkus, Paris, March 9, 1949," CIAM Collection B5, Frances Loeb Library, GSD Harvard, Cambridge.

Gropius, Walter. "Letter to Forbat, March 20, 1952, Am 1970–18," Forbat Archive, Arkdes Stockholm.

Gropius, Walter. "Letter to Mr. Wells Coates, cc. Giedion and Sert, December 22, 1949," 42/SG/34/54, gta/ETH.

Gruen, Victor. "The Charter of Vienna," Victor Gruen Papers: Box 48, Folder 5, Library of Congress, Washington.

GSD, Walter F. Bogner, C. H. Burchard. "Arch. 2b. Problem II, A Commercial Center for Hingham, Mass. 1945–46," GSD Student CA 182, Frances Loeb Library, GSD Harvard, Cambridge.

GSD, Prof. Gourley, Mr. Goodwin. "Problem L2. Shopping Center. Arch. 2–2ab. Fall Term 1957–58," GSD Student CA 184–185, Frances Loeb Library, GSD Harvard, Cambridge.

Hovens Greve, Hans, Wim Wissing. "Contribution to: The Core or Physical Heart. CIAM 8, July 1951," g18, Het Nieuwe Instituut, Rotterdam.

Le Corbusier. "Presentation in Venice, Trincanato 2. Attività scientifica/2/011," Archivio Progetti IUAV, Venice.

MARS. "DRAFT, Letter to CIAM Groups, 'CIAM Summer School: London 1949'," SG-19-31b, gta/ETH.

MARS. "Letter, November 24, 1949," 42-JT-4-215, gta/ETH.

MARS Group. "CIAM Summer School 1949. Program for a New Elephant and Castle," 42-JT-3-203, gta/ETH.

MARS Group. "CIAM Summer School. Information Sheet," 42-JT-3-219, gta/ETH.

MARS Group. "Letter to Giedion May 14, 1948," 42-SG-19-4, gta/ETH.

Norberg-Schulz, Christian. "Commission 3A (Young Architects), Report on Architectural Education," CIAM 8, Report of Hoddesdon Conference, 1951, p. 113, BIB 200583, CCA Library, Montreal.

Norberg-Schulz, Christian. "Eduard Neuenschwander, 'TEAM 1,' May 1, 1951," 42-x-150, gta/ETH.

Norberg-Schulz, Christian. "Eduard Neuenschwander, 'TEAM 2', February 1952," 42-SG-39-62, gta/ETH.

Norberg-Schulz, Christian. "Eduard Neuenschwander, 'TEAM 3', September 1952," 42-WM-X-1, gta/ETH.

Norberg-Schulz, Christian. "Letter to Giedion, Oslo, February 5, 1951," 42-SG-X-133, gta/ETH.

Norberg-Schulz, Christian. "On the Creation of Junior Groups, Sigtuna June 26, 1952," 42-JT-10-70, gta/ETH.

Opbouw group. "CIAM 8 Describing the Core of Pendrecht, Responsible Rapporteur: W. Wissing," g. 18, Bakema Archive, Het Nieuwe Instituut, Rotterdam.

Paci, Enzo. "Relationism and Architecture," Trincanato 2. Attività scientifica/2/014, IUAV University Archive, Venice.

PAGON. "Tveten Panel, 1951," NAMT.ako061, The National Museum of Art, Architecture and Design, Oslo.

PAGON Group. "Notes, Norway, Lapad Congress July 10 1956," 42-JT-15-339/340, gta/ETH.

Rogers, Ernesto Nathan. "Architectural Education, First Session, CIAM 8, 1951," 42-JT-7-473/475, gta/ETH.

Rogers, Ernesto Nathan. "Letter to Le Corbusier, June 13, 1950, D2-19-265-001, Le Corbusier Archive, Paris. AM1970–18–162," Forbat Archive, ArkDes Archive, Stockholm.Sert, Josep Lluís. "Introduction to the Urban Design Conference," April 9, 1956, Rare NAC 46 Harv 1956, Frances Loeb Library, GSD Harvard, Cambridge. And in "Urban Design," *Progressive Architecture* (August 1956): 97–112.

Sert, Josep Lluís. "Letter to Jaqueline Tyrwhitt, October 1, 1951, CIAM Collection, C10, Frances Loeb Library," GSD Harvard, Cambridge.

Sert, Josep Lluís. "Letter to Tyrwhitt, September 7, 1951, CIAM Collection_Correspondence 1951 July–September, C9," Frances Loeb Library, GSD Harvard, Cambridge.

Sert, Josep Lluís. Tyrwhitt, "The Shape of American Cities, June 1958," TjJ/38/9/10, RIBA, London.

Sert, Josep Lluís, Prof. Carlhian, "Problem VII: Preliminary Study for the Redevelopment of Times Square,- Studio #1 Urban Design, Fall Term, 1954–55, Arch, 2–4a," p. 2, GSD Students, CC098, Frances Loeb Library, GSD Harvard, Cambridge.

Smithson, Alison, Peter Smithson. "Letter August 23, 1957, TTEN0002, Team 10 Smithsons," folder 16, Het Nieuwe Instituut, Rotterdam.

Tange, Kenzo. "The Core. Its Social and Historical Background, June 1951," 42-JLS-17-60, gta/ETH.

Tyrwhitt, Jaqueline. "The Core of the City, December 15, 1952," Toronto University, for the Commerce Journal, TjJ/38/9/3, RIBA Archive, London.

Tyrwhitt, Jaqueline. "Document, September 1974," Tyrwhitt TjJ/38/1, RIBA Archive, London.

Tyrwhitt, Jaqueline. "Document, TjJ/38/9/10," RIBA Archive, London.

Tyrwhitt, Jaqueline. "Ideal Cities and Utopias, January 1952," TJJ/16/3, RIBA, London.

Tyrwhitt, Jaqueline. "Letter to Sert, September 22, 1951," CIAM Collection, C9, Frances Loeb Library, GSD Harvard, Cambridge.

Tyrwhitt, Jaqueline. "New Towns for Defence – The Urban Constellation," Progressive Architecture, June 1951 (Part of an address given to the AIA at Chicago, May, 1951), TjJ/38/7/2/1, RIBA Archive, London.

Tyrwhitt, Jaqueline. "Principles of Town Planning, Lecture 10: The Urban Constellation and the Core of the City," University of Toronto, 1951, TjJ/16/1, RIBA Archive, London.

Tyrwhitt, Jaqueline. "Slides for the Public Lecture on 'The CORE', March 1953," University of Toronto, TjJ/18/4, RIBA Archive, London.

Tyrwhitt, Jaqueline, Josep Lluís Sert. "The Shape of American Cities, June 1958," p. 6, TjJ/38/9/10, RIBA Archive, London.

Wogenscky, André. "Letter from to Sert, Paris, April 9, 1953," BAKE0153, g21, Bakema Archive, Het Nieuwe Instituut, Rotterdam.

Index